THIS BOOK IS INSCRIBED
TO MY TWO SONS
WINSTON AND JOHN

CONTENTS

THE REMINISCENCES OF LADY RANDOLPH CHURCHILL

BY

MRS. GEORGE CORNWALLIS-WEST

𝔉llustrated

NEW YORK
THE CENTURY CO.
1908

THE DE VINNE PRESS

CONTENTS

vii

CONTENTS

LIST OF ILLUSTRATIONS

LIST OF ILLUSTRATIONS

x

LIST OF ILLUSTRATIONS

xi

LIST OF ILLUSTRATIONS

PREFACE TO BOOK

In studying the prefaces to various contemporary Memoirs, I find that most of them are apologetic in tone, and I ask myself . . . why? If a book needs an apology ought it to be written?

Having been favored by Providence with delightful and absorbing experiences, having traveled all over the world, and met many of the most distinguished people of my generation, why should I not record all that I can about them, and about the stirring things I have seen, or shared in doing?

I have done so. But there may be some to whom these Reminiscences will be interesting chiefly in virtue of what is left unsaid.

J. C. W.

Salisbury Hall, St. Albans, England, 1908

REMINISCENCES OF
LADY RANDOLPH CHURCHILL

REMINISCENCES OF
LADY RANDOLPH CHURCHILL

CHAPTER I

EARLY RECOLLECTIONS—PARIS 1869

MY father was for three years American Consul at Trieste, and Italy thus colored my first impression of life, although I was born in Brooklyn, in the State of New York. Italian skies gave me my love of heat and of the sun, and a smiling, dark-eyed peasant nurse tuned my baby ears to the harmony of the most melodious of all languages. Until the age of six I spoke hardly anything but Italian. My father, Leonard Jerome, a Princeton graduate and the most enterprising of nine brothers, soon wearied of the tranquil life of a Mediterranean town, and returned to America with my mother and three small children, all girls, one of whom died a year or two later. On our journey back I remember how, as we crossed the Mont Cenis in a *vettura,* the deep snow filled my childish mind with awe and astonishment. But this was a sight I was soon to become familiar with in my own country.

3

For four or five years my family lived in New York, where my father, in making and unmaking several fortunes, and at one time virtually possessing the whole of the Pacific Mail Line, found plenty of scope for his ambitions and his active brain. For a short period he was co-editor of the "New York Times" with Mr. Henry Raymond. He founded Jerome Park and the Coney Island Jockey Club, the first of the two great American race-courses, and with his friend August Belmont made good his claim to being called "the father of the American turf."

Then came the period of the Civil War. That great struggle, which for four years devastated my country and sacrificed a million men in the cause of freedom, passed our nursery unmolested, and I remember nothing about it except that every little Southerner I met at dancing classes was a "wicked rebel," to be pinched, if possible; while the words of the bitter parody which we used to sing to the tune of "Maryland, My Maryland" come back to me to-day.

Besides the 4th of July celebrations of fire-crackers, and memories of burnt fingers, and St. Patrick's Day processions when the streets were filled yearly with an ever-increasing crowd of Paddies and Biddies, one vivid recollection of an important event strikes across my mind. I remember our house in Madison Square draped from top to bottom in white and black, and the whole of New York looking like one gigantic mausoleum. It was the funeral of President Lincoln.

Next came a few uneventful years of lessons, with matinées at the opera "to improve our minds," sleighing and skating for pleasure, and on red-letter days a drive

4

to Jerome Park on my father's coach, where, tiny mite
that I was, I always occupied the seat of honor next him.
Sometimes from afar I could see the blue and white of
his racing colors come in first, which was a great excitement. On one occasion I was hoisted upon the back of
his most famous race-horse—the celebrated "Ken-
tucky," whose sire "Lexington" and dam "Magnolia"
by "Glencoe," were of the best blood in England. Ken-
tucky was never beaten, but came to an untimely end,
being burned to death on his way to California, my father having sold him for the then fabulous sum of
$40,000. Unlike most American children, we were sel-
dom permitted to go to boy and girl dances, but a photograph I have of myself at the age of ten, dressed as a
vivandière, reminds me of a fancy ball given by Mr.
Belmont to which I was allowed to go. For days I did
not sleep with the excitement of anticipation, but on the
eventful night I was found in a flood of tears, the explanation being that I did not look "at all as I thought I
was going to"—a situation which, alas! has often repeated itself.

We spent several delightful summers at Newport,
where my father had built a charming villa more in ac-
cordance with one's idea of a seaside residence than the
gorgeous white marble palaces which are the fashion
nowadays. There we were allowed to run wild and be as
grubby and happy as children ought to be.

Mrs. Ronalds, who was as gifted as she was lovely,
and shared with Mrs. Ritchie (now Mrs. Adair) the
reputation of being the reigning beauty, gave me a species of small dog-cart and two donkeys which rejoiced
in the names of "Willie" and "Wooshey." With the

cart filled with half a dozen children, and urged by a stick, at the end of which was "the business end of a tin tack," christened the "Persuader," Willie and Wooshey were gently made to tear up and down Bellevue Avenue at the risk of our necks and every one else's. The cart and its occupants soon became a terror to the smart folk in their silks and feathers who drove majestically by. These were delightful days.

In 1867, owing to my mother having become ill, we sailed for Europe in order that she might consult the celebrated American physician Dr. Sims, in Paris. I little thought I was fated not to return to my native land until 1876, when I had already been married two years. Finding that the educational advantages were greater in Paris than in New York, we decided to remain there. On regaining her health, my mother went out a great deal in French society, where her beauty attracted much attention, *la belle Américaine* at that time having all the charm of novelty.

THE last flicker of the candle, the last flame of the dying fire, is ever the brightest; and so it was with Paris in 1869.

Never had the Empire seemed more assured, the court more brilliant, the fêtes more gorgeous. The light-hearted Parisians reveled in the daily sights of royal processions and cavalcades. The Bois de Boulogne and the Champs Elysées, where we were living at that time, were crowded with splendid equipages. I remember often seeing the Empress Eugénie, then the handsomest woman in Europe, driving in her daumont, the green and gold liveries of the postilions and out-

"THE MISSES JEROME AS CHILDREN

riders making a brave show. Nor were four horses and postilions the privilege of royalty alone. Princess Metternich, the wife of the Austrian Ambassador, often went out in similar style. The beautiful Madame de Canisy, and the Duchesse de Mouchy, the Empress's greatest and perhaps only intimate friend, and a host of court ladies habitually drove out in great state, and helped by the magnificence of their appearance to give to Paris that air of elegance and distinction which could neither be surpassed nor emulated by any other capital in Europe. Even among those who had forebodings of the gathering storm, no one had descried the black shadow cast on the blue sky by the approaching figure of Bellona, her fierce eyes fixed on happy, smiling, tranquil France.

Although I was not old enough to go into society, being still troubled with governesses, the echoes of the Tuileries fêtes and of the gay social life of Paris were heard in our house, and eagerly listened to by my curious and greedy ears. The Emperor Napoleon III was credited with a great liking for Americans, and he certainly showed his partiality by having many invited to the official festivities. Among them was my eldest sister, who made her début at one of the Tuileries balls. Notwithstanding her awe at the magnificence of the palace, and her confusion at having to walk up the grand staircase between the Cent-Gardes in her first low frock, she was able to give me afterward a graphic description of the scene, which made a deep impression on me. Unlike the procedure at the Court of St. James, no procession was formed. When the company was assembled, the doors were flung open, and "*Sa Majesté*

9

l'Empereur" was announced. Then after a pause, *"Sa Majesté l'Impératrice!"* who that evening appeared a resplendent figure in green velvet, with a crown of emeralds and diamonds, spiked with pearls, on her small and beautifully shaped head. The Emperor and Empress walked round the circle of courtesying and bowing guests, addressing a few words here and there, and then proceeded to the ball-room. Besides the great functions at the palace, smaller and more informal dances were given. These were the *petits Lundis,* which had been instituted ten years before, and at which the Prince Imperial, although only a boy, was allowed to appear and amuse himself, perhaps with a view to forming his manners, and giving him that ease in society in which foreign royalties excel. All the most beautiful and charming women of Paris, including many attractive foreigners, were asked. Court ceremonial and etiquette were dispensed with, which added greatly to the enjoyment of the evening. After one of these petits Lundis, which had been unusually animated (owing to its being Twelfth Night, when a magnificent "Gâteau des Rois," with presents for the ladies, had been the event of the evening), Count Hatzfeldt, late German Ambassador to England, who was then Secretary to the Embassy in Paris, and a frequenter of our salon, prophetically sounded the first note of trouble to come. "I never saw their Majesties in better spirits than they were last night," he remarked, "and God knows where they will be next year at this time." In the light of subsequent events, we were much impressed by his having said this, although I cannot believe that he really knew much.

The celebrated beauties, most of them in the zenith of

10

their fame, with whom the Empress loved to surround herself, and whose portraits adorned the walls of her boudoir in the Tuileries, were conspicuous at these small dances. The Marquise de Gallifet, wife of the General, and her sister Madame Cordier, formerly Mesdemoiselles Lafitte, one fair, the other dark, would sometimes dress alike, making a lovely contrast. The Comtesse de Pourtalès, whose bewitching face and fascinating manner won all hearts, also concerned herself so seriously with politics that she became the social link between the two camps of Legitimists and Bonapartists. Comte de Pourtalès, being of Swiss origin, had no compunction in becoming an Imperialist, and they were great favorites at the Tuileries. Madame de Pourtalès later showed her gratitude and devotion to the fallen monarchs by interceding for them with M. Thiers for the restoration of some of their property. Having visited them at Chiselhurst in the dark year of 1873, and realizing their poverty, which was known to few, Madame de Pourtalès never rested till she had succeeded in her task.

As a girl I remember seeing her at the opera, a vision of beauty in a cloud of tulle, with her soft brown hair, lovely, expressive eyes, and radiant smile. Later, when as a married woman I had the pleasure of knowing her, I always found a pleasant welcome at her house in the rue Tronchet, on my visits to Paris; and from the charm of her beauty and personality, and the vivacity of her conversation, could easily understand the sway she held over society. To this day, although a grandmother of many years' standing, she is still a beautiful woman, and no Frenchman can speak of *"La belle Mélanie"* without saying, *"Elle est étonnante."* For so many years did these beautiful women reign supreme that envious rivals christened them *"La vieille Garde,"* perverting the old saying with malicious aptness.

At this period Princesse Mathilde, who had a fine house in the rue de Courcelles, used to give cotillions, at which the *colletmonté* and aristocratic families made their appearance in greater numbers than at the Tuileries: the noble faubourg, satisfied that her mother was a Princess of Würtemberg, while her uncle was the Czar Nicholas I, did not look upon her as a parvenu and an interloper.

Princesse Mathilde, undoubtedly the most brilliant and intelligent woman of the Second Empire, had done the honors at the Elysée, in 1848, for her cousin Louis Napoleon, then President of the Republic. Her marriage to Count Anatole Demidoff, Prince of San Donato, had not been a success as every one knows, and after some scenes of great violence on his part, she separated from him, supported in this step by her uncle Nicholas I, who also forced his subject Count Demidoff to give her a large income, which it is said amounted in the course of sixty years to twelve million francs.

The Princess loved to surround herself with all those possessing wit or talent, and her salon had a world-wide reputation, comparing easily with the famous salons of the eighteenth century, with the added attraction and glamour of royalty and great wealth. That these sacred portals were opened for anything so frivolous as a dance was to please the Prince Imperial and the Empress's nieces, the Mesdemoiselles d'Albe. It was there that some of the young and pretty Americans in Paris, including my sister, now Mrs. Moreton Frewen, had

MISS JENNIE JEROME, AS A VIVANDIÈRE, AT TEN YEARS OF AGE

the privilege of meeting such men as Dumas, Sardou, Théophile Gautier, Baudry, and many other habitués of the house.

Among the celebrated women of Eugénie's circle none took so prominent a place as Princess Pauline Metternich, the wife of the Austrian Ambassador. Though she was only twenty-two when she first arrived in Paris in 1860, her wit, vivacity, and extraordinary "chic" (the only word which really describes her) placed her at once among the leaders of what was undoubtedly the most brilliant court in Europe. Her life is too well known for me to dilate on it, her repartees and bon mots were on every one's lips, her dresses were the models all tried to copy, and her company was eagerly sought for by the greatest in the land. Apart from other interests, her predilection for the stage was perhaps her ruling passion. She was never so happy as when organizing theatricals, and she was the ruling spirit of all the entertainments of that kind given at Compiègne, where, whether as a black devil dancing in a ballet before the whole court, or dressed as a coachman singing sprightly verses, she was the cynosure of all eyes. Her success was enhanced by the fact that Octave Feuillet wrote the verses, while Viollet-le-Duc was stage-manager. Notwithstanding these frivolities, Princess Metternich always remained *grande dame*. After the fall of the Empire, on returning to Vienna, she took her legitimate place at court, where she soon gained the same social ascendancy that she had held for ten years in the French capital. A real patron of art and music, it was owing entirely to her influence, as is well known, that "Tannhäuser" was given in Paris in 1861, although it was a gigantic failure. The French not having aspired in those days to anything so complex as Wagner, it must be put down to her credit that she understood and appreciated him twenty years before they did.[1] Smetana's "Verkaufte Braut," given in London for the first time in 1907, was brought out in Vienna some years ago under the auspices of Princess Metternich.

In 1888 the Viennese wrote a couplet in her honor which runs:

> Es giebt nur a Kaiserstadt;
> Es giebt nur a Wien;
> Es giebt nur a Fürstin:
> Es is die Metternich Paulin.

The following letter, which I received from her *apropos* of the "Puppenfee," which I wanted to give in London, proves what a born stage-manager she was. Her directions are most clear and lucid, and show how great an interest she still takes in theatrical matters:

LETTER FROM PRINCESSE METTERNICH

VIENNE, le 8 Juin, 1891.

CHÈRE LADY RANDOLPH,

Je reçois à l'instant la lettre dans laquelle vous me faites part de votre désir de représenter la pantomime ballet "Puppenfee" pour une œuvre de charité mondaine. J'en suis très flattée car c'est nous qui en sommes les auteurs, la "Puppenfee" ayant été donnée pour la première fois chez nous à la campagne en Bohème. Je vais demander au maître de ballet de l'Opéra de m'envoyer le libretto avec toutes les indications voulues. Quant

[1] See "Les Femmes du Second Empire," by F. Loliee.

aux costumes rien de plus simple, car vous pouvez prendre tout ce que vous voulez. Il faudra seulement pour les pas seuls, avoir une Japonaise, une Espagnole, une Styrienne ou Tyrolienne, une Chinoise et un bébé, de ceux qui disent "Papa" et "Maman." Pour le reste, laissez libre cours à votre fantaisie. Le reveil des poupées s'opère au coup de minuit lorsque le magasin est fermé, et quand, reveillée par le sabbat, la marchande arrive, elle s'évanouit de frayeur, ayant été entrainée dans les rondes folles des poupées devenues vivantes. En revenant de son évanouissement elle trouve tout rentré en bon ordre, et les poupées sont redevenues immobiles. Alors la marchande s'avance vers la rampe et fait comprendre par gestes aux spectateurs qu'elle a été évidemment le jouet d'un rêve!

Le sujet est bien simple, comme vous voyez, et il n'a pas fallu beaucoup d'imagination pour le trouver!

Recevez, chère Lady Randolph, l'assurance de mes sentiments les meilleurs et les plus affectueux.

P. METTERNICH.

Foremost among the social lights of the Second Empire was Boson de Talleyrand Périgord—Prince de Sagan—now Duc de Talleyrand. With the Duc de Morny and the celebrated Count Gramont-Caderousse, he kept Paris society in a ferment of amazement and excitement. His name, his fêtes, and his extravagances were on all lips. When I first met the Prince after the war, in 1872, he must have been about forty-five. He was a remarkable-looking man, with snow-white, curly hair, which stood out like a lion's mane, and through which he had a habit of passing his fingers. With a well set-up figure, irreproachable clothes, a white carnation in his buttonhole, and an eye-glass to which was attached a black moiré ribbon which became the fashion, he was undoubtedly the ideal Parisian beau, *le dernier cri.* As such he was caricatured in the press and on the stage *ad infinitum.* A kindly man, he deserved a better fate than was meted out to him in his domestic circle, where his differences with the Princess were for many years public property. A descendant of the famous diplomat, the Marquis de Talleyrand, he was heir to a dukedom and vast estates in Germany as well as in France, where he owned the historical Château de Valançay on the Loire. Although he did not succeed to his estates until stricken in years and in health, he had already anticipated most of his inheritance, and had dissipated enormous sums.

He was the originator of the Auteuil race-course and the Cercle de la rue Royale. He was a patron of the drama, and many artists owed their success to his timely aid. If he had faults, he was, I fancy, as much sinned against as sinning. Struck down with an attack of paralysis, he was taken by the irony of fate to his wife's house, where he had not lived for many years and which he had sworn never to re-enter. He is still living there, the Princess having died a few years ago. Many a pleasant party did he organize for my sister and me. I also remember a picnic to St. Germain when, as Mr. James Gordon Bennett was driving us back on his coach, we came to grief near the Arc de Triomphe and were nearly killed. I used sometimes to ride with my father and the Prince in the Bois. Mounted on a seemingly fiery chestnut, I fancied myself vastly.

In the month of November, 1869, the Empress went to Egypt to open the Suez Canal; the Emperor for state reasons remained in France. The imperial progress

created the greatest enthusiasm. Her Majesty left Port
Saïd for Ismailia on board the *Aigle,* which had been
sumptuously fitted up for her; sixty vessels followed in
the wake. Cleopatra sailing up the "river of Cydnus" to
meet Mark Antony in all the color and glory of Eastern
pomp paled in comparison, while "for her own person"
Eugénie, like Cleopatra, "beggared all description."
The most lavish expenditure and extraordinary display
marked every step. All vied in doing honor to the brilliant and beautiful Empress who, imposing and serene,
was then poised—for a final moment, had she but known
it—at the summit of her fortune.

The late Duc d'Albe, her favorite nephew, was in her
suite, and related to me a few years ago the details of
this wonderful journey. The Empress, as she stepped
off the vessel on reaching Ismailia, found all the carriages awaiting her painted in the imperial colors, with
green and gold liveries and the gold bees; and even her
villa there was furnished in facsimile of her rooms
at the Tuileries, that she might feel "at home." I believe that the same compliment was paid to Queen Victoria when she and the Prince Consort visited the French
court in 1855 for the Exhibition.

Verdi composed "Aïda" for the opening of the Canal,
and in honor of the Empress, who was present at the first
performance in Cairo.

During her absence in Egypt, the Emperor gave what
was fated to be the last of his famous parties, or *séries* as
they were called, at Compiègne, at which Princesse Mathilde helped to do the honors. It was much smaller than
usual, on account of the Emperor's bad health and political worries. Among those invited were my mother and

sister. Hunting, shooting, and dancing were some of the amusements provided. There was a *grande chasse,* or stag hunt, on the first day, at which all the guests appeared, riding or driving. Those who hunted wore the royal colors, the men in green coats and the gold hunt buttons, the ladies in flowing green habits and three-cornered hats. The stag on this occasion was brought to bay in a lake, the Prince Imperial giving him the *coup de grâce.* At night there was a *curée aux flambeaux* in the courtyard of the château, the whole party assembling on the balconies in the glare of the innumerable torches. The carcass of the deer lay in the center, covered with its skin; the *hallali* was sounded; at a signal the hounds were unleashed, and in a moment every vestige of the stag had disappeared.

The next day an expedition was organized to see the Château de Pierrefonds, a distance of nine or ten miles: the party went in *chars-à-bancs* under the guidance of M. Viollet-le-Duc, the celebrated architect, who had just completed its restoration. Compiègne, where Joan of Arc was taken prisoner, and which was rebuilt by Louis XV and decorated by Napoleon I, seemed modern in comparison with this huge castle, with its battlemented walls and medieval arrangements.

After a tour of inspection under the guidance of Viollet-le-Duc, the day ended with tea in the beautiful armory of the castle from which the Emperor presented each lady with a souvenir in the shape of a small weapon.

One day there was a Cabinet Council, and the guests were exhorted to be discreet in their amusements and not disturb his Majesty. Who knows what fateful questions were discussed? Times were disquieting, and the

MRS. LEONARD JEROME, MOTHER OF
LADY RANDOLPH CHURCHILL

pourparlers going on with Prussia were anything but pleasant. The Government was in direct conflict with the Opposition. Maréchal Bazaine, who had come from Paris for this Council, had a few weeks previously made great military preparations for preventing the Opposition members from meeting to fix a date other than that settled by the Government for the assembling of the Chambers. The Emperor himself, anticipating trouble, had gone to Paris. Fortunately all passed off quietly, and the troops were not called out. But it gives one an idea of the volcano on which the Empire and the new Ollivier Ministry were living. At this visit to Compiègne Bazaine was accompanied by his wife, a Mexican lady, who created a sensation by appearing in a gown of vivid scarlet with gloves to match. This was thought *très Anglais,* as no one in France wore such brilliant colors.

Every night from sixty to a hundred guests sat down to dinner, the Emperor never permitting it to last more than three quarters of an hour. Sometimes magnificent gold plate adorned the table, sometimes precious *biscuit de Sèvres.* Before dinner the company assembled in two long lines. The Emperor took in Princesse Mathilde, sitting opposite her at the center of the table, a few seats of honor being reserved on each side, while the rest placed themselves as they wished, the ladies choosing the gentlemen to take them in, according to the custom of Compiègne. After dinner there was dancing, in which the Prince Imperial, then only thirteen, was allowed to join till ten o'clock, when his tutor would approach him, saying, *"Monseigneur, votre chapeau,"* which meant going to bed. At the close of the visit there was a grand lottery in which all tickets were prizes. The Emperor

2

stood near two great urns from which the numbers were drawn, and as each guest received one he wished him *"Bonne chance."* Some little juggling must have gone on, for my mother and the American minister, Mr. Washburne, won valuable pieces of Sèvres china, whereas the presents for the younger people were less costly. My sister, much to my envy, was given an inkstand shaped like a knotted handkerchief filled with napoleons, upon which the Emperor remarked, *"Mademoiselle, n'oubliez pas les Napoléons!"*

CHAPTER II

IN the spring of 1870 Paris was full of unrest and rumors of war. Prussia on several occasions had been more than aggressive and had heaped insults on France. Prévost Paradol, the brilliant journalist and writer, whose daughter was a playfellow of mine, described the two countries as "running on the same lines, collision being inevitable." It was said that the Emperor was credulous and that Bismarck was unscrupulous; the latter wanted war, and what he wished generally happened. In Prussia also disturbing rumors had been rife for some time; as an instance of this a story is told of General Blumenthal shooting in Norfolk in 1869 with Lord Albemarle, who remarked that he would like to see the Prussian manœuvers. "It is not necessary to come to Prussia," said the General; "we will have a review for you in the Champ-de-Mars."

The Hohenzollern incident was the last straw, and it provoked France beyond endurance. Prince Leopold of Hohenzollern, a tool of Bismarck, became a candidate for the throne of Spain. It was looked upon as *"une sanglante injure pour l'Empereur Napoléon."* Excited by the press, the whole country clamored for war. According to history, peace might have been maintained had it not been for the rashness and violence of the Duc

25

de Gramont, then Minister for Foreign Affairs, and the ineptitude and blunders of M. Emile Ollivier, whose famous phrase, that he took upon himself and his colleagues the responsibility of the war *d'un cœur léger,* will ever be associated with his memory. Conciliation having been rendered impossible, on the 19th of July, 1870, war was declared, to the sorrow of the Emperor, who, very ill at the time and on the eve of a serious operation, had done all he could to avert it. I shall never forget the excitement. Crowds paraded the streets with cries of *"A Berlin!"* The war, the war—there was no other topic. Utter strangers would stop to discuss the situation. The confidence in the generals and the army was immense. It was to be one long but straight march to Berlin; not a soul doubted it. Of course our sympathies were French, and I felt that I hated *"Ces sâles Prussiens"* as much as did any of the inhabitants of the doomed city.

Exciting incidents crowded on us. One day we saw Capoul the celebrated tenor, and Marie Sass of the Opêra, on being recognized in an omnibus, made to stand on the top and sing the "Marseillaise," an ever-growing crowd joining in the chorus. One night we went to the opera in walking dresses, with our hats in our hands, in case there was any trouble and we might have to walk home, which proved to be the case. It was a strange performance, as the singers were constantly being interrupted and made to sing patriotic songs. We found the greatest difficulty in getting home, owing to the streets being filled with huge crowds marching to the cry of *"des chassepots, des chassepots."* Poor fellows, they soon had them, and all the fighting they wanted.

26

July and August were anxious months for us. With keen interest we followed with maps and flags the incidents of the war. One day the Emperor was leaving Paris for Metz to join his army of 380,000 men, which, to his dismay, proved to muster only 220,000 badly equipped troops. Another day came; it was the details of Saarbrück and the *baptême de feu* of the Prince Imperial; or, again, of Maréchal Lebœuf's resignation and Maréchal Bazaine being made Generalissimo, which, according to M. Barthélemy Saint-Hilaire, would give confidence to the country. But, alas! news of fresh defeats was continuous; the rapidity with which disaster after disaster befell the French army seemed incredible.

Soon our maps of France were bristling with the hated Prussian flag, and one heard nothing but cries of *"Nous sommes trahis."* On one or two occasions great victories were bruited about; in the twinkling of an eye the whole city would be decorated, flags flying from every window, and signs of rejoicing everywhere, only to be taken in a few hours later, and blinds pulled down, as the truth filtered out, and the glorious victory became a ghastly defeat, such as Weissemburg, Wörth, or Gravelotte, with more cries of betrayal from the bewildered Parisians.

As the war advanced, all the foreigners who could leave Paris departed. We were advised to go, but unfortunately my mother was laid up with a very severe sprain, and could not put her foot to the ground, and so we tarried. Besides, we were incredulous of the Prussians ever reaching Paris, and every day we put off our departure. Our house became the rendezvous of the few of our French friends who had not gone to the front.

27

Our principal visitor was the Duc de Persigny, who, with his family, had been on intimate relations with us for some years. Persigny, a short, dapper-looking little man with a piercing eye and a pleasant manner, was Louis Napoleon's bosom friend and companion, Victor Fialin. He shared his fortunes at Strasburg in 1836 and at Boulogne in 1840. Imprisoned for a time at Doullens, when released he took an important part in the Coup d'État. He reaped the benefit of his devotion to the Bonapartist cause when Louis Napoleon became Emperor. His Majesty, when describing his Ministry one day, said laughingly: "How can you expect my government to get on? The Empress is a Legitimist; Morny is an Orleanist; Prince Napoleon is a Republican; I am a Socialist—only Persigny is an Imperialist, and he is mad!" When later on Persigny was made a duke, he married the daughter of the Prince de la Moskowa, whose maternal grandfather had been the famous Maréchal Ney.

The Duchesse de Persigny was, to say the least of it, eccentric, and many were the stories related of her while her husband was Ambassador to England, somewhere in the sixties. Her unpunctuality was notorious. One evening there was an official dinner at the Embassy for the Lord Mayor. The guests, who had been waiting some time for her appearance, were told that "Her Grace was in her bath," and presently she appeared with her beautiful, fair hair (of which she was very proud) still wet and hanging down her back. *"Pardonnez moi, mes amis,"* she exclaimed with her slight stammer, *"c'est cet imbécile de Persigny qui ne m'a pas fait dire l'heure."* The Duchess's temper was somewhat quick, on one occa-

DUC DE PERSIGNY

sion, at a children's dance in Paris, I have a vivid recollection of her boxing my ears because I could not dance the mazurka.

She was a great Anglomaniac, and Chamarande, their country place, was entirely furnished after the English fashion, and as in those days the taste was early Victorian it was not attractive. Several rooms were copied from Balmoral, and rejoiced in tartan curtains and carpets, at which the art-loving Frenchmen opened their eyes. On the other hand, bedrooms, with their English writing-tables and comfortable arm-chairs, were a revelation of what such rooms should be.

In August, 1870, the Empress—who had been made Regent and was living at St.-Cloud—was often visited by M. de Persigny, who brought us all the latest news which grew more and more ominous until one day he rushed in crying, *"Tout est perdu; les Prussiens sont à nos portes!"* and imploring us to fly, otherwise it would be too late. With much difficulty and discomfort and many heartburnings we prepared to depart and go to Deauville.

Trains were running most irregularly and were few and far between. As it turned out, the one we elected to go by was the last to leave. No luggage was allowed us but what we could carry. A few clothes were tied up in sheets and table-cloths, and so we left. My mother had to be carried, as she was too lame to walk.

While at Deauville a friend of ours, M. de Gardonne, called on us unexpectedly at the hotel and asked if he might spend the day in our rooms—in fact, hide there. He begged that on no account were we to mention his name or let any one know we had seen him. Naturally

31

we thought this very strange, and my mother grew suspicious; but he impressed upon us that it was for "state reasons," of which we should hear later. After dinner, when it was quite dark, he departed as mysteriously as he had come. Two days later we were thrilled to hear of the Empress's escape from Paris, accompanied by Dr. Crane, Dr. Evans (the American dentist), and Madame Lebreton, our friend M. de Gardonne having helped to make the arrangements. The Empress came to Deauville unknown to all, went on board Sir John Burgoyne's yacht, which had been lying in the harbor, and after a rough crossing landed at Ryde in the Isle of Wight. The perils of this flight, less hazardous and certainly more successful than the flight of Varennes, have been greatly exaggerated.

Meanwhile the Emperor, after Bazaine's defeat at Gravelotte and other disasters, repaired to Sedan, where, after the battle, on his own authority, he raised the flag of truce. According to his posthumous memoirs, Napoleon III "understood the gravity of the responsibility which he was incurring and foresaw the accusations that would be raised against him." As an example of these, the letter on the following page, which I have in my possession from General Palikao, his late Minister of War, is of interest.

The Comte de Palikao, formerly General Moutauban, took part in the 1860 expedition to China. He was said to have acquired his title (the name Palikao being derived from a town in China) from the fact that he had presented the Empress Eugénie with some splendid black pearls, looted during the sack of the Summer Palace in Peking.

LADY RANDOLPH CHURCHILL

OSTENDE, le 21 Octobre, 1870.

MON CHER DUC,

Je suis arrivé à Ostende depuis quatre jours, et j'y ai trouvé votre addresse chez nos amis communs les Dureau.

Depuis notre séparation le 7ème, je suis en Belgique et je vous aurais demandé de vos nouvelles depuis cette époque si j'avais su où vous envoyer une lettre. Je saisis donc avec empressement l'occasion qui m'est offerte par la rencontre de cet excellent préfet d'Orleans, pour venir causer quelques instants avec vous.

Menacé le jour du 4 Septembre dans ma liberté, j'ai quitté le même soir, et je suis venu me réfugier d'abord à Namur où j'ai été rejoint par ma femme et mes filles 24 heures après mon départ.

Le but principal de mon voyage à Namur était de me rapprocher de Sedan, pour savoir le sort de mon fils qui me donnait de vives préoccupations. Après plusieurs jours de recherches j'ai fini par savoir que mon fils, après avoir été blessé à Sedan, et avoir eu un cheval tué, était prisonnier à Cologne, n'ayant pas voulu accepter pour son compte la capitulation.

J'ai quitté Nemours pour Spa; ce dernier séjour n'étant plus habitable pendant l'hiver, je suis venu me fixer à Ostende pour attendre les évènements dont je ne puis prévoir l'issue.

Combien je voudrais, mon cher Duc, avoir une plume assez habile pour vous retracer toutes les impressions par lesquelles j'ai passé depuis ce fatal Sedan. Je suis venu à me demander comment un pareil désastre a pu se produire, sans que le principal auteur de ce lugubre drame ne se soit pas enseveli sous les cadavres de son armée!

Je croyais qu'il était plus facile de mourir que de se déshonorer. . . .

La mort de l'Empereur à Sedan sauvait et la France et son fils, la capitulation a tout perdu.

33

Aujourd'hui que la France est devenue la proie des Vandales étrangères et de l'intérieur, comment pourra se terminer cette désolation de notre malheureux pays!—à moins d'une guerre générale, qui devrais apporter une diversion dans la politique prussienne, je ne vois pas de quel côté nous pourrons nous tourner. L'Angleterre parait nous avoir abandonnée, et cependant les circonstances qui avaient cimentées notre alliance de 1856, peuvent se reproduire pour Elle, mais alors elle ne pourra plus compter sur notre concours. Nous sommes tombés bien bas!

J'avais offert mes services au gouvernement de la défense nationale mais j'ai retiré mes offres dès que j'ai vu le gouvernement appeler, à la honte éternelle de la France, un Garibaldi pour la défendre.

D'un autre côté les accusations de trahison atteignent tous les généraux qui ont servi l'Empire, je n'ai pas voulu mêler mon nom à toutes ces ignominies.

Adieu, mon cher Duc, si vous voulez me donner de vos nouvelles, ma famille et moi nous en serons bien heureux . . . car nous avons tous la reconnaissance du coeur.

Tout à vous,

GENERAL DE PALIKAO.

In view of this somewhat cruel letter, I cannot refrain from quoting General Changarnier, who, although at one time hostile to the Emperor, spoke of him thus: . . . "And he has been called 'Coward'! When I remember that this man, tortured by a horrible disease, remained on horseback at Sedan an entire day, watching disappear the prestige of France, his throne, his dynasty, and all the glory reaped at Sebastopol and in Lombardy, I cannot control myself."

And again, Colonel Fabre says: "The Emperor remained passively for two hours under the fire of shells, seeing many of his officers killed round him, before he reëntered Sedan."

In October, not being able to return to Paris, we migrated to England, which I now saw for the first time. A winter spent in the· gloom and fogs of London did not tend to dispel the melancholy which we felt. Our friends scattered, fighting, or killed at the front; debarred as we were from our bright little house and our household gods, it was indeed a sad time.

Among the refugees who came to London was the Duc de Persigny. Broken-hearted, ill, and penniless, our poor friend was put to many straits to eke out a living, selling his plate and the little he had been able to bring away with him. His devotion to Napoleon III never altered, although the Emperor was often irritated with him and evidently, from the following letter, thought he interfered indiscreetly:

WILHELMSHÖHE, le 7 Janvier, 1871.

MON CHER PERSIGNY,

J'ai reçu votre lettre du 1 Janvier, et je vous remerçie des vœux que vous faîtes pour un meilleur avenir. Sans vouloir entrer dans la discussion des idées que vous émettez, je vous dirai que rien de bon ne peut sortir de cette confusion qui résulte d'efforts individuels, faits sans discretion et sans autorisation. Je trouve en effet singulier qu'on s'occupe de l'avenir de mon fils sans se préoccuper de mes intentions.

Je sais que vous avez écrit à M. de Bismarck qui m'a naturellement fait demander si cela était avec mon autorisation et comme étant d'accord avec moi. Je lui ai fait répondre que je n'avais autorisé personne à s'occuper de mes intérêts et de ceux de mon fils sans mon consentement.

Croyez, mon cher Persigny, à mon amitié,

NAPOLEON.

The letter was written from Wilhelmshöhe and given to me by M. de Persigny as an autograph of the Emperor, the Duke adding at the same time that it compromised no one but himself.

There is good reason to believe that the letter referred to a scheme for placing the Prince Imperial on the throne during the Emperor's captivity, with the Empress as Regent.

Persigny died in 1872, preceding by one year his imperial master.

That autumn and winter (1870–71) London society was much entertained and a little scandalized by the doings and sayings of two pretty and lively refugees from Paris. The Duchesse de Carracciolo and the Comtesse de Béchevet, with their respective husbands and a few Frenchmen who preferred shooting birds in England to being shot at in France, took a place in the country. Many were the stories told of practical jokes and unorthodox sporting incidents, the ladies astonishing the country yokels by shooting in kilts and smoking cigarettes, a thing unheard of in those days. All London laughed at the misfortunes of M. de Béchevet, who, being ill, was persuaded by one of the guests, admirably disguised as a doctor, that he was dying. Another guest, travestied as a priest, received his last confession, which was eagerly listened to by the rest of the party, hidden behind curtains, their peals of laughter resuscitating the dying man.

While we were in London, and during the siege, my father, who had just arrived from America, arranged to go to Paris with General Sheridan. They got permission to see Mr. Washburne, the American Minister, who had been through the whole siege. They were blindfolded and taken through the Prussian lines, and a few days later saw the great columns of the victorious army roll down the Champs-Elysées. My father on his return gave me a graphic description of the triumphal entry and of the vivid scene impressed on him—how the masses of infantry, most of them wearing spectacles, marched by the Arc de Triomphe, which was barricaded, and through the deserted streets of the once gay city singing "Die Wacht am Rhein." Many were the stories of individual suffering and despair, of hair-breadth escapes and brave deeds, told him by the besieged.

That summer I paid a first visit to Cowes. In those days it was delightfully small and peaceful. No glorified villas, no esplanade or pier, no bands or "nigger minstrels," no motors or crowded tourist steamers—"no nothing," as the children say. The Royal Yacht Squadron Club lawn did not resemble a perpetual garden party, or the roadstead a perpetual regatta. Yachts went in and out without fear of losing their moorings, and most of them belonged to the Royal Yacht Squadron. People all seemed to know one another. The Prince and Princess of Wales and many foreign royalties could walk about and amuse themselves without being photographed or mobbed, and many were the gay little expeditions to Shanklin Bay, Freshwater, or Beau-lieu, where they threw off all ceremony and enjoyed themselves like ordinary mortals.

Ever since those early days Cowes has always had so great an attraction for me that, notwithstanding its gradual deterioration, I have rarely missed a yearly visit. My first ball in 1873 was at the Royal Yacht Squadron Castle, an entertainment long since abandoned, but then an annual event during the Cowes regatta week. It was there that I had the honor of being presented to the present King and Queen, and made the acquaintance of Lord Randolph Churchill.

In August, 1871, the Emperor Napoleon III and the Empress Eugénie, who were living at Camden House, Chiselhurst, came to Cowes on a short visit. One day a gentleman called, but finding us out, left a card saying he would come again. "Le Comte de Pierrefonds"— who could it be? We asked the Empress's private secretary, M. Pietri. *"Mais c'est l'Empereur,"* he said laughing. Shortly afterward we were asked by their Majesties to go for an expedition round the Island. The party consisted of the Emperor and Empress, the Prince Imperial, the Empress's nieces the Mesdemoiselles d'Albe (afterwards Duchesse de Medina Coeli and Marquise de Tamamis), and Prince Joachim Murat, the Duc d'Albe (Carlos), a few Spaniards, and the suite, which was composed of one or two faithful followers. The expedition was rather a failure, owing to the roughness of the sea, most of the party seeking "the seclusion that the cabin grants." The Mesdemoiselles d'Albe were desperately ill, and lay on the deck in a state of coma. But the Empress enjoyed the breeze. The Prince Imperial, full of life and spirits, chaffed every

38

one, some of his jokes falling rather flat on the Spaniards, who were feeling anything but bright, and evidently thought it no laughing matter. I can see now the Emperor leaning against the mast, looking old, ill, and sad. His thoughts could not have been other than sorrowful, and even in my young eyes he seemed to have nothing to live for.

AFTER two years' absence (having left for two weeks, as we thought at the time), we returned to Paris, to find our house, goods, and chattels intact, with the exception of the cellar, which had been visited by a shell from Mont Valérien. But what changes in Paris itself! Ruins everywhere: the sight of the Tuileries and the Hôtel de Ville made me cry. St.-Cloud, the scene of many pleasant expeditions, was a thing of the past, the lovely château razed to the ground. And if material Paris was damaged, the social fabric was even more so. In vain we tried to pick up the threads. Some of our friends were killed, others ruined or in mourning, and all broken-hearted and miserable, hiding in their houses and refusing to be comforted.

The statues at the Place de la Concorde representing the most important towns of France,—Strasburg, Lille, Nancy, Orléans,—swathed in crape, in which some are still draped on the anniversary of Sedan, reminded one daily, if one had needed it, of the trials and tribulations France had just gone through. Only the embassies and a few foreigners, principally Americans, received or entertained. The Misses King (one of them became Madame Waddington, wife of the Ambassador to England) gave small parties. Mrs. John Munroe, the wife of the

American banker, also gave dances for her daughters, who eventually married, one Mr. Ridgeway, well known in Paris and the hero of Bourget's "M. Cazal," the other Baron Hottingue. A few opened their houses, but the French on the whole were shy of going out at all, and if Paris had any gaiety left in those days, it was owing to her cosmopolitan character. As time has gone on, with the fall of the Empire and the advent of the Republic, society in Paris has become a thing of the past. Broken up into small coteries and cliques, each, a law unto itself, thinks the others beneath contempt. The old nobility, which was beginning to get accustomed to the Empire, and was peeping shyly out of its faubourg, has retired into it more pertinaciously than ever. Where there is no recognized head or "fount of honor," so to speak, there can be no recognized grades, and with the exception of a small group, Paris society in the present day, as compared with the past, is like a ship without a rudder.

Among our compatriots who were more or less settled in Paris, our greatest friends were perhaps the Forbeses of New York. Two of the daughters eventually married Frenchmen, one the Duc de Praslin, head of the house of Choiseul, and the other M. Odilon Barrot, son of Louis Philippe's Minister.

My sister and I and Countess Hatzfeldt were once invited by the Duc de Praslin to visit his beautiful Château of Vaux-Praslin. Our host took us all over the huge building, pointing out everything of historical interest, until we came to an ornamented door, before which he paused, but did not enter. *"La chambre du feu Duc de Praslin,"* he said in a grim voice, and then passed on. This was the room of the late Duke his father, who

LEONARD JEROME

had murdered his wife, a deed which filled the civilized world with horror, and which undoubtedly precipitated the revolution of 1848. The Duchess's unfounded jealousy of their French governess drove the Duke to this terrible act. On our way home we discussed the details with bated breath—how the Duchess had first been stabbed, then smothered under the canopy of the bed, which the Duke pulled down on her; how the Duke was tried by his peers and sentenced to death, but the night before the execution was found dead in his cell, friends having smuggled in poison to him. It was averred, later, that the story of his death was not true, and that in reality he had escaped and lived in exile for many years. At the trial the French governess pleaded her own cause so eloquently, that she left the court without the slightest aspersion on her character. She went to America and married the Rev. Henry M. Field, brother of Cyrus W. Field of Atlantic Cable fame. By the way, the first time the cable was laid by the *Great Eastern* it broke in mid-ocean, and my father, who was much interested in the scheme, lent his steam-yacht the *Clara Clarita* which went out and recovered it. The yacht was afterward sold to the Government. I remember well being taken, as a great treat, on the yacht on its trial trip, and my poor mother's face of dismay at the fittings of pale blue velvet and silver! My father, in his extravagant manner, had left it all to the upholsterer.

In the autumn of 1873, I recollect going to Bazaine's trial at Versailles. A long, low room filled to suffocation with a curious crowd, many of whom were women, a raised platform, a table covered with green baize and holding a bottle of water, a few chairs ar-

3

ranged in semicircles, completed the *mise-en-scène,* which seemed rather a poor one for the trial for life or death of a Marshal of France. The Duc d'Aumale, who was president, having seated himself at the table, Bazaine was brought in. All eyes turned on him, and some of the women jumped on their chairs, leveling their opera-glasses at the unfortunate man. This was promptly put a stop to by the gendarmes present, who pulled the offenders down unceremoniously by their skirts. *"Fi donc!"* I heard a gendarme say, *"c'est pas gentil";* nor was it.

Bazaine sat impassive even while Maître Lachaud, his advocate, making a curious defense at one moment pointed with a dramatic gesture to the accused, exclaiming *"Mais, regardez-le donc! Ce n'est pas un traitre, c'est un imbécile!"*

How the mighty had fallen! I thought of him and his wife in the glittering throng of Compiègne only three years before, and of him again as commander-in-chief of a huge army, which now he was supposed to have betrayed and sold. I say supposed, for although he was found guilty and condemned to death (which was commuted to twenty years' imprisonment) there were many who believed in him and thought him a hero. His permitted escape on the 9th of August, 1874, from the Ile Ste. Marguerite had the elements of the grotesque about it, and if he was a martyr, I doubt if posterity will place a halo round his head.

CHAPTER III

MARRIAGE AND LONDON LIFE

"THE course of true love never runs smooth," as we all know, and my engagement to Lord Randolph Churchill was no exception to the rule. The Duke of Marlborough, my prospective father-in-law, would not consent to our marriage until Randolph had got into Parliament. Moreover, the wish to test the stability of our affections may not improbably have lurked in the recesses of the Duke's mind, for I am bound to admit that we had arrived at our momentous decision without much delay.

During the year of our engagement, I remained with my family in Paris and had to content myself with flying visits from my *fiancé,* with whom, however, I kept up an animated correspondence. He tried to initiate me in the mysteries of English politics, of which I was at that time in blissful ignorance. I looked forward greatly to the impending General Election, which, apart from the dignity Randolph was to acquire by becoming a member of Parliament, meant the end of our long probation.

In one of Randolph's letters of that date (1874), he says in speaking of Mr. Disraeli, for whom he had a profound admiration:

I advise you to get a copy of to-day's "Times" if you can, and read Disraeli's great speech. He has made a magnificent one to the Conservatives of Glasgow . . . it is a fine specimen of perfect English oratory.

I remember in our letters a great controversy on my having used the word "prorogued" in a wrong sense, *apropos* of Bazaine's trial. Much to Randolph's indignation, I had quoted in my defense the opinion of the Comte de Fénelon, a young Frenchman of our acquaintance whom I thought in virtue of his descent, a good authority. From Blenheim, Randolph writes:

. . . Hang *le petit Fénelon* . . . little idiot! What do I care for him—He may be a very good authority about his own beastly language but I cannot for a moment submit to him about English. Whether you use the word prorogation as a French or an English one I don't know. In the former case, as the word is a Latin one and as there can be no doubt as to its meaning, I apprehend you are wrong, but still would not attempt to lay down the law to you on the meaning of any French word. If you use it as an English word you are undoubtedly not only using an inaccurate expression, but a meaningless and unintelligible one. To prorogue, means to suspend something for a definite time to be resumed again in exactly the same state, condition, and circumstances. Therefore to talk about proroguing the Marshal's powers, would mean that they were to be suspended for a certain time and then resumed again exactly as before. Parliament is prorogued, *L'Assemblée* is prorogued; that does not in the least mean that the powers of either are lengthened or increased in any way but that they are temporarily suspended. Whatever words the French papers may use, I have never seen any English paper use the word in any other sense, and in any other sense it cannot possibly be used.

46

LORD RANDOLPH CHURCHILL IN 1874

And in a further letter he ends:

I am looking forward particularly to utterly suppressing and crushing *le petit Fénelon*. We must really tho' drop this argument when I am with you, as it is likely to become a heated one, I fear. We will therefore "prorogue" it.

IMMEDIATELY after my marriage in April, 1874, I settled in London, to enjoy my first season with all the vigor and unjaded appetite of youth. After the comparatively quiet life of Paris, we seemed to live in a whirl of gaieties and excitement. Many were the delightful balls I went to, which, unlike those of the present day, invariably lasted till five o'clock in the morning. Masked balls were much the vogue. Holland House, with its wonderful historical associations and beautiful gardens, was a fitting frame for such entertainments, and I remember enjoying myself immensely at one given there. Disguised in a painted mask and a yellow wig, I mystified every one. My sister who was staying with us, had been walking in the garden with young Lord ——, who was a *parti* and much run after by designing mothers with marriageable daughters. Introducing him to me, she pretended I was her mother. Later in the evening I attacked him, saying that my daughter had just confided to me that he had proposed to her, and that she had accepted him. To this day I can see his face of horror and bewilderment. Vehemently he assured me that it was not so. But I kept up the farce, declaring that my husband would call on him next day and reveal our identity, and that meanwhile I should consider him engaged to my charming daughter. Deficient in humor and not overburdened with brains, he could not take the joke, and left the house a miserable man.

Generally speaking, there is no doubt that English people are dull-witted at a masked ball, and do not understand or enter into the spirit of intrigue which is all-important on such occasions. One reason may be that both sexes are masked in England—whereas abroad this is not the practice, nor would it be understood. The license a man might take if his identity were to remain unknown would never be tolerated. Besides, it stands to reason that unless one of the two remains unmasked there cannot be much mystifying. Some women refuse to say anything but "Yes" and "No" in a falsetto voice, and think they have had a glorious time as long as their identity is not discovered. "You don't know me. You don't know me," was the parrot cry of one lady. "And I don't want to," said Lord Charles Beresford, fleeing from her, "if you 've nothing else to say."

Another masked ball was given by M. and Mme. de Santurce, the head of the Murietta family. They had a charming house in Kensington, like many others long since closed. Madame de Santurce, a beautiful woman of the Spanish type, was very popular, and entertained lavishly at Wadhurst, their country place in Sussex. Some years later, being there with Randolph, an amusing incident occurred at which we all laughed heartily. Thought-reading was the fashionable amusement of the moment, and one evening Lady de Clifford, a very pretty and attractive woman, insisted on making Randolph, who was reading peacefully in a corner, join in the game. Having duly blindfolded him, she led him into the middle of the room and made various passes with her hands, saying, "Don't resist any thought which comes into your head; do exactly what you feel like doing. *I* am willing you." Without a moment's hesitation Randolph threw his arms round the lady, and embraced her before the whole company. To her cries and indignant remonstrances he merely replied, "You told me to do what I felt like doing—so I did."

The London season of thirty years ago was far more prolonged and its glories more apparent than they are now. It was looked upon as a very serious matter which no self-respecting persons who considered themselves "in society" would forego, nor of which a votary of fashion would willingly miss a week or a day. The winter session which usually assembled in February, as it does now, and sat for six weeks, brought to London the legislators and their families; but from October to February the town was a desert. Religiously, however, on the first of May, Belgravia—the Belgravia described by Lord Beaconsfield—would open the doors of its freshly painted and flower-bedecked mansions. Dinners, balls, and parties succeeded one another without intermission till the end of July, the only respite being at the Whitsuntide recess. A few of the racing people might go to Newmarket for a week, but the fashionable world flocked only to the classic races—the Derby, Ascot, and Goodwood.

Parties were arranged for Hurlingham to see the pigeon-shooting, or for the fashionable flower-shows then held at the Botanical Gardens, or again to Wimbledon to see the shooting for the Elcho Shield, which in those days was a feature of the London season. To be

Commandant of the Camp was a coveted post, and I remember Lord and Lady Wharncliffe living in large tents and entertaining for a whole fortnight in the most sumptuous manner. We used to drive down on coaches in Ascot frocks and feathered hats, and stay to dinner, driving back by moonlight.

Chiswick House, which was let at that time by the late Duke of Devonshire to the Prince and Princess of Wales, was the scene of many garden-parties and dinners. One night we dined there to meet two Russian Grand Dukes. My elder sister, who had arrived from Paris and was staying with us, was also invited. We were pressed to play the waltzes of Waldteufel, whose lovely music was only just beginning to be known in England, although he had for years been band-master at the Tuileries. When the royalties were departing the company stood on both sides of the hall, the Prince and Princess of Wales gracefully bowing and saying a few words to each guest as was their wont. The Russian Grand Dukes, on the other hand, marched out without so much as a look or a bow to the courtesying ladies. This was very much commented on and murmurs of "Cossacks!" and *"Grattez le Russe,"* were heard on all sides.

The French Embassy was a great feature of that season. Sosthènes de La Rochefoucauld, Duc de Bisaccia, had been appointed Ambassador to London, and he and his wife (Princesse Marie de Ligne) were immensely liked, the prestige of his great name adding luster to the importance of his post. Their dinners and balls were most sumptuous, everything being done on a princely scale. On state occasions their gala coach vied

in splendor with the finest English equipages, the purple
and red liveries of the La Rochefoucauld family having
rarely seen the light of day since the reign of Louis
XVIII. Much to every one's regret the Duke was re-
called after a few months. Appointed by Marshal
MacMahon, he so far forgot that he was Ambassador of
the Republic as to make a speech in the Chamber during
a week's leave in Paris, in which he warmly advocated
the reëstablishment of the Monarchy!

I think the sight which impressed me the most was
Rotten Row, the wonder and admiration of foreigners,
whose Prater, Pincio, Unter den Linden, or Allée des
Acacias, were but a faint copy. Its glories are, alas! a
thing of the past. In 1874, between the hours of twelve
and two, the Park was still the most frequented place
in London, the fashionable world congregating there to
ride, drive, or walk. It was a brilliant and animated
scene which filled the foreigner with admiration and
envy, no capital in Europe being able to compete with it.

The claim to the finest horsemanship in the world has
with justice been awarded to English men and women.
Mounted on thoroughbred hacks, the ladies wore close-
fitting braided habits, which showed off their slim figures
to advantage. The men, irreproachably attired in frock-
coats, pearl-gray trousers, and varnished boots, wore the
inevitable tall hat, a great contrast to the negligé Rough
Rider appearance of the present day, when all elegance
is proscribed in favor of comfort. For two hours a
smartly dressed crowd jostled one another, walking
slowly up and down on each side of the Row. Well-ap-
pointed vehicles of all kinds made the Park look gay,
from the four-in-hand coach and pony-carriage to the

now obsolete tilbury, with its tiny groom clinging like a limpet behind. In the afternoon the stately barouche made its appearance, with high-stepping horses, be-wigged coachmen, and powdered footmen in gorgeous livery. A few of these still survive, but formerly they were the rule rather than the exception. One day much excitement was caused by the sight of a man galloping furiously up and down in pursuit, so it seemed, of the Heir Apparent. It was found out afterward that he had no nefarious intentions, but unfortunately he went a little too close, and cannoning against the royal person-age, knocked him over. This incident gave rise to an amusing popular song called "The Galloping Snob of Rotten Row."

Up to 1834 carriages were allowed in the Row, but now its tanned roadway is kept entirely for riders. The Duke of St. Albans, Hereditary Grand Falconer, how-ever, has the privilege of driving through the Row if he chooses. This reminds me of a story told of Lord Charles Beresford, who accepted the wagers of some friends that he would drive up the Row without being molested by the police. But on the day fixed for the experiment, the friends, who had repaired thither *en masse,* looked in vain for him until in the much-abused driver of a water-cart, which was careering up and down splashing every one, they spied the laughing counte-nance of the triumphant Lord Charles.

It may not be generally known that what is now called Rotten Row was in old days termed "The King's Old Road" and "The King's New Road," Rotten Row being probably derived from "Route du Roi." For more than two centuries Hyde Park has been a rendezvous for exercise and social intercourse. Pepys says in his gossipy diary: "April 30th, 1661. I am sorry that I am not at London, to be at Hide-Parke to-morrow, among the great gallants and ladies, which will be fine." And again: "April 16th, 1664. To Hide-Parke, where I had not been since last year; where I saw the King with his periwigs, but not altered at all; my Lady Castlemaine in a coach by herself, in yellow satin and a pinner on; and many brave persons. And myself being in a hackney and full of people, was ashamed to be seen by the world, many of them knowing me." And again: "March 19th, 1665. Mr. Povy and I in his coach to Hide-Parke, being the first day of the tour there. Where many brave ladies, among others, Castlemaine, lay impudently upon her back, in her coach, asleep, with her mouth open."

Having been brought up in France, I was accustomed to the restrictions and chaperonage to which young girls had to submit, but I confess to thinking that as a married woman I should be able to emancipate myself entirely. In matters of propriety, however, London was much more strict and conventional than it is now. A lady never traveled alone without taking her maid with her in the railway carriage. To go by oneself in a hansom was thought very "fast"—not to speak of walking, which could be permitted only in quiet squares or streets. As for young girls driving anywhere by themselves, such a thing was unheard of.

Etiquette and the amenities of social life were thought much more of than they are now. The writing of ceremonious notes, the leaving of cards, not to speak of *visites de digestion,* which even young men were supposed to pay, took up most afternoons. There was little or none of that extraordinary restlessness and craving for something new which is a feature of to-day, necessarily causing manners to deteriorate, and certainly curtailing the amenities of social life on which past generations set such store. A nod replaces the ceremonious bow, a familiar hand-shake the elaborate courtesy. The carefully-worded beautifully-written invitation of thirty years ago is dropped in favor of a garbled telephone message, such as "Will Mrs. S. dine with Lady T. and bring a man, and if she can't find one she must n't come, as it would make them thirteen"; or a message to a Club, "Will Mr. G. dine with Lady T. to-night? If no, will he look in the card-room and see if any of her lot are there, and suggest somebody." Life, however, seemed to be as full as it is now, although people did not try to press into one day the duties and pleasures of a week, finishing none and enjoying none. The motor and the telephone were unknown, and the receipt of the shilling telegram was still unusual enough to cause feelings of apprehension. There was none of that easy tolerance and familiarity which is undoubtedly fostered by the daily, not to say hourly, touch and communication of modern society.

The strict observance of Sunday filled me with awe and amazement. I had lived most of my life in Paris, where everything gay and bright was reserved for that day, and could not understand the voluntary, nay, deliberate gloom and depression in which every one indulged. There was then no Queen's Hall to while away a wet afternoon and improve one's knowledge of good music. The fashion of going to the country for the week-end

LADY RANDOLPH CHURCHILL.

was not known, whereas now motors have made the country so accessible that the eyes of all sensible people are open to the folly of wasting days when not obliged in a hot, evil-smelling and noisy metropolis.

Innumerable are the country-house parties with golf, lawn-tennis and the river to amuse and keep one out of doors. Mothers with broods of marriageable daughters find this kind of entertainment a better market to take them to than the heated atmosphere of the ball-room, which the desirable *partis* shun for the greater attraction of air and exercise.

Gardening, too, has become a craze. The lovely gardens which formerly were left by their owners to bloom unseen are now sought after, and reveled in. Every one aspires to be a Miss Jekyll or a Mrs. Boyd, and the rival merits of Japanese, Friendship or Rock Gardens form a favorite subject of discussion.

It was not until well on in the eighties that people began to give dinner parties on Sundays. Very few had out their carriages, and as Randolph objected to the practice our modest brougham was replaced by the common cab.

On one occasion we dined at Marlborough House. As it was a very hot night in July, and the party a small one, the Prince of Wales accompanied his departing guests to the door. At that moment a footman in stentorian tones announced, "Lady Randolph Churchill's carriage stops the way," whereupon a decrepit Rosinante, dragging the most dilapidated of four-wheelers, well filled with straw, crawled up to the door. As I prepared to get in, our royal host chaffingly remarked that my conscience was better than my carriage.

Not to be outdone, I retorted: "Is it not, Sir, the Queen's carriage? How can I have a better?" [1]

Speaking of cabs reminds me that it was always said that the late Lord and Lady Salisbury, who were not given an adequate allowance in the early years of their marriage, and who, as every one knows, increased their income by the work of their pens, went about habitually in four-wheelers. Lady Salisbury, it is added, used to stick straws in her ball dress to draw attention to the parsimony with which they were treated.

Thirty years ago there were very few Americans in London: Miss Consuelo Ysnaga, afterwards Duchess of Manchester; Miss Stevens, now Lady Paget; and Mrs. William Carrington, were among those I knew.

In England, as on the Continent, the American woman was looked upon as a strange and abnormal creature, with habits and manners something between a Red Indian and a Gaiety Girl. Anything of an outlandish nature might be expected of her. If she talked, dressed and conducted herself as any well-bred woman would, much astonishment was invariably evinced, and she was usually saluted with the tactful remark, "I should never have thought *you* were an American," which was intended as a compliment.

As a rule, people looked upon her as a disagreeable and even dangerous person, to be viewed with suspicion, if not avoided altogether. Her dollars were her only recommendation, and each was credited with the possession of them, otherwise what was her *raison d'être?* No distinction was ever made among Americans; they were all supposed to be of one uniform type. The wife and

---

[1] Public conveyances were dubbed the Queen's carriages.

daughters of the newly-enriched Californian miner, swathed in silks and satins, and blazing with diamonds on the smallest provocation; the cultured, refined and retiring Bostonian; the aristocratic Virginian, as full of tradition and family pride as a Percy of Northumberland, or a La Rochefoucauld; the cosmopolitan and up-to-date New Yorker: all were grouped in the same category, all were considered tarred with the same brush.

The innumerable caricatures supposed to represent the typical American girl depicted her always of one type: beautiful and refined in appearance, but dressed in exaggerated style, and speaking—with a nasal twang —the most impossible language. The young lady who, in refusing anything to eat, says, "I 'm pretty crowded just now," or in explaining why she is traveling alone remarks that "Poppa don't voyage, he 's too fleshy," was thought to be representative of the national type and manners.

So great in society was the ignorance even of the country that it was thought astonishing if an American from New York knew nothing of one from San Francisco, as though they came from neighboring counties. On the Continent the ignorance was still greater—many went so far as to include South America. I remember once a Frenchman asking if I knew a certain Chilian lady, and when I replied in the negative, he exclaimed, *"Mais n'êtes vous pas toutes les deux Américaines?"*

American men were myths, few being idle enough to have leisure to travel. But they were all supposed to be as loud and vulgar as the mothers were unpresentable, and the daughters undesirable—unless worth their weight in gold.

A great deal of water has flowed under the bridge since those days. The steady progress of American women in Europe can be gauged by studying their present position. It is not to be denied that they are sharing many of the "seats of the mighty," and the most jealous and carping critic cannot find fault with the way they fill them. In the political, literary, and diplomatic world they hold their own. The old prejudices against them, which arose mostly out of ignorance, have been removed, and the American woman is now generally approved of.

In those days Parisian fashions made their appearance in London about two years after they were the mode in Paris. In the matter of dress the Englishwomen have so improved of late years that it is difficult to realize how badly and inappropriately they used to attire themselves. Having formed my opinion by what I had heard abroad, I fancied that they generally wore a muslin and a sealskin—and perhaps I was not far wrong; but the genial climate of England, with its variation of from fifteen to twenty degrees in a day, might be offered as an excuse.

What would now be thought proper only for a dinner could then be worn at Ascot. I remember appearing on the Cup Day in my wedding-dress of white satin and point lace, with roses in my bonnet. On the other hand, black was alone thought possible for a lady to wear at the play, and once when I appeared in pale blue, Randolph implored me before starting to change it, as it was "so conspicuous."

The late Lord Dudley, like Napoleon I, disliked black and dark colors, and never allowed any member of his family to wear them. Not knowing this, I went to a ball

His Grace~John, Duke of Marlborough, Marquis of Blanford Earl of Marlborough, Baron Churchill of Sandridge and Baron Churchill of Aimouth, Captain General of all Her Majestys Forces, Master General of the Ordnance, One of ye Lords of Her Majestys most Honourable Privy Council, and Knight of the most Noble Order of the Garter. Her Majestys Ambassader Extraordinary and Plenipotentiary to the States General of the United Provinces and General of the Confederate Armies.

HIS GRACE, JOHN, DUKE OF MARLBOROUGH

at Dudley House in what I thought a particularly attractive costume—dark blue and crimson roses. To my discomfiture my host came up to me and nearly reduced me to tears by asking why I came to his ball in such a "monstrous dress." An otherwise most kind and attentive host, he certainly was an autocrat in his own house respecting dress. At Witley Court, his famous place in Worcestershire, when there was a shooting party he would come to breakfast in a velvet coat, and insisted on his guests wearing shoes and morning coats instead of the hobnailed boots and rough and often weather-beaten tweeds donned by the sportsmen of to-day.

There is no doubt that even in sporting pursuits elegance in dress was thought more of than comfort. In looking at the old pictures of the Prince Consort, it seemed strange that he could stalk in the costume he is invariably represented as wearing—tight-fitting trousers and a long cutaway coat, not to mention a flyaway felt hat, and a plaid on his shoulders by way of cape.

Before leaving the subject of dress, it is only fair to recognize that Englishwomen have set the fashion to all the world in country clothes. There they are at their best, and their practical and sensible garments, now so widely adopted by all, were a revelation to me, with my Louis XV heels and plumed hats. When I first came to England and was taken for walks in the country, I had many bitter experiences with long gowns and thin paper-like shoes, before realizing the advantage of short skirts and "beetle-crushers."

Even Englishwomen, however, have had to wait for the evolution of fashion in that respect. A granddaughter of Sir Hugh Hume Campbell, a Scotchman of the

4

old régime, told me once how shocked and horrified he was the first time he saw her in an ulster. He dubbed it "fast and mannish," only one remove from bloomers, and declared that no grandchild of his, or even any lady, who wore one should be allowed to enter his house. "Mr. Punch," who at that time caricatured women smoking cigarettes in short tailor-made dresses and hard pot hats as something improbable, nay, impossible, little knew what a prophet he was. It is not to be denied that smoking is much on the increase among women in England, and it is now more or less an accepted fact, and is tolerated even in the most old-fashioned houses. This has its advantages, making life more sociable, as men seek their own dens less, knowing that they can have their cigarettes in the company of the ladies.

In the early fifties it was supposed to be the height of ill-breeding and vulgarity for a man to be seen smoking a cigar in the street, and the smoking-room in a country-house was generally some miserable room considered too unattractive for anything else, and as far removed from the living-rooms as possible. Now the warmest and brightest is surrendered.

An old story is told of Lord —— who was an inveterate smoker. While staying at Windsor in the lifetime of the Prince Consort, he was one day discovered in his bedroom, lying on his back, smoking up the chimney. This was repeated to Queen Victoria, and thenceforward, it is said, a smoking-room was provided.

Although women smoke in restaurants it is unlikely that the practice will spread farther, for in Russia where they smoke more than in any other country with the exception of Austria, a lady who would indulge in

Her Grace the Dutchess of Marlborough

HER GRACE, SARAH JENNINGS, FIRST DUCHESS OF MARLBOROUGH

thirty or forty cigarettes a day will not smoke in a public place, such as a street or railway-station. In the most aristocratic Austrian circles, on the other hand, ladies are frequently seen smoking cigars at balls and receptions.

When one sees the number of restaurants there are at the present day, crowded with well-dressed and often well-known people, it seems incredible that thirty years ago none existed. Sometimes Randolph and I would be passing through London in August, and our house being closed we were sorely put to it to know where to dine. The only possible place was the St. James's Hotel, now the Berkeley. There, if necessity took you, you could get, in a small, dingy dining-room lighted with gas, an apology for a dinner. Smoking was never allowed, and two people of opposite sex seen together were looked at very much askance. Later the Bachelors' Club and the New Club at Covent Garden became the fashionable resorts at which to dine, although to do so anywhere but in a private house was thought quite "emancipated."

Small dances were given at the New Club, at one of which, Count Kinsky being the host, the Prince of Wales, the ill-fated King of Portugal then Duke of Braganza, the King of Greece, and the unfortunate Archduke Rudolph of Austria were present. It was most animated, and we danced till the early hours of the morning to the music of the Tziganes, then a new importation. An American young lady was so carried away with the excitement of the moment that she was heard calling the King of Greece, with whom she had been dancing, a "bully King"—much to his amusement. I often met the King in later years at Aix-les-Bains.

He was then extraordinarily like his sister Queen Alexandra, and had the same voice. At one time he was much interested in a playhouse which was being built at Athens, to be called the National Theater, and discussed the project at length with me. Madame Duse, happening to be at Aix at the time, was very anxious to inaugurate it. I spoke to the King on her behalf, and was instrumental in bringing about the interview between them. Unfortunately nothing eventually came of it, as Madame Duse fell ill. It was a great pity that the finest actress alive should have missed this opportunity of opening the finest theater in the most classic of all cities. Although very attractive, she is a woman of moods, and a difficult person to cultivate. But genius excuses everything.

In those days it would have been absolutely impossible for ladies to appear in public places in full dress. Now people dine at restaurants attired as for a ball, with jewels and tiaras. Once at the Carlton Hotel I saw a large party of well-known people having supper in the public room, who, from their costumes, had evidently been performing in tableaux vivants. It was a comical, if not very edifying, sight to see Boadicea, with her shield and spear, her hair hanging to the ground, sitting beside a youth travestied as a cherub, with a wreath of roses on his foolish head, while Madame de Pompadour in powder and patches faced them with Julius Cæsar! Another night it was a wedding party which held high revels in the same place. The young, well-born, and handsome couple were to be married the next day, and had chosen this form of public amusement to celebrate their last hours of "single blessedness." Each sat at a

GEORGE, FOURTH DUKE OF MARLBOROUGH, AND HIS FAMILY

In his volume " Sir Joshua Reynolds," Mr. William B. Boulton says: " There are many interesting stories told about this picture. When Sir Joshua went down to Blenheim to paint in the younger members of the group, the little Lady Anne Churchill, a child of four, on being brought into the room, drew back, caught hold of the dress of her nurse, and cried, ' I won't be painted!' The watchful painter immediately transferred a note of the natural attitude of the child to the canvas, where we see her clutching the dress of her eldest sister, just as he had done with the obstreperous young Russell in the Bedford group. To account for this attitude, he placed her next eldest sister with a mask before her face, as if frightening the younger child."

long table decorated with white flowers, the prospective bride with her girl friends, the bridegroom with his boon companions. As the dinner progressed and the fun increased, the throwing of notes and flowers to one another occasioned shrieks of laughter, which startled and amused the general company, not to speak of the waiters, who were having provided for them a show for which they were not asked to pay.

One custom which has changed very much is the short interval thought necessary before a married couple can appear after their "honeymoon." Two or three days is all that is now required after the wedding; whereas formerly it was supposed to be quite extraordinary, if not actually improper and embarrassing, to mix with your fellow-creatures for at least a month. Shortly after my marriage, I was presented to the Czar, Alexander II, at a ball given in his honor at Stafford House. On being told that I had been married only a few weeks, he exclaimed, fixing his cold gray eyes on me with a look of censure, *"Et ici déjà!"*

I had many new experiences in those early years, not the least trying being my attempt at housekeeping, which was very erratic, owing to the ignorance I often had cause to bemoan. At the first dinner party we ever gave the chef we had brought from Paris became "excited," and, to my consternation, I saw the entrée, in the shape of patties, floating in the soup, whereas the poached eggs intended for it appeared in solitary grandeur. These are things never to be forgotten by a young housewife.

Although Randolph did not trouble the House of Commons very much at that time, being satisfied with a perfunctory attendance, he delighted in the society of politicians and men older than himself. Lord Beaconsfield, then Mr. Disraeli, sometimes dined with us. On one occasion Randolph and I were discussing the evening, after our guests had departed, and he commented on Mr. Disraeli's flowery and exaggerated language saying, "When I offered him more wine, he replied, 'My dear Randolph, I have sipped your excellent champagne, I have drunk your good claret, I have tasted your delicious port, I will have no more.'" This I found amusing, as having sat next to him at dinner I had particularly noticed that he drank nothing but a little weak brandy and water. Mr. Disraeli was always kind and talked to me at length, which occasioned much chaff among my friends, who invariably asked me what office I had got for Randolph. He was very fond of dragging in French words, a language he spoke with a weird accent. I remember once his saying to me, speaking of a prominent politician of the day, Sir ——, a great friend of ours: "I think him very gross, like an episeer" (*épicier*), at which pronunciation I could hardly keep from laughing. Sometimes he was rather cross, and if bored or vexed, did not hesitate to let people know it. On one occasion when Lady Lonsdale (now Lady de Grey) gave an evening party at Carlton House Terrace, a lady whose antics were generally a source of amusement ambled up to Lord Beaconsfield, and tapping him archly with her fan, made some foolish remark. Turning a stony stare on her, he said in an audible voice to his neighbor, "Who is that little ape?"

CHAPTER IV

BLENHEIM

MY first visit to Blenheim was on a beautiful spring day in May, 1874. Some of the Duke's tenants and Randolph's constituents met us at the station to give us a welcome, and taking the horses out of the carriage, insisted on dragging us through the town to the house. The place could not have looked more glorious, and as we passed through the entrance archway, and the lovely scenery burst upon me, Randolph said with pardonable pride, "This is the finest view in England." Looking at the lake, the bridge, the miles of magnificent park studded with old oaks, I found no adequate words to express my admiration, and when we reached the huge and stately palace, where I was to find hospitality for so many years, I confess that I felt awed. But my American pride forbade the admission, and I tried to conceal my feelings, asking Randolph if Pope's lines were a true description of the inside:

> "See, sir, here's the grand approach;
> This way is for his grace's coach:
> There lies the bridge, and here's the clock;
> Observe the lion and the cock,
> The spacious court, the colonnade,
> And mark how wide the hall is made!

75

The chimneys are so well design'd
They never smoke in any wind.
This gallery 's contrived for walking,
The windows to retire and talk in;
The council chamber for debate,
And all the rest are rooms of state."
"Thanks, sir," cried I, " 't is very fine,
But where d' ye sleep, or where d' ye dine?
I find by all you have been telling,
That 't is a house, but not a dwelling."

The imperious Sarah, known to her contemporaries as "Great Atossa,"

Who with herself, or others, from her birth
Finds all her life one warfare upon earth,

demolished the older and probably more comfortable hunting lodge which stood in the forest. Tradition asserts that it occupied the site of the "Bower" in which "Fair Rosamond" hid her royal amours. To this day "Rosamond's Well," concealed among the trees, is the object of a favorite walk. Pope also took exception to the noble bridge which in his day spanned the narrow river only, the large lake through which it now runs having been made later.

How strange life in a big country-house seemed to me, who until then had been accustomed only to towns! The Duke and Duchess of Marlborough lived in a most dignified, and, indeed, somewhat formal style. Everything was conducted in what would now be considered a very old-fashioned manner. At luncheon, rows of entrée dishes adorned the table, joints beneath massive silver covers being placed before the Duke and Duchess, who each carved for the whole company, and as this included governesses, tutors, and children, it was no sinecure.

Before leaving the dining-room, the children filled with food small baskets kept for the purpose for poor cottagers or any who might be sick or sorry in Woodstock. These they distributed in the course of their afternoon walks.

When the house was full for a shooting-party, even breakfast was made a ceremonious meal, and no one dreamed of beginning until all had assembled. The ladies would be dressed in long velvet or silk trains, and I remember one morning laughing immoderately when Lady Wilton (the second wife of the "wicked" Earl, as he was called), on appearing in an electric blue velvet and being asked who made it, she said with conscious pride, "It 's a Stratton," [1] as who would say, "It 's a Vandyke." On the other hand, luncheon for the shooters was not in those days the glorified affair it is at present. People were quite content with something cold, eaten in haste, often not under cover, instead of the carpeted tent and elaborate feast provided nowadays, hot, from the soup to the coffee. There is no doubt the present generation treat a country-house more or less like a hotel, coming and going as they like, to suit their own convenience, and seldom consulting that of their hosts.

In those days, the guests having been duly told by which train to come, were expected to arrive by it, unless a very good excuse was forthcoming. They used to sit solemnly through an elaborate tea, exchanging empty civilities for an hour or more, until the hostess (who

---

[1] Mrs. Stratton was one of the fashionable dressmakers of the day.

wore a lace cap if middle-aged, then about forty) gave the signal to rise, uttering the invariable formula, "I am sure you must need a little rest." The guests, once immured within their rooms, were not to reappear until the dining-hour. However little they wanted rest, however bored by their own society, or disturbed by the unpacking maid, there they were supposed to remain. Sometimes it was the hostess who suffered. A friend of mine, a rather shy lady, who was entertaining a prim Princess, timidly proposed after half an hour of uphill small talk, to take her to her rooms. "Thank you," said the Princess in icy tones, looking at her watch, "it is now half-past five. I will go to my room at seven."

Nous avons changé tout cela. Nowadays some of the modern hostesses do not take the trouble to communicate at all in respect of trains and such details. The guests find their own way, and choose their own time, at their own sweet will and proper responsibility. Perchance the host and hostess are not even at home to welcome their guests. They may be hunting, golfing or motoring, and excuses when they do appear are thought hardly necessary by them or by their guests.

When the family were alone at Blenheim, everything went on with the regularity of clockwork. So assiduously did I practise my piano, read, or paint, that I began to imagine myself back in the school-room. In the morning an hour or more was devoted to the reading of newspapers, which was a necessity, if one wanted to show an intelligent interest in the questions of the day, for at dinner conversation invariably turned on politics. In the afternoon a drive to pay a visit to some neighbor, or a walk in the gardens, would help to while away some

VIEW OF BLENHEIM PALACE

GATEWAY AT BLENHEIM

part of the day. After dinner, which was a rather solemn full-dress affair, we all repaired to what was called the Vandyke room. There one might read one's book, or play for love a mild game of whist. Many a glance would be cast at the clock, which sometimes would be surreptitiously advanced a quarter of an hour by some sleepy member of the family. No one dared suggest bed until the sacred hour of eleven had struck. Then we would all troop out into a small anteroom, and lighting our candles, each in turn would kiss the Duke and Duchess and depart to our own rooms.

The Duke was extremely kind, and had the most courteous and *grand seigneur* appearance and manner; his wife, Frances Anne, Duchess of Marlborough, my mother-in-law, was a very remarkable and intelligent woman, with a warm heart, particularly for members of her family, which made up for any overmasterfulness of which she might have been accused. She ruled Blenheim and nearly all those in it with a firm hand. At the rustle of her silk dress the household trembled. An amusing instance occurs to me of the way in which her opinion was consulted even by distant members of the family. Jane, Duchess of Marlborough, who was the third wife of the sixth Duke, a simple and amiable woman, asked the Duchess what redress she could get for not being invited to Court balls, although she attended the Drawing Rooms. The Duchess advised her to write to the Lord Chamberlain on the subject. A few days later she received a gushing letter from Jane, Duchess, thanking her for her advice, which had been most efficacious. "I am told it was a clerical error," she added, "although I cannot see what the clergy have to do with it."

Owing to the admirable taste and knowledge of the present Duke, people who visit Blenheim to-day and see its pictures, tapestries, and art treasures, can scarcely believe that it has been shorn of many of its glories. When I first went there the far-famed Sunderland Library was still in existence. The beautiful old leather bindings decorated as nothing else can the immense long gallery with its white, carved book-cases and vaulted ceiling. Cabinets of Limoges enamels gave the old-world look and Renaissance coloring to the Duchess's sitting-room. There, too, were the "Marlborough gems," besides rooms full of priceless Oriental, Sèvres, and Saxe china. And what of the four hundred and fifty pictures all recklessly sold regardless of the remonstrances and prayers of the family and without a thought of future generations! Little did Lord Cairns think when he made his Act affecting the sale of heir-looms that it could be stretched to such a point. No doubt a certain number could have been spared, such as Rubens's "Progress of Silenus," "Lot and his Daughters," and a few others which, though works of art, were startling, to say the least, and, oddly enough, hung in the dining-room. If familiarity breeds contempt, it also engenders indifference, and the most prudish of gover-nesses, sitting primly between her charges, never seemed to notice these pictures, nor did any members of the family.

The best twenty-five pictures of the collection alone were valued at £400,000 [$2,000,000]. Of these the "Madonna Ansidei," by Raphael, which had been given by the King of Prussia to John, Duke of Marlborough, was purchased for a sum of £70,000 [$350,000] by the National Gallery; also a portrait of Charles I by Van-

THE ENTRANCE HALL, BLENHEIM

dyke for £50,000 [$250,000]. Rubens's portrait of himself with his wife Helen Forment and infant, and another of his wife and son, were sold for £50,000 [$250,000] to the late Baron Alphonse de Rothschild. Several family portraits, notably "The Fortune-Teller" (Lord Henry and Lady Charlotte Spencer) by Sir Joshua Reynolds, were sold. Luckily the famous Marlborough Family, also by Sir Joshua, was not allowed to go.

Many interesting stories are told about this picture. "When Sir Joshua went down to Blenheim to paint in the younger members of the group, little Lady Anne Churchill, a child of four, on being brought into the room, drew back, caught hold of the dress of her nurse, and cried, 'I won't be painted!' The watchful painter immediately transferred a note of the natural attitude of the child to the canvas, where we see her clutching the dress of her eldest sister, just as he had done with the obstreperous young Russell in the Bedford group. To account for this attitude, he placed her next eldest sister with a mask before her face, as if frightening the younger child. This incident is borrowed from an antique gem, but it is as good an illustration as another of Reynolds's facility and resource.

"It is said, too, that while he was painting the picture at Blenheim he dropped his snuff about, and the Duchess, anxious for her carpet, sent a footman to sweep it up. 'Go away,' said the painter, with a proper sense of his dignity, 'the dust you make will do more harm to my picture than my snuff to the carpet.'"

It surprises me that in Mr. Boulton's book upon Sir Joshua Reynolds, from which the above is quoted, he should have overlooked the interesting point that the young Marquess of Blandford standing near his father is holding in his arms one of the ten red jewel cases which contained the celebrated Marlborough gems. The Duke himself, who during the latter part of the eighteenth century formed one of the finest collections of gems, intaglios and cameos ever made in England, has in his hand his favorite sardonyx with a cameo head of Augustus. This gem was sold later on for £2,350 [$11,750].

Tourists, with whom most show-places in England are infested, abounded at Blenheim, and at certain times of the year and for several days in each week one had, for a little privacy, to take refuge in one's own rooms. Occasionally, for fun, some of us would put on old cloaks and hats, and, armed with reticules and Baedekers, walk round with the tourists to hear their remarks, which were not always flattering to the family. One day we nearly betrayed ourselves with laughter at one of my compatriots exclaiming before a family picture: "My, what poppy eyes these Churchills have got!"

Foreigners visiting Oxford would often come over to see Blenheim. The famous tapestries, representing the victorious battles of the first Duke, and given to him by various towns, were always an object of great interest. On one occasion a Frenchman, who had been listening in sullen silence to a glowing account of the French defeats, could stand it no longer. Thrusting his stick through a bit of the tapestry representing a *fleur de lis* flag and trophies in the possession of the British, he tried to tear it up, shouting with rage, *"Ce n'est pas vrai! ce n'est pas vrai!"* To this day the long rent can be seen.

This reminds me of my father-in-law's favorite anecdote in respect to Blenheim. I think it was his grand-

86

HIS GRACE, GEORGE CHARLES, SEVENTH DUKE OF MARLBOROUGH

father who had as his guest the French Ambassador of the day, evidently a man who was somewhat cynical, not to say disagreeable, for he kept asking the Duke most unnecessary questions as to who had given this and who had given that. "The house, the tapestries, the pictures—were they all given? And the Raphael— Was that the gift of the King of Prussia? Was there anything that had *not* been given?" The Duke, slightly annoyed, said at last: "If your Excellency will come with me, I will show you one of the glories of Blenheim which has not been given." Taking his visitor outside, he pointed to the stone trophies and the effigy of Louis XIV which adorn the south front of the house, "These," he said, "were *taken,* not *given,* by John, Duke of Marlborough, from the gates of Tournai." When the Emperor Frederick, while Crown Prince, once came to stay at Blenheim, he was delighted with this story. He was a very charming man and during the few days he was there made himself most agreeable. Absolutely simple in his manners and tastes, English life seemed rather luxurious to him. I remember his face of astonishment when he saw at breakfast a gold tea-service which was produced in his honor. "Ach! much too good, much too good," he kept saying, and every morning he spoke of its magnificence.

Among the many new acquaintances I made was that of the Duchess of Cleveland, widow of the third Duke, one of the *grandes dames* of a former generation. She had a liking for Randolph, and asked him to bring me to see her. She was very kind although she received me in a ceremonious manner, not shaking hands but courtesying. A woman of caustic wit, many stories are told of her and her imperious ways. The family doctor having written to her "My dear Duchess," she wrote back, "Sir, I am *not* your dear Duchess." Her successor, the late Duchess of Cleveland (Lord Rosebery's mother), was an equally interesting character whose energy was remarkable. When long past seventy, she was still an habitué of the Row, never missing her morning gallop. Not long before her death she went to India accompanied only by her servants.

A delightful man who came to stay at Blenheim, was Sir Alexander Cockburn, Lord Chief Justice of England. But he was dangerous! One day out shooting, while I was walking with him from one covert to another, he let his gun off by accident. Luckily the shot went over my head. "I must be careful," he said placidly. I fled. I remember asking him what had been the most amusing experience of his legal career. In reply he told me the story of a young barrister who came into court late, having evidently, from his appearance, dined well but not wisely, the night before. Sir Alexander reprimanded him, asking what excuse he could offer. "None," retorted the culprit, "unless it is that I had the honor of dining with your lordship last night, and bad wine tells on an empty stomach." This anecdote may not be original, but Sir Alexander Cockburn told it to me as such.

When one night the snipe, which abound at Blenheim, ran short, the Lord Chief Justice, to his annoyance, was given only half of one. On leaving, he wrote in the Visitors' Book some lines to the effect that he would share almost everything in life, even his wife (he not having one), but *not a snipe!*

HER GRACE, FRANCES ANNE, DUCHESS OF MARLBOROUGH

CHAPTER V

IN 1876 we decided to go to America. Owing to Randolph having championed his brother Lord Blandford in an unfortunate affair in which the latter was implicated, he had had serious differences of opinion with various influential people, and he felt in need of a little solace and distraction. So, in company with Mr. Trafford and the late Lord Ilchester, we made a flying trip, going first to Canada, where we seemed to spend most of the time eating melons and having cold baths, so overpowering was the heat. We saw Niagara, of course, and made a visit to Newport. Although the life there was a great contrast to that of Cowes, savoring more of town than of country, we found it one of the most fascinating of seaside places, and the hospitality and kindness shown us by the friends of my family were most gratifying. We also went to Saratoga, where the beauty of the ladies, and the gorgeousness of the dresses, astonished the men of our party. Having found the hotel at that place absurdly expensive, I asked my father to remonstrate with the proprietor, who replied: "The lord and his wife *would* have two rooms, hence the expense."

From there we went to the Philadelphia Exhibition which occupied us for several days, and was the source

5

of great interest and amusement. We were accompanied by my uncle, the late Mr. Lawrence Jerome, father of the present District Attorney of New York, William Travers Jerome. While there, my uncle, who is remembered as one of the wittiest men of his day, kept us in transports of laughter. When we stopped at different stalls, he would come up to us as though we were strangers, and taking up some article or new invention, would extol its merits in such an inexpressibly funny manner and language that a crowd soon collected, many ending by buying the article. Mr. Jerome would then receive with pride a commission from the delighted shopman. During our stay we had occasion to meet several prominent Philadelphians. I remember one in particular, who entertained us vastly, by remarking to Mr. Trafford that Randolph was a "bright fellow," but it was a pity he had such an "English accent." The same man asked me if I knew Cyrus B. Choate, and when I answered in the negative, exclaimed, "Not know Cyrus B. Choate! Why, he is one of our most magnificent humans!" We left Philadelphia with regret, and, staying only a few days in New York, returned to England, feeling in spite of our short stay invigorated and refreshed by contact with the alert intellects of my compatriots.

On our arrival in London we found that the Duke of Marlborough had been appointed Viceroy of Ireland. This post Lord Beaconsfield had pressed him to accept, thinking that it might distract his thoughts from certain family worries which at that time were weighing rather heavily upon him. Hating to be parted from Randolph, his father and mother persuaded him to go with them to

DUBLIN CASTLE, THE OFFICIAL RESIDENCE OF THE LORDS LIEUTENANT

Ireland. Not being in favor with the Court, from which London society took its lead, we were nothing loath to go. Randolph was to act as unpaid private secretary to the Duke. This unofficial post proved to be of the greatest interest and value to him, diverting his mind from the frivolous society to which he had till then been rather addicted and which now had ceased to smile upon him.

Accompanying the new Lord Lieutenant, we took part in the State Entry into Dublin, which was conducted with the usual military display, and viceregal etiquette. The Duke in uniform rode with a glittering staff round him. The rest of the family, in carriages with postilions and outriders, drove through the crowded streets to the black and grimy old Castle, which for centuries has witnessed these processions come and go.

In view of the repeated attacks made during the last century on the Irish Viceroyalty, it is strange that it still exists and is apparently flourishing. In the old days of slow travel and no telegraph, when it took a week to get to Dublin, things were very different, and one can understand the pomp and circumstance with which the representative of the Sovereign necessarily surrounded himself. In India, the Eastern mind has to be impressed with the glamour of royalty. In the distant colonies, Canada, Australia, New Zealand and others, Government House is a great feature, and the governors are men of responsibility. But what is the *raison d'être* of the Dublin Court, which is within a few hours of London and in direct communication by telegraph and telephone with Downing Street? The Lord Lieutenant, however intelligent and ambitious he may be, who is not in the Cabinet is but a figurehead, a purveyor of amusements for the Irish officials and the Dublin tradespeople, on whom he is obliged to lavish his hospitality and his money, with no return and no thanks. The wives of the Viceroys labor in good works, each in turn vying with the other in charitable ardor. But these philanthropic works could be carried on just as well if they did not emanate from the Castle. The ingratitude of the people must be very disheartening to each successive Viceroy. However popular the Lord Lieutenant and his wife may have been, however successful their attempts to cajole, conciliate and entertain—though out of their private means they may have spent money like water—in a week all is forgotten. The new régime is paramount: *Le roi est mort: vive le roi!* If the Lord Lieutenant carries out with tact and success the policy of the Government, the credit is taken by the Ministry. If, on the other hand, the policy is a failure, he gets the blame, or, worse still, is repudiated in the House of Commons and told that the opinion of the Lord Lieutenant is of no account. It is a marvel to me that any one can be found to accept so ungrateful a post. The Duke of Marlborough was preceded by the Duke of Abercorn, whose delightful personality and extraordinary good looks were long remembered. "Old Magnificent," as he was called, was very fond of effect, and when making his State Entry into Dublin insisted on the ladies of his family wearing long flowing veils, that streamed behind as they drove in the procession through the streets. Stories are told of his having the Drawing Room stopped while he combed and scented his beard, disarranged by the chaste salutes of the débutantes, who, if they were pretty, were made to pass the dais again. Of late years the Dublin Drawing

Rooms have become so conventional that they no longer afford the amusement they once provided. In old days St. Patrick's Ball, which always takes place on the 17th of March and marks the close of the season, was a regular bear garden, at which sentries were needed to prevent the company from appropriating the plate as well as the food. People picnicked sitting on the floor of the supper rooms. As for the clothes, they were fearfully and wonderfully made! Curtains often did duty for trains. I have myself seen a lady in a black dress with a white train, and, in order to carry out the magpie effect, one shoe was white, the other black!

Randolph and I, with our boy Winston, took up our abode at the Private Secretary's lodge in the Phœnix Park. I found the Irish life very pleasant with its various occupations and amusements, and I delighted in the genial character and ready wit of the people. During the three years we lived there I cannot remember meeting one really dull man. From the Lord Chief Justice to the familiar carman, all were entertaining.

Momentous political work was going on. The Government was struggling with the feeling of revolt which at that time was smoldering beneath the surface, besides trying to cope with a famine which was breaking out. The Duchess of Marlborough at this juncture came forward with her usual energy and started an Irish Relief Fund, which ultimately reached the figure of £135,000 [$675,000]. This sum was distributed in such a practical and businesslike manner that even the Nationalist Press was obliged to praise these viceregal endeavors. The success of the scheme added greatly to the Duchess's popularity, and to that of the Lord Lieutenant. Queen Victoria, whose sympathy and appreciation were always very keen in any matters connected with charity, was greatly pleased, and complimented the Duchess in the accompanying letter:

WINDSOR CASTLE. April 19, 1880.

DEAR DUCHESS,

I, as every one is, am filled with admiration at the indefatigable zeal and devotion with which you have so successfully laboured to relieve the distress in Ireland. I am therefore anxious to mark my sense of your services at this moment when alas! they will so soon be lost to Ireland, and wish to confer on you the Third Class of the Victoria and Albert Order. I will wait till you come over to invest you with it.

Believe me always,

Yours affectly,

VICTORIA, R. I.

The Duchess was very proud of this letter, and her grandson, the present Duke, told me a somewhat pathetic incident in connection with it. A little while before her death she sent for him and gave it to him "to be kept in the archives of Blenheim," adding, "I may seem a useless old woman now, but this letter will show you I was once of some importance and did good in my day."

Hunting became our ruling passion. Whenever I could "beg, borrow or steal" a horse I did so. We had a few hunters of our own which we rode indiscriminately, being both of us light-weights. Some of my best days with the Meath and Kildare hounds I owed to a little brown mare I bought from Simmons at Oxford, who negotiated the "trappy" fences of the Kildare country, and the banks and narrow doubles of Meath as though

LADY RANDOLPH CHURCHILL IN RIDING COSTUME

to the manner born. Many were the "tosses" I "took," as the Irish papers used to describe them, but it was glorious sport, and, to my mind, even hunting in Leicestershire later on could not compare with it. With the exception of the Ward Union Stag Hounds and the Galway Blazers, I think we hunted with nearly every pack of hounds in Ireland.

Colonel Forster, who was then Master of the Horse, as he had been to several previous viceroys, was a beautiful rider, and many were the pleasant hunting days we had together. I remember once he, Randolph and I sallying forth, each on a gray,—mine, which I afterward sold to the King of the Sandwich Islands, had a tail like a shaving-brush, looking for all the world like one of Leech's pictures. The trio fancied themselves, to say the least of it, and vast sums would not have bought us at our own estimation. But alas! in a very short time our pride had a fall in every sense. Colonel Forster's horse lamed itself early in the day; Randolph's animal, after refusing for half an hour to face a yawning chasm, was pushed into it by its irate owner, while mine was caught broadside by a heavy gate I was going through, and horse and rider were upset in the adjoining deep ditch. Luckily I fell clear, but it looked as if I must be crushed underneath him, and Randolph, coming up at that moment, thought I was killed. A few seconds later, however, seeing me all right, in the excitement of the moment, he seized my flask and emptied it. For many days it was a standing joke against him that *I* had had the fall, and *he* the whisky!

The ready wit of the Irish is proverbial and we had many opportunities of judging of it during our stay.

One day we met our friend Colonel Forster being driven to a meet in an Irish car. He was laughing heartily and told us that he had just passed a young man riding who evidently fancied himself, from the way he was first gazing at his boots, then smoothing his coat and patting his waistcoat. "Who is it?" inquired Colonel Forster. "Ah, bedad, Colonel, I 'm thinking that maybe he is not knowing it rightly himself, by the way he is looking at himself," answered the car driver. Another witty carman was driving a relation of mine to a meet of the Ward Union Hounds, who, fearing to be late, pressed him to whip up his horse. "D' ye see that?" said the jarvey, pointing to a monument in Glasnevin Cemetery, which they were passing. "That was put up to the gintleman I was driving the last time I sthruck th' auld mare!"

Returning from Punchestown races once, the crowd was so great that the viceregal carriage got blocked, when some one, pointing at the aide-de-camp in full uniform and cocked hat who was sitting opposite the Lord Lieutenant, shouted, much to the poor man's confusion, "Faith, it 's the Captain that 's doin' the escortin' and chaperonin' to-day!"

Every sportsman knows what it is to ride over a country while looking out of the window on a railway journey. How bold one is! How small the fences seem! and how one wishes with Jorrocks that one could be "a heagle a-soaring o'er the 'ounds!" Colonel Forster who was traveling was vaguely tapping with his fingers on the arm of his seat, when a stranger, who was at the opposite window suddenly said, "You were wrong—you should have 'trigged' at that fence," meaning that if the Colonel was hunting, which he of course thought he *must be,* the horse would have kicked back, and this ought to have been illustrated by two taps of his fingers, not one.

At that time the great excitement in the hunting field was the advent of the Empress Elizabeth of Austria, who had taken a place in Meath for a few months. The whole country was agog, and crowds used to flock to the meets to catch a glimpse of her. The Empress, although her reputation for physical endurance and love of riding was great in the sporting world, astonished every one by the indefatigable life she led. Arriving at Summerhill, from Vienna, without a break she donned a habit in the train, got on a horse, and before going into the house went for a school over a small course which had been specially prepared by her orders. Lord Langford, the owner of Summerhill, had, with much care and at considerable expense, furnished a boudoir for her which was hung in blue damask, and decorated with pictures and china. However, before the Empress had been there twenty-four hours, disdaining such feminine frivolities, she converted it into a gymnasium, in which to exercise daily before going out hunting. With a wonderful figure and a beautiful seat on a horse her Majesty made a fine appearance. She rode gallantly and knew no fear, but her riding was of the *haute école* order, and like most women she could seldom make a horse gallop. This was a source of perpetual worry to her hard-riding pilot, Captain Bay Middleton, whose "Come on, Madam, come on!" was constantly heard in the field. The Empress wore the tightest of habits buttoned down and strapped in every direction, the safety skirt not having as yet made its appearance. She found herself in many a ditch, and whether she fell clear of her horse or not, it was impossible for her to stand up until the buttons and straps had been unfastened. Under the circumstances it was a marvel that she did not hurt herself. It was her invariable custom to ride with a large fan, which she held opened between her face and the crowd, whether against the rays of the sun or the gaze of the people I never made out. Another curious habit of hers was to use small squares of rice paper in the Japanese fashion instead of pocket-handkerchiefs; by these she could be traced for miles, as in a paper chase.

Much to the chagrin of the Viceregal Court the Empress never came near it, not wishing to lose a single day's sport while in the country. But all those who came in contact with her were fascinated by her graciousness and her imposing beauty. It is sad to think that one who had never harmed any one, and was beloved by all in her own country, should have met a tragic end at the hands of an obscure miscreant.

The following year the Viceroy had occasion to entertain the Archduke Rudolph, who had come to Ireland on a short visit. At a grand ball given in his honor in St. Patrick's Hall an unfortunate occurrence happened. The Lord Mayor of Dublin being present, and being in his own province, had an arm-chair on the dais next to the Viceroy, but by some oversight none was placed for the Archduke. This gave great offense, and to add to the "tempest in a tea-cup," the Lord Mayor was made to take precedence of the Heir Apparent of Austria and Hungary, and went in to supper before him. Next day many apologies were offered and the viceregal staff were properly trounced, but the royal visitor, unap-

THE MARQUIS OF LONDONDERRY

peased, departed. Who could have prophesied that he, too, in a few years would come under the ban, and share the evil fate of the House of Hapsburg?

During the three years of the Duke of Marlborough's tenure of office we saw a good deal of Ireland, as he took various places. At Knockdrin Castle, in Westmeath, where we stayed for a few months, we enjoyed the hunting, for the foxes were as wild there as the people were untamed. We thought nothing of going to the meet fifteen or twenty miles on an outside car, and often rode our horses to a standstill in very long runs. After one of these I remember shocking the Lord Lieutenant's local guests by falling asleep during dinner.

One winter my father-in-law had Lord Sligo's place at Westport, County Mayo, where the snipe-shooting afforded excellent sport. Among the works of art in the house was a celebrated statue of a tinted Venus, whose blue eyes and golden locks were rather too realistic to my mind for true beauty. In our walks we had many opportunities of seeing the heartrending poverty of the peasantry, who lived in their wretched mud hovels more like animals than human beings. Alas! I fear these deplorable conditions must ever prevail in Ireland, where neglect and misery have rooted the people in their shiftless and improvident habits. No philanthropic scheme seems really to touch them.

We also visited Galway and Connemara, whose melodious name prepared one for the beauty of its scenery, enhanced as it was by the delights of trout-fishing. Muckross Abbey, on the Lake of Killarney, famed alike for its shooting and its scenery, had been taken by Lord and Lady Wimborne, with whom we often stayed.

From there we sometimes went over to Kenmare close by, one of the show-places of Ireland, where the details of the house were carried out in such perfection that even the door-handles were made of old watchcases.

But this magnificence was exceptional and I was often reminded of the descriptions in "Charles O'Malley" of the improvidence and extravagance of the Irish. Sometimes on the roadside one might see a splendid gateway, whose stone pillars and iron-wrought gates stood in solitary grandeur leading to nothing, all the money having been spent on the approach, and none being left for the house.

Among the most delightful personalities I met during those three years was Father Healy, vicar of Bray near Kingstown. He was one of the most celebrated Irish wits of the day, and his genial manner and kind heart made him a most pleasant companion. He and Mr. Isaac Butt often dined with us at our little house in the Phœnix Park.

Mr. Butt was very friendly, not to say homely, but although he could tell a good story in an amusing way, I confess I thought him rather too serious, constantly dwelling on the miseries and oppression of his countrymen. He would appeal to me as an American to agree with him and when in rash moments I did, would then declare I was a Home Ruler. The words "Home Rule" were the invention of Butt. He thought the old cry of "Repeal" would frighten the English, while the phrase Home Rule would commend itself to every one as reasonable and innocent. The echoes of our conversations would sometimes reach the ears of the Viceroy, and be thought great heresy.

LADY RANDOLPH CHURCHILL

Of our many *habitués,* besides Professor Mahaffy of Greek fame, Dr. Nedley another Irish wit, Lord Morris, and Lord Ashbourne (Lord Chancellor of Ireland), Lord Justice FitzGibbon was the most intimate. It was there that the friendship began which lasted to the end of Randolph's life. FitzGibbon had a house at Howth, where every Christmas he assembled a select number of boon companions—Randolph invariably being of the number.

LORD Randolph Churchill was obliged to be in London a good deal during this time to attend to his parliamentary duties. The letters he wrote to me in Ireland were full of politics.

S. JAMES' CLUB. PICCADILLY. W.

January 28, 1878.

I missed the afternoon post because the discussion lasted till eight o'clock. I am sure the debate will be very stormy. I am in great doubt what to do. I think I could make a telling speech against the Government, but old Bentinck got hold of me to-day and gave me a tremendous lecture. Of course I have my future to think of, and I also have strong opinions against the Government policy. It is very difficult. I shan't decide till the last night of debate, which won't be till next Monday or Tuesday, so my departure for Ireland will be postponed.

Northcote made a very feeble speech to-night and the country every day gets more and more against the Government. Russia's terms of peace are monstrous, but after all it concerns Austria so much more than us, and if she won't move we are practically powerless.

I had a pleasant evening last night at Dilke's. . . . Harcourt,

111

G. Trevelyan, Dicey, editor of "The Observer," and Sir Henry Maine. Harcourt was very amusing. You need not be afraid of these Radicals, they have no influence on me further than I like to go, but I hate the Government. . . .

My visits to London at that time were few and far between, but on one of these, in the summer of 1878, I had the privilege of going with a few other ladies to the "Peace with Honor" banquet which was given in the Wellington Riding School in honor of Lord Beaconsfield and Lord Salisbury on their return from their successful participation in the Berlin Conference. I went with the Duchess of Wellington, arm-chairs being placed in the center of the huge building. It was a wonderful sight, and the enthusiasm was boundless when Lord Beaconsfield, looking like a black sphinx, rose to speak. It was on that occasion that, pointing with a scornful finger at Mr. Gladstone, he declared that he was "inebriated with the exuberance of his own verbosity."

The following year, the Duke of Marlborough having given up the Viceroyalty and left Ireland for good, we also departed, returning to London.

In the summer of 1881 Randolph and I went again to the United States on a short visit. When in New York we heard of the Phœnix Park murders. The Kilmainham Treaty had just been arranged, Parnell having promised to put down outrage. Mr. Forster had resigned, and Lord Frederick Cavendish had been appointed Chief Secretary for Ireland in his place. I remember a reporter calling at my father's house in Madison Square and telling me the news. We were

THE MARCHIONESS OF LONDONDERRY

greatly shocked and could hardly believe it until it was confirmed the next day. I had never met Lord Frederick Cavendish, but Mr. Burke, the other victim, who with his sister lived at the Under Secretary's lodge in the Phœnix Park, we knew quite well. The outcome of this dastardly deed was of course the Prevention of Crimes Act, which was passed at once.

Curiously enough, I had occasion later to see the murderers, just before their condemnation. Although we had left Ireland, I rarely missed paying a visit, either to the Castle during the season, or to the Viceregal Lodge for the Punchestown races.

I was staying in Dublin for the Horse Show when I met an official of Kilmainham Gaol, who, owing a debt of gratitude to Randolph, wanted to show me some civility, and therefore thought of nothing better than to invite me to see Kilmainham and the murderers. I confess that I did not feel any great desire for this entertainment, but being told that it was nearly impossible to get permission to see them, and that without exception no one was allowed in the prison, I began to feel more interested. Under the seal of the greatest secrecy I found my way to the gaol, where I met Mr. ――. He took me into a small room and told me to stand behind his chair while he interviewed the prisoners one by one. They looked apprehensively toward me, but my friend reassured them by saying they need not mind as I was a relation. He only kept them a minute or two putting some trivial questions. The youngest of them, as he was passing out, suddenly turned and asked me to help his wife if he "had to go." This depressed me dreadfully, nor were my spirits raised by being taken round the prison by the Governor, whom Mr. —— had somehow "squared." The tier upon tiers of tiny cells, each containing a miserable-looking man, the food brought in baskets which I saw prodded through and through with swords for fear that something might be smuggled in them, were a more than unpleasant sight. I saw Carey, the informer, who was occupying the same room in which Parnell had been imprisoned. Carey was in his shirt-sleeves and glared at us. Just as I was going to leave and while standing in the middle of the building, talking to the Governor and Mr. ——, an electric bell rang and a warder came running up and whispered something to the Governor. He became rather pale and passed his news on to my friend, who seemed equally disturbed. They both looked at me, and when I asked what had happened, the Governor said the Inspector-General was coming to pay a surprise visit to the prison and was at that moment at the gates, and that if I were found there without a permit signed by the Lord Lieutenant, they would get into great trouble. "Well, let me fly," I exclaimed. "Impossible," they cried; "there is no outlet." "Well, hide me." "You can't hide in a prison!" "One moment," said the Governor hesitatingly, "would you mind a cell?" "Of course not," I replied, and forthwith I was hurried into a cell—a black cell, as being safer from the Inspector's prying eyes. The door was shut on me, and I felt not "on velvet," but *in* velvet of the blackest dye. After a time the velvet became thick black wool, and I was certain it was closing round me. Hours seemed to pass and I began to think I was forgotten. My mind wandered from black wool to rats—and I felt sure I saw little beady eyes looking at me, when the door opened just in time to save me from screaming. I was in that cell twenty minutes at the outside, but it was enough of such an experience. Later I could not help laughing to think of the face of the Inspector—an acquaintance, by the way —had he happened to visit my dungeon. I kept my counsel for more than three years after the execution of those wretched men, and never mentioned my visit to a soul for fear of doing harm.

Under such terrorism did every one live at that time in Ireland that Lord Spencer, who was then Viceroy, never moved without an escort of Constabulary even when hunting. It was comical to see them in full uniform, their swords bounding in the air as they careered over the fences after the sporting Lord Lieutenant.

During the Jubilee year of Queen Victoria I revisited the Viceregal Court when Lord Londonderry was Viceroy. Ireland was again suffering under the Crimes Bill, which had been carried by the closure. Mr. Balfour (than whom, with his back to the wall, there is no better fighter) was Chief Secretary, and was beginning that policy of repression which only a strong man could have carried out. There was much unrest in the country and the air was full of disquietude and rumors. The Government no doubt was again going through anxious times, but the visitors at the Castle saw only the sunny side. The festivities of the Dublin season were taking place with perhaps even more animation than usual, owing to the popularity of the Lord Lieutenant and Lady Londonderry, who was not only a perfect hostess, but the most indefatigable worker in the many charitable schemes she had set on foot. Later, when having

6

left Ireland she returned to London, her salon became and has continued to be a political center, of which she is the presiding genius. An omniverous reader, blessed with a retentive memory, her conversational powers are great, and her influence and interest in the political world have been most valuable to her family and friends. If her receptions are perhaps too crowded, the battalions of a large Conservative Party are to blame. Everything that year was dubbed "Jubilee," from knights and babies to hats and coats. "God save the Queen" was heard *ad nauseam* on every conceivable occasion, until the tune became an obsession. This led to a practical joke at the Castle which caused much amusement. One morning, speaking of the Jubilee craze, I pretended that I had received as an advertisement a "Jubilee bustle"which would play "God save the Queen" when the wearer sat down. This, of course, created much curiosity and laughter. Having promised to put it on, I took my hosts into my confidence. An aide-de-camp was pressed into the service, and armed with a small musical box was made to hide under a particular arm-chair. While the company was at luncheon I retired to don the so-called "Jubilee wonder," and when they were all assembled I marched in solemnly and slowly sat down on the arm-chair where the poor aide-de-camp was hiding his cramped limbs. To the delight and astonishment of every one the National Anthem was heard gently tinkling forth. Every time I rose it stopped; every time I sat down, it began again. I still laugh when I think of it and of the astonished faces about me.

CHAPTER VI

THE new Parliament of 1880 found us established with our household gods in the little house we had taken in London in St. James's Place. It was next door to Sir Stafford Northcote, then leader of the Opposition. Little did the kind old gentleman realize at that time his proximity to the hornets' nest which was being built by the Fourth Party.

Randolph had been reëlected for Woodstock, defeating the Liberal candidate, Mr. W. Hall. The contest was not an exciting one, although many of the constituents were dissatisfied and full of grumblings and complaints. They fancied themselves neglected, from the owners of Blenheim being absent in Ireland for so many years. Nevertheless, I was confident that we should win, having too many good friends in the constituency to fear a rebuff.

Randolph, whose interest in politics had become very keen during his stay in Ireland, now became entirely absorbed by them. During this session the Bradlaugh incident arose in which he took so prominent a part. I, too, caught the fever, and went frequently to the House of Commons, listening with growing interest to the debates. The Ladies' Gallery, for which one ballots,

119

and the Speaker's Gallery, to which one is invited by the Speaker's wife, were not in those days the fashionable places of resort they have since become. Only a few ultra-political ladies frequented them. In the Speaker's Gallery, Mrs. Gladstone, picturesque and dignified, always occupied a reserved seat, from which she was seldom absent. Miss Balfour, too, was generally there. Mrs. Cavendish Bentinck, a tall, handsome woman, whose flashing eyes and raven locks had gained for her among her friends the name of "Britannia," and whose son married Miss Livingston of New York, was also an *habitué* and literally seemed to live there. Later, Mrs. Chamberlain joined the group. But the gay butterflies of society thought it too serious a place for them. Now, however, this has quite changed. The present generation are full of the desire of being, or appearing to be, serious. To be beautiful and rich is not sufficient; the real social leaders of to-day are not content with these accidents of birth and fortune. They aspire to political influence, or to be thought literary and artistic, and society follows the lead. For an interesting debate, or to hear a popular politician, they will make strenuous efforts to get into the Speaker's Gallery. On such an occasion, many of the youngest and prettiest women in London can be found there. Hidden in Eastern fashion from masculine sight, fifty or more will sometimes crowd into the small, dark cage to which the ungallant British legislators have relegated them. The ladies in the first row, in a cramped attitude, with their knees against the grille, their necks craned forward, and their ears painfully on the alert if they wish to hear anything, are supposed to enjoy a great privilege. Those in the second

row, by the courtesy of the first, may get a peep of the gods below. The rest have to fall back on their imagination or retire to a small room in the rear, where they can whisper and have tea. Some take the opportunity to polish off their correspondence, hoping, perhaps, that these letters, written on House of Commons paper, may convey a political flavor to the unpolitical recipients. Silence is supposed to be *de rigueur,* but the thread of many an interesting speech has been lost in the buzz of stage whispers and the coming and going of restless ones. "Is that Mr. ——?" exclaims a pretty blonde to her neighbor. "Do lend me your glasses. Yes, it is he. I wonder if he would dine with me to-night." (" 'Sh!" comes from a relative of the man who is speaking.) "We are thirteen—so tiresome. I think I must send him a note by the usher." (" 'Sh!") "I can get the answer at once—*so* convenient." (" 'Sh!" " 'Sh!") *"Who* is that odious woman hushing me? *Darling,* keep my chair; I will return in a moment," and amid a jingling of beads and chains and a *frou-frou* of silk petticoats, the fair one flies to scribble her note. Meanwhile the front row settles down once more to the speech to which they are listening. "What an immoral argument! Just like a Radical's impudence to say such things!" exclaims in no dulcet tones a Conservative peeress, who would be better occupied waking up her lord in the Upper House, than crowding out the wife of some Member of Parliament in the Lower.

"Be careful!" says her neighbor; "his wife is next to you."

These are specimens of the remarks one sometimes hears. I remember an enthusiastic wife whose husband was making an important speech, betraying her too intimate knowledge of it by giving her unwilling listener the best points beforehand. Next to speaking in public oneself, there is nothing which produces such feelings of nervousness and apprehension as to hear one's husband or son make a speech. There is no doubt, however, that the frequent recurrence of it minimizes the ordeal, particularly if the speakers are sure of themselves. In this respect I can claim to being specially favored, though Randolph, even after years of practice and experience, was always nervous before a speech until he actually stood up. This subject reminds me of a painful sight I once saw at a big political meeting. A young member of Parliament with more acres than brains, who sat for a family pocket borough, was making his yearly address to his constituents. Shutting his eyes tight and clenching his hands, he began in a high falsetto voice: "Brothers and sisters, Conservatives!" and for thirty minutes he recited, or rather gabbled, the speech he had learned by heart, while his wife, with her eyes riveted on him, and with tears pouring down her cheeks from nervousness, unconsciously, with trembling lips, repeated the words he was uttering.

Those years (1880–84) of political activity when the Fourth Party was at its zenith, were full of excitement and interest for me. Our house became the rendezvous of all shades of politicians. Many were the plots and plans which were hatched in my presence by the Fourth Party, who, notwithstanding the seriousness of their endeavors, found time to laugh heartily and often at their own frustrated machinations. How we used to chaff about the "goats," as we called the ultra-Tories and followers of Sir Stafford Northcote! Great was to be their fall and destruction.

Sir Henry Drummond Wolff, whom I had met at Cowes before my marriage, was a godsend if anything went wrong, and a joke from him saved many a situation. With a pink-and-white complexion that a girl might have envied, and a merry twinkle in the eyes which hid behind a pair of spectacles, he was the best of company. But I confess I thought rather dangerous his habit of treating the most serious questions in a flippant manner, and of turning everything into ridicule. Sometimes, to hear him and Randolph discussing the situation, the uninitiated might have thought the subject was a game of chess. It is sad to think that Fortune has been so little kind to Sir Henry, for, notwithstanding his many services to the State and his private life of unselfishness and abnegation, cares and misfortunes have come heavily upon him in his old age.

Sir John Gorst—then Mr. Gorst—was a very different type of man from Sir Henry Wolff. His stern countenance belied him, and he could make himself very pleasant. I remember his defending me in some trivial case in the County Court, and winning it; the appearance of a Queen's Counsel in silk gown and wig creating a sensation. Randolph accompanied us, and we drove away in a four-wheeler, feeling very triumphant until the wheel came off, and we were ignominiously precipitated into the street.

Sir John had a music-loving soul, and many were the occasions when he and I and Arthur Balfour went off to the "Monday Pops," to listen to the sweet strains of Joachim and Norman Neruda. My fashionable and frivolous friends, spying the three of us walking together, often teased me about my "weird" companions, one solemn with beard and eye-glass, the other esthetic with long hair and huge spats. Mr. Balfour's knowledge of music was remarkable, considering the little time he was able to devote to it, and he was no mean performer at the piano, reading and playing classical music. We often played Beethoven or Schumann together. But it was not without difficulty that he could get away from his parliamentary duties, which increased yearly, and often I was disappointed of his company, as shown by the following letter:

1883   House of Commons.

MY DEAR LADY RANDOLPH:

I am groaning and swearing on this beastly bench: while you are listening to Wagnerian discords, I am listening to Irish grumblings—there is a great deal of brass in both of them; otherwise there is not much resemblance! I *am* sitting next ——, I *might* be sitting next you! I am an unhappy victim. However, there is no choice. Monday night is a most unlucky one for Richter: the Irish have a talent for turning everything into an Irish debate; and when the Irish speak I must answer, as I have just been endeavoring to do!

Your miserable servant,

ARTHUR JAMES BALFOUR.

As regards the Fourth Party, I was full of grievances against Mr. Balfour. He never seemed quite certain whether he belonged to it or not; it depended how Randolph, Wolff, and Gorst were behaving, how much his uncle, Lord Salisbury, remonstrated, or how political events were shaping themselves for the party. If badly,

Mr. Balfour would, as I often had reason to tell him, *"retirer son épingle du jeu,"* and repudiate with indignation the idea that he was a member of it. This did not prevent him, however, from secretly hankering after the "wicked" three, whose company had for him all the fascination of forbidden fruit. Be it as it may, History, that often untruthful jade, will probably write him down as the fourth member of the party, although he may have only coquetted with it. A contemporary says of him, "An apostle of modern intelligence, a depositary of universal knowledge, a standard of mental infallibility, Mr. Balfour would have constituted an important Party in himself if he had not been a chosen vessel designed by nature, by culture, and by the eternal fitness of things to be the Fourth Party's fourth man."

During the time that Randolph and his friends were struggling in Opposition, Sir William Harcourt, Sir Charles Dilke, and Mr. Joseph Chamberlain came frequently to our house. This was looked upon with much disapproval by the "goats," who regarded these politicians as very dangerous company for young people properly imbued with true Conservative principles. The Duke of Marlborough, my father-in-law, was particularly incensed, and took Randolph seriously to task for having had Mr. Chamberlain to dinner—"a man who was a Socialist, or not far from one; who was reputed to have refused to drink the Queen's health when Mayor of Birmingham," etc. "How could the influence of such a man be anything but pernicious?" Indeed, London society thought as much, and since we were not in favor at Court at that time, this association with advanced Radicals was made another subject of grievance against us. Randolph, however, pursued the even tenor of his way, and I am glad to think that, notwithstanding their sometimes very acute political differences, he remained to the end of his life an ardent admirer and friend of Mr. Chamberlain.

Sir William and Lady Harcourt used to give the most delightful dinners and parties at their house in Grafton Street, restricted enough in numbers to make conversation possible. Unlike the present day, people were content to remain where they were being entertained, and were not troubled with anxiety to be seen at half a dozen places in the course of one evening. The pleasantest people in London were to be met there, attracted not only by Sir William's wit and conversation, but also by Lady Harcourt's geniality and her art of making every one feel at home. I was always proud to think that the daughter of that most illustrious historian, Motley, was a compatriot. I remember at one of these dinners having an amusing passage-at-arms with my host, Sir Charles Dilke, and Mr. Chamberlain. At that period I had taken up painting very violently, martyrizing many models, paid and unpaid, covering miles of canvas with impossible daubs, and spending a small fortune in paints and pigments. My first picture, a life-size copy in oils of Sant's "Inexorable" was to my discomfiture mistaken by an admiring friend for a brilliant piece of wool-work! My three Radical friends having been told of my artistic efforts, chaffingly implored me to hand them down to posterity by painting their portraits. "Why refuse to paint us?" "Where can you find more attractive or noble models!" "Come, here is a chance to immortalize yourself and us."

SIR CHARLES DILKE

SIR WILLIAM HARCOURT

JOSEPH CHAMBERLAIN

"Impossible," I cried. "I should fail; I could never paint you black enough."

I used to accompany Randolph to most of his political gatherings in the country. We would stay with some local magnate, who probably would be taking the chair at the meeting. Men on those occasions fare better than their women folk, for, on the plea of having to prepare speeches, they can seek the solitude of their rooms. Not so the wife, who has to sit, perhaps for hours, talking platitudes to the wives and daughters of the political supporters who have been invited to meet her. But their desire to please, and the hospitality they so cordially extend to one, make up for it. On these social-political experiences, the late Lord Goschen, a personal friend, often compared notes with me.

HOUSE OF COMMONS, S. W.

17th August.

DEAR LADY RANDOLPH:

I telegraphed to you yesterday to Penn, that I am extremely sorry that I could not accept your fascinating invitation. That is to say, this was the substance of the telegram: I did not put it so warmly to the telegraph clerk. We have a party of friends coming to us in the country to-day, so that I am due at home to entertain them—we are further from London than you, but not too far to get friends for the Sunday. I indeed want fresh air and a "rest from the House and all its inmates."

We hang on here in a deplorable condition, without amusements, and without ladies, without any interests except the dying interests of a dull Session. Sometimes a stray woman appears on the terrace, but what is that among so many? "Souls" and bodies have equally vanished. I wonder which Mr. Russell has said or written what about me, where? Anyhow, I do not know that I possess the particular characteristics you mention. But if I did, I should certainly not think you "one of my failures" . . . for your extracted talk has always interested me extremely, so much so that there is not a woman in London I like more to take into dinner if I get the chance. As I know that you and all Americans hate compliments I must apologize for the last sentence.

The division bell is ringing and disturbs my memories. Please remember that my pen is only dipped in a House of Commons inkstand, and not in such a romantic inkstand as that which emanated from your first literary earnings.[1] So you must forgive me if I have written a mere Philistine letter.

Yours very sincerely,

GEORGE G. GOSCHEN.

Of all the statesmen I have met, I think the late Lord Salisbury and Mr. Gladstone were the pleasantest companions at dinner. Both had the happy knack of seeming vastly interested in one's conversation, whatever the subject, or however frivolous. There was no condescension or "tempering of the wind to the shorn lamb" about it. At the same time, I must own that any feeling of elation for having had, as one considered, a success was speedily destroyed; for the next woman, whoever she might be, who had the privilege of sitting beside either of these great men, would receive exactly the same courteous attention. As for Mr. Gladstone, having once started him on his subject, an intelligent "Yes" or "No" was all that was required. But if you ventured a remark (to which he listened in grave silence), he had a discon-

---

[1] Speaking once of a common friend who was famous for his epistolary style, I had related to Lord Goschen how I had sent this friend a present of an inkstand (paid for out of my first literary earnings) as a gentle hint that I wished for a letter from him

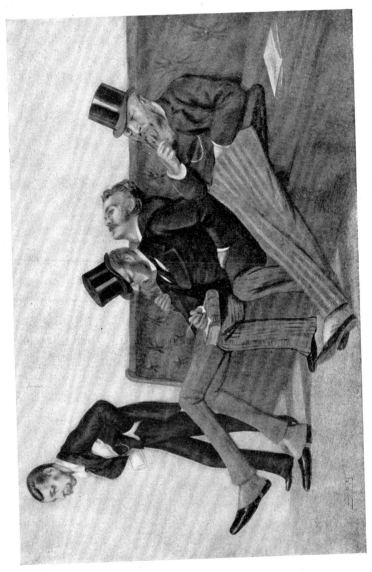

"THE FOURTH PARTY" (IN THE HOUSE OF COMMONS)

From left to right the persons are Lord Randolph Churchill, Mr. Arthur Balfour, Sir Henry Wolff, Mr. (later Sir) John Gorst

certing way of turning sharply round, his piercing eye fixed inquiringly upon you, and his hand to his ear, with the gesture so well known to the House of Commons. His old-world manner was very attractive, and his urbanity outside the House remarkable. On one occasion I had been at the House hearing Randolph make a fiery attack on him, which he answered with equal heat and indignation. The hour was late, and Randolph and I had just time to rush home and dress to dine at Spencer House with Lord and Lady Spencer. The first person I met as I went in was Mr. Gladstone, who at once came up and said: "I hope Lord Randolph is not *too* tired after his magnificent effort." What an object lesson to those foreign politicians who would look upon it as an insult to be asked to meet in the same house!

The autumn of 1883 was marked by the formation of the Primrose League, which subsequently proved to be an event of great political importance, and a tower of strength to the Conservative Party.

The Fourth Party, with the exception of Mr. Balfour, and the addition of Sir Alfred Slade, had drawn up the statutes and ordinances of this new political society, which was to "embrace all classes and all creeds except atheists and enemies of the British Empire." Sir Henry Wolff, who had originated the idea from seeing Conservatives wearing primroses on the anniversary of Lord Beaconsfield's death, came to Blenheim, where I was staying at the time, to initiate us.

All the female members of the family who happened to be there were enrolled as dames, and were given a badge and a numbered diploma. Mine was No. 11. The Duchess of Marlborough was made President of the

Ladies' Grand Council, which was being formed. I must say we laughed immoderately over the grandiloquent names—the "Knights Harbingers" (or "Night refugees," as we dubbed them), the "Ruling Councillors," the "Chancellor of the League," "Dames," "Dame President," "Habitations," and what not. We criticized freely the Brummagem gaudy badges and "ye ancient" diplomas printed on vellum. Little did we know the power the League was to become. As a "dame," I was determined to do all I could to further its aims. The first years of its existence were a struggle. The wearing of the badge exposed one to much chaff, not to say ridicule; but we persisted. Recruits joined "surely, if slowly," and to-day, after twenty-one years of existence, the League can boast of having 1,703,708 knights, dames, and associates upon its rolls, and of having materially helped to keep the Conservative Party in power twenty years.

For many years I worked strenuously on behalf of the League. I became the "Dame President" of many Habitations, and used to go all over the country inaugurating them. The opening ceremonies were often quaint in their conceptions, a mixture of grave and gay, serious and frivolous—speeches from members of Parliament, interspersed with songs and even recitations, sometimes of a comical nature. The meeting would end with the enrolment of converts.

A strange medley, the laborer and the local magnate, the county lady and the grocer's wife, would troop up and sign the roll. Politics, like charity, are a great leveler. The late Lady Salisbury, when President of the Ladies Executive Council of the Primrose League, once at a committee meeting rebuked a member who thought that a certain form of entertainment to be held at one of the Primrose League Habitations, though attractive to the masses, might be thought slightly vulgar. "Vulgar? Of course it is vulgar," exclaimed the President; "but that is why we have got on so well."

Among the many entertainments of this kind, I particularly remember going with Mr. Balfour to Manchester just before the general elections of 1886 to open a large Habitation. A few days later, on the seventh of June, Mr. Gladstone was defeated on his Home Rule Bill. In view of this, I permit myself to give my remarks on the occasion, as they proved prophetic.

Trembling with excitement, my notes hidden in my fan, I said:

"I am proud to have the privilege of inaugurating this most important Habitation. It is not necessary for me to dilate on the usefulness of the Primrose League. We have had ample proof of the great work it did at the recent General Election (1885), and we shall soon have an opportunity of showing to our opponents that not only is its power undiminished, but that it is increased tenfold. But to make this a certainty, I think that every member of the Primrose League must put his or her shoulder to the wheel. When Mr. Gladstone appears in his new rôle of undertaker, let us hope that, with the exception of a few hypocritical mourners, he may be left to bury his doomed Bill alone. When that melancholy rite is accomplished, and he appeals to the country, I trust with all my heart that it will answer with one voice in favor of that Party which is pledged to support all that is dear to England—religion, law, order, and the unity of the Empire." The local press were good enough to add that "Lady Randolph was ably supported by Lord Salisbury's nephew, Mr. Balfour, M.P.!"

The year 1883 saw us in a new house in Connaught Place. "Tyburnia," our friends called it, as on the railings opposite our windows, which faced Hyde Park, there was a small tablet to mark the site of Tyburn Gate. Often I thought of the thousands of poor wretches who had been hanged there, and sometimes wondered if the house would be full of wailing ghosts: but frankly I never saw or heard one.

I was very much occupied that winter furnishing, and disposing in the new house what my brother-in-law Blandford used to call my "stage properties." In a former house which we had bought shortly after our marriage, I had, in my ignorance of the climate, covered the walls with silks and stuffs, and nearly cried with dismay when I saw the havoc wrought upon them by the fogs and smuts of the dirtiest of towns. My dearly bought experience stood me in good stead when furnishing again. The paneling and clean white paint, which is so popular to-day, formed the principal decoration of our next dwelling, which, by the way, was the first private house in London to have electric lights. We had a small dynamo placed in a cellar underneath the street, and the noise of it greatly excited all the horses as they approached our door. The light was such an innovation that much curiosity and interest were evinced to see it, and people used to ask for permission to come to the house. I remember the fiasco of a dinner party we gave to show it off, when the light went out in the middle of the feast, just as we were expatiating on its beauties, our guests having to remain in utter darkness until the lamps and candles, which had been relegated to the lower regions, were unearthed. The electric light did not prove to us an unmitigated blessing, inasmuch as Randolph, having spoken enthusiastically in the House of Commons in favor of an Electric Lighting Bill, felt he could no longer accept the gift of the installation which by way of an advertisement a company had offered to put into our house, free of cost. Unfortunately, there being no contract, we were charged double or treble the real price. It is curious how fond one can become of inanimate objects apart from their intrinsic value. We had many nice bits of old furniture which we had picked up in Dublin, where they had found their way from the dismantled houses of impecunious Irish landlords. Things could be bought cheaply in those days, the artistic craze being confined to the eclectic few. Now collecting millionaires have bought up nearly everything, and what is left is held at fabulous prices. On the other hand, owing to the taste of the present day, the "House Beautiful" is now within the reach of all. We are far from the heavy and uncomfortable monstrosities of the Early Victorian epoch. Taste and common-sense, with a desire for knowledge, even if allied to a limited purse, will go farther nowadays to please the eye of the senses than the riches of a Crœsus spent for him by upholsterers. Once the eye is accustomed to the purest styles and perfect models, it unconsciously rejects base imitations and inharmonious lines; just as the man who lives surrounded by fine pictures even if he be not an artist, retains an impression of the warmth and beautiful coloring of the masterpieces.

7

I remember coming across some large painted panels which I found in an old shop in the City. Although grimy and in a deplorable condition, I thought I detected in them real merit. My sojourn at Blenheim among those glorious pictures, I suppose, had educated my eye. The owner wanted some £300 for them, for which they were to be restored and put into good order. Full of my *trouvaille,* I rushed home with a glowing tale, in the hopes of persuading Randolph to buy them. I found him with Mr. Balfour and Sir Henry Wolff, discussing the merits of "Elijah's Mantle," which he had just written for the "Fortnightly." The laughter it provoked reached my ears as I subsequently sat in my drawing-room looking at its bare walls, which, alas! had to remain so. "Three hundred pounds—preposterous! Besides, we cannot afford it"—so Randolph settled the question. I reluctantly gave up the panels, which were sold shortly afterward, and turned out to be Morland's, worth to-day perhaps £7000 or £8000!

London was very animated that season. Randolph's growing prominence in the political world was attracting considerable attention in the social, and we were bombarded with invitations of every kind. The fashionable world, which had held aloof, now began to smile upon us once more. Most people in the course of a lifetime get to know the real value of "the Mammon of Unrighteousness," but few learn their lesson so early. We both profited by it. Personally I would never give up anything by which I really set store for the sake of its unsatisfactory approbation.

A curious phase had come over society. Publicity be-

ARTHUR JAMES BALFOUR

came the fashion, although it was mild in comparison with that which exists to-day. People live much more before the public than they did. Privacy seems a luxury no one is allowed to indulge in—even the most uninteresting must be interviewed; their houses, their tastes, their habits, photographs of themselves in their sanctum, all are given to the "man in the street." The craze for exhibiting the photographs of "Ladies of Quality," as they would have been called in the eighteenth century, was a novelty which brought forth much comment. The first time mine found its way into a shop, I was severely censured by my friends, and told I ought to prosecute the photographer.

So great was the license allowed to the public that some ladies who had taken London by storm were publicly mentioned as "Professional Beauties." Conspicuous among them were Mrs. Langtry and Mrs. Wheeler. A fierce war of opinion as to their rival merits raged about them.

Artists extolled Mrs. Langtry's classical Greek profile, golden hair, and wonderful columnlike throat, graced with the three *"plis de Vénus,"* which made her an ideal subject for their brushes and chisels. So great was the enthusiasm created by the beauty of the "Jersey Lily," as she was called, that in the height of the season I have seen people standing on chairs in the Row to get a peep at her. Professor Newton on one occasion lectured at King's College on Greek art. Mrs. Langtry, as a living exponent of the classical type which the professor was describing, sat in a prominent place facing the audience. In one of his letters to me while I was in Ireland, Randolph writes: "I dined with Lord Wharncliffe last night, and took in to dinner a Mrs. Langtry, a most beautiful creature,—quite unknown, very poor, and they say has but one black dress."

Mrs. Wheeler was quite different with dark hair and deep gray-blue eyes, which held you by their gentle, appealing expression. She was very fascinating.

For a time no party was considered complete or successful without these ladies. People would receive invitations with "Do come; the P. Bs. will be there." This meant the certain attendance of society. On which a poet (saving the mark!) of the day wrote the following verses:

First Lady Dudley did my sense enthral,
    Whiter than chisel'd marble standing there,
The Juno of our earth, "divinely tall,
    !And most divinely fair."

And next with all her wealth of hair unroll'd,
    Was Lady Mandeville, bright eyed and witty;
And Miss Yznaga whose dark cheek recall'd
    Lord Byron's Spanish ditty.

The Lady Castlereagh held court near by,
    A very Venus, goddess fair of love,
And Lady Florence Chaplin nestled nigh,
    Gentle as Venus' dove.

As gipsy dark, with black eyes like sloes,
    A foil for Violet Lindsay, sweetly fair,
Stood Mrs. Murietta, a red rose
    Was blushing in her hair.

And warmly beautiful, like sun at noon,
    Glowed with love's flames our dear Princess Louise,
Attended by the beautiful Sassoon,
    The charming Viennesse!

GEORGIANA, COUNTESS OF DUDLEY

LADY RANDOLPH CHURCHILL

Then Lady Randolph Churchill, whose sweet tones
  Make her the Saint Cecilia of the day;
And next those fay-like girls, the Livingstones,
  Girofla-Giroflé!

And then my eyes were moved to gaze upon
  The phantom-like, celestial form and face
Of the ethereal Lady Clarendon,
  The loveliest of her race.

The beauteous sister of a Countess fair,
  Is she, the next that my whole soul absorbs,
A model she for Phidias, I declare,
  The classic Lady Forbes.

Although London has always been famous for the beautiful women of all nationalities that one can see there, I doubt their having been surpassed since the eighties. To pick and choose among such a bevy is somewhat of an invidious task. I can think of few nowadays who could really compare with the Duchess of Leinster and her sister Lady Helen Vincent, Lady Londonderry, Lady Dalhousie, Lady Lonsdale (better known as Lady de Grey), Lady Ormonde who has the cameo-like features of her mother, the beautiful Duchess of Westminster, Lady Mary Mills, and Lady Gerard. Mrs. Cornwallis-West, whose daughters have inherited her beauty, held her own with the best of them. It was difficult to find a fault in her bright, sparkling face, as full of animation as her brown eyes were of Irish wit and fun. She had a lovely complexion, curly brown hair, and a perfect figure. Undoubtedly, however, the one who will be handed down to posterity as the most beautiful woman of her generation is Georgiana Lady Dudley, whose imposing presence and small aristocratic head still command admiration.

Among royal ladies no one can dispute the palm being given to her Majesty Queen Alexandra.

CHAPTER VII

GASTEIN—LORD RANDOLPH'S LETTERS FROM INDIA

IN July, 1883, an otherwise pleasant season was suddenly turned into grief and mourning for us by the death of my father-in-law. Randolph had dined with him the previous night, when he appeared quite in his usual health. At eight o'clock next morning we heard a knock at our bedroom door, and a footman stammered out "His Grace is dead!"

It was naturally a great shock to Randolph, who was much attached to his father, and saw him constantly. I regretted the Duke very much: he had always been most kind and charming to me. If he seemed rather cold and reserved, he really had an affectionate nature. Although his children were somewhat in awe of him, having been brought up in the old-fashioned way which precludes any real intimacy, they were devoted to him. The Duke was greatly interested in politics, and was a Tory of the old type, holding in abhorrence anything approaching change. He was one of the strongest opponents of the "Deceased Wife's Sister" Bill, and only a few days before his death, owing to his efforts, the Third Reading of the Bill had been defeated by a narrow majority.

After a few days spent at Blenheim, we left for Gastein, taking our boy Winston with us. There we led the "simple life" with a vengeance, but after the rush of

London, and the gloom of the preceding weeks, the peace and quiet were not unpleasant.

In our walks we frequently met Bismarck with his big boar-hound, two detectives following him closely. One day as he was walking rather slowly we tried to pass him, whereupon, much to my annoyance, the detectives rushed forward in a most threatening manner. I had no idea we looked like anarchists.

Beyond climbing the mountains and taking the baths, there was little to do. We made the acquaintance of Count Lehndorff, who introduced us to an old Gräfin, who lived in a villa called "La Solitude." This lady was a great friend of the Emperor William I, and invited us one day to tea to meet him. The Emperor was a fine-looking man, notwithstanding his age, and he had that old-world manner which is as attractive as it is rare. He was full of gaiety, and chaffed some of the young people present. It was a mystery to me how he survived what he ate and drank, although he was doing a cure. He began with poached eggs, and went on to potted meats and various strange German dishes, added many cups of strong tea, and ended with strawberries, ices, and sweet, tepid champagne. We talked *banalités;* it was not very exciting.

We spent the winter following the Duke's death more or less at Blenheim under the new régime. My brother-in-law, who had now succeeded to the family honors, was most kind and hospitable, and insisted that nothing should be altered as regarded us. He even persuaded Randolph to revive his harriers. I thoroughly enjoyed the hunting, and was given the proud post of whipper-in. But I own to my discomfiture that I could never remember the names of the hounds; to me they all looked alike. Randolph, on the contrary, knew not only their names, but their characteristics, and spent many hours at the kennels.

In November, 1884, wanting a rest from the arduous political work he had been indulging in, Randolph decided to go to India for a few months. He had been speaking at a good many meetings all over the country, at Edinburgh, at Blackpool, to his own constituents at Woodstock, and finally in a regular campaign in Birmingham, where on one occasion occurred the celebrated Aston Riots, which were organized by Mr. Chamberlain's agent, a Mr. Schnadhorst. How the meeting was broken up, the speakers (Sir Stafford Northcote, Colonel Burnaby, Lord Randolph, and others) fleeing for their lives, is a matter of history. Notwithstanding Randolph's righteous indignation at such treatment, particularly from a friend, even though a political opponent, he made it up with Mr. Chamberlain before leaving for India. Amiable letters passed between them, and they shook hands. While Randolph was on the high seas, the Aston Riots question, which had already been discussed at length in the House of Commons, came up again. In view of the reconciliation which had just taken place, I was rather disappointed to hear Mr. Chamberlain warmly backing up his constituents. It may have been necessary from his point of view, but I agree with M. de Camors—"*La politique desséche le cœur.*" Sometimes, indeed, I think politics a "sorry game." Too often its attributes are callousness and ingratitude, tricks and treachery. In any other "walk of life" these things would not be tolerated for a moment.

The press in those days attacked Randolph most viciously on every possible opportunity. Mr. Buckle, the editor of the "Times," who was by way of being a friend of ours, often, if not invariably, wrote slating articles on him. One night I met him at the Speaker's after a particularly poisonous leader had appeared in the morning "Times." Coming up, he half-chaffingly asked me if I intended to speak to him, or if I was too angry. "Angry? Not a bit," I replied. "I have ten volumes of press-cuttings about Randolph, all abusive. This will only be added to them."

I sometimes wonder if the power of the press is not greatly exaggerated. I have always observed that it has to follow a popular movement, not lead it, and great abuse of a public man only seems to help him to office. At the last General Election (1906), with few exceptions the whole press of England preached protection, and yet free trade won all along the line. In all political matters indeed one may say with Omar Khayyám:

> "I heard great argument
> About it and about: but evermore
> Came out by the same door where in I went."

Randolph remained in India four months, enjoying himself immensely. He wrote me glowing accounts of his travels and all that he was seeing. These letters made me greatly regret that I had not been able to accompany him.

GOVERNMENT HOUSE,
BOMBAY, January 1, 1885.

WE got here Tuesday morning early, after a very pleasant voyage across the Indian Ocean. I found the Governor's carriage waiting at the dock, and we came up here. Sir James Fergusson is most kind and pleasant and so are all the Staff. I have not done any sight-seeing yet, except going into Bombay and walking about the streets and looking at the people, an endless source of interest. It would be quite useless my endeavoring to describe to you my impression of this town. The complete novelty and originality of everything is remarkable, and one is never tired of staring and wondering. I cannot tell you how much I am enjoying myself or how much I wish you were with me. The Bombay Club asked me to a dinner but I declined, as there would have been speeches and more or less of a political demonstration against the Ripon Party, which would never have done. I did not come out to India to pursue politics or to make speeches.

January 9.

WE have been going about a great deal, seeing various things and people. Sir Jamsetjee Jeejeebhoy, a great Parsee, took us to see the Towers of Silence, where they place all the dead Parsee bodies to be eaten by vultures. I was asked to write my opinion of their process in their books, and composed a highly qualified and ambiguous impression which would have done credit to Gladstone.

Last night we dined at the Byculla Club with several gentlemen, when an American lady gave us some very dull recitations from Tennyson; we were all much bored. I had a long interview with eight of the leading native politicians on Wednesday morning on Indian politics, in which they set forth with great ability their various grievances. We leave to-night for Indore, and after that go to Jaipur, Agra, Delhi and Lucknow, which last place we hope to reach about the 21st. From there I go to spend a week or ten days with Colonel Murray in the district which he administrates, somewhere on the borders of Nepaul. We shall be in camp, and moving about every day, and I shall be able to see something of the details of Indian administration and also lots of sport; but of this last I shall be a spectator rather than an actor. You have no idea how extraordinarily polite people are out here, and what trouble they take to amuse me.

THE RESIDENCY,

INDORE, January 14.

WE were met at the junction for Indore by Captain F., of Holkar's service, who informed us that Holkar was away from his capital and was ill, but would come to a station near and meet us; and presently there we found him, drawn up with all his Court. We had an interview of about half an hour, while the other unfortunate passengers were kept waiting. He was most gracious and very intelligent, and when we left he embraced me! At Indore we found his son, also drawn up, and more pow-wow. In the evening fireworks, Hindu drama, Nautch, conjurers, &c. All very Hindu and delightful the first time one sees it, but I can quite imagine that after a time it would pall. In the morning Holkar sent us out cheetah-hunting for black buck; however, the cheetah was sulky and would not run well, so did not catch one. We then took our rifles, and I shot three and Thomas [1] two.

IN CAMP,

DUDNA, February 1.

HERE we are in camp in the middle of an immense forest at the foot of the Himalayas. We have been leading a very enjoyable life since we left Lucknow and Colonel Murray. Out all day careering round on elephants after game, sleeping in tents at night, always at a different place, always hungry for breakfast, very hungry for dinner—two sensations to me which have the attraction of novelty. The whole thing is a charming change after racketing about in railways from town to town. We have not seen much game I must admit, as it is far too

[1] Private Secretary.

154

THE BRIDGE AT BLENHEIM

early in the year and, no grass being burnt and much water being about, the wild animals are very widely scattered, and shots are few and far between; though yesterday we hunted one leopard which ultimately escaped after being much fired at and, I think, grievously wounded. I shot a very nice swamp deer and Thomas a nilghai or blue bull. We also shot pea-fowl, bustards, and partridges and every variety of bird. We have fifteen elephants, and these creatures are an unfailing source of interest and amusement. I think an elephant is the best mode of conveyance I know. He cannot come to grief; he never tumbles down nor runs away (at least, not on the march); nothing stops him; and when you get accustomed to his pace he is not tiring. You would not believe what steep places they get up and down or what thick, almost impenetrable, jungle they go through. If a tree is in the way, and not too large a one, they pull it down; if a branch hangs too low for the howdah to go under, they break it off. They are certainly most wonderful animals, and life in many parts of India would be impossible without them. The scenery all round here is lovely—very wild and with splendid woodland effects. We have spent more days in camp here than we meant, which has altered our plans a little, but I like so much seeing the country and the people.

What explosions there are in London! I think it very amiable of the dynamite people to blow up the House of Commons when we are all away; they might have chosen a more inconvenient moment.

GOVERNMENT HOUSE,
CALCUTTA, February 8.

I HAVE had the great good fortune to kill a tiger. It was our last day, and the party proposed to shoot ducks and snipe; but for that I did not much care and suggested that I and a Mr. Hersey (an English gentleman who is living in the district) should go into the forest on the chance of seeing deer and perhaps getting a sambur-stag, while the others went to shoot ducks. This was agreed to, and the others bet fifty rupees they would have the heaviest bag. Well, Hersey and I, each on an elephant and accompanied only by two other elephants, were beating an open space in the forest when I came upon the recently killed carcass of a hog, half devoured. Hersey, when he saw it, declared it was quite fresh, and that the tiger must be close by. You may imagine the excitement. We beat on through the place and then came through it again, for it was very thick high grass. All of a sudden out bundled this huge creature, right under the nose of Hersey's elephant, and made off across some ground which was slightly open. Hersey fired, and missed. I fired and hit him just above the tail. (A very good shot, for he only showed me his stern, and he was at least forty yards off.) Hersey then fired his second barrel, and broke his shoulder, which brought him up (literally with a round turn). He took refuge in a patch of grass about fifty yards from us where we could just see bits of him. Heavens, how he growled and what a rage he was in! He would have charged us but that he was disabled by Hersey's last shot. We remained still, and gave him four or five more shots, which, on subsequent examination, we found all told; and then, after about five minutes' more awful growling, he expired. Great joy to all. The good luck of getting him was unheard of at this time of year; the odds were a hundred to one against such a thing. He was a magnificent specimen, nine feet seven inches in length, and a splendid skin—which will, I think, look very well in Grosvenor Square. This is certainly the acme of sport. I never shall forget the impression produced by this huge brute breaking cover; or, indeed, the mingled joy and consternation of the other party when they saw him—for they had to pay up fifty rupees. They had got a black buck and a blue bull, and thought they had certainly won.

LORD RANDOLPH CHURCHILL

Tigers in the Zoo give one very little idea of what the wild animal is like.

GOVERNMENT HOUSE,

CALCUTTA, February 10.

I HOPE to leave Bombay March 20th and return *via* Marseilles, in which case I should be back in London about the 11th or 12th of April.   I do not think I shall be able to stop in Paris, as I guess the House of Commons will be just reassembling after Easter, and it would be a good moment to drop in upon that body.   It is extremely pleasant here.   The Dufferins are very kind and easy-going; the Staff, too, are amiable; and Bill Beresford does everything he can for one.   Yesterday the Government telegraphed to Dufferin to despatch a brigade of Indian troops and thirty miles of railway plant to Suakim.   Great preparations at once made; late at night comes an order from London countermanding the whole thing.   Dufferin, diplomatist as he is, could not conceal his disgust at this vacillation when they handed him the telegram on our return from dinner.   I telegraphed to Borthwick, and I hope I put the fat in the fire.

REWAH, February 17.

I GOT a telegram from Wolff yesterday, through Pender, saying that affairs were pressing and a crisis impending and inquiring when I was coming back.   *Mais je connais mon Wolff;* he has crisis on the brain and, in any case, no political contingency will hasten my return by an hour.   I expect the Government will try and get put out and the Tories will try to come in; I wish them joy of it.

On Sunday morning General Roberts turned up, and we had a jolly day; lots of talk.   The General is all I had imagined him to be.   He is very keen on taking me up the frontier to Peshawar and Quetta.   It would be most pleasant if it could come off, and one would learn a great deal about that most mysterious problem, "the dangers of the Russian advance"; but there is no chance of it.

BENARES, February 24.

THIS place is the most distinctly Hindu city I have yet seen; old and curious in every part. We are leaving for one of the Maharajah's palaces, or villa rather. We are extremely *bien logés et nourris*, with a retinue of servants and carriages at all times ready. There is an old Rajah, Siva Prasad, an interesting and experienced old man who acts as guide; he speaks English perfectly though at the top of his voice, and indulges in endless dissertations on Indian politics. Yesterday morning we started off to see the Maharajah's royal palace of Ramnugger. Very great reception; all the retainers, elephants, horses, &c., together with army—the latter about 100 strong—drawn up in a long avenue from the gates to the door. The army gave a royal salute, and the band played "God save the Queen," which I had to receive with dignity and gravity; rather difficult! The Maharajah's grandson, a boy of ten, met us at the door, and his son a man of thirty, half way up the staircase; such are the gradations of Oriental etiquette. The Maharajah was not there, as he is old and infirm, and was keeping himself for the evening. Then Nautch girls and mummers, which, so early in the morning, were out of place; and so on.

Later we took a boat, came down the Ganges, and saw all the Benares people bathing—thousands. As you know, this is part of their religion. The water is very dirty, but they lap up quantities of it, as it is very "holy"; also there were to be seen the burning Ghats, where all the dead are cremated. There were five bodies burning, each on its own little pile of fagots; but the whole sight was most curious and I am going again this morning to have another look. Benares is a very prosperous city, as all the rich people from all parts of India come here to spend the end of their days. Any Hindu who dies at Benares, and whose ashes are thrown into the Ganges, goes right bang up to heaven without stopping, no matter how great a rascal he may have been. I think the G. O. M. ought to come here; it is his best chance.

In the evening the Maharajah gave a party to all the native notabilities of the city; great attendance of Baboos. Many of them speak English, and some appear to be very clever men, but I have had so much *pow-wow* that I did not talk to them much. I discovered a great scandal here the evening of my arrival. I found the magistrate and police were impressing Bheesties, or water-carriers, for service in the Soudan; great consternation in the profession, and all the Bheesties were hiding and were being actively hunted up by the police. I investigated the matter, questioned the head of the police, and went and saw three of the victims for the Mahdi. The poor creatures fell at my feet in the dust, screaming not to go. I was very angry, and telegraphed to Sir Alfred Lyall, the Lieutenant-Governor of the North West Provinces, and an inquiry is being made which will, I hope, save these unfortunate persons from a service to them terrible. This little incident of our rule goes far to explain why we make no progress in popularity among the people.

JAIPUR, March 3, 1885.

WE only remained at Delhi two days as the hotel was piggy, and we moved to the Club at Agra, which is very comfortable, with excellent food and wine. This also gave us opportunity of seeing the "Taj" by moonlight, which we were not able to do last time, and which is an unequalled sight. Also we went to dine at the house of a native judge—a very interesting and clever man; we met a most curious collection of native notabilities. The natives are much pleased when one goes to their houses, for the officials out here hold themselves much too high and never seek any intercourse with the native out of official lines; they are very foolish.

8

We go on to-night to Baroda, where the Guicowar is organising a tiger hunt. I almost think I am getting a little tired of traveling, and shall be glad to find myself on board ship.

As appears from these letters, Lord Randolph's relations with Lord and Lady Dufferin were of the most cordial kind, and this friendship stood him in good stead when shortly after his return to England he was appointed to the India Office. Many years later as I was passing through Paris, Lord Dufferin, who was then Ambassador there, showed me much kindness. Referring to his relations with Randolph while Viceroy in India, he says in the following letter:

BRITISH EMBASSY,

PARIS, March 14, 1895.

MY DEAR LADY RANDOLPH,

I have been so sorry not to be able to come and see you; but ever since your arrival I have been laid up almost continuously with what they call here "*la grippe*," and I have only just begun to go out. I would so like to be allowed to come and pay you a visit. I suppose like most ladies, you are in late, or would you prefer me to come at an earlier hour?

Of course there is nothing that Lady Dufferin and I would not be anxious to do to make your stay in Paris as little sad and irksome as possible. As I am sure you must know, I had the greatest regard and personal affection for your husband.

He quite won my heart when he paid us a visit in India, and when afterwards he became Secretary of State, I found him more courteous, more considerate, more full of sympathy, than any of those with whom I had previously worked. In short, it is impossible to say what a pleasure it was to me to have been associated with him in the Government of India. He always came to see me when he passed through Paris, and it was a renewed delight to have a chat with him. . . .

Believe me, my dear Lady Randolph,

Yours most sincerely,

DUFFERIN AND AVA.

CHAPTER VIII

OFFICE AND RESIGNATION

IN the absence of Lord Randolph in India, the political horizon had grown very dark for the Liberal Government, which fell shortly after his return (1885). The triumphant Fourth Party now reaped the reward of their labors, all being included in the new Administration. Great was the excitement and many the *pourparlers* at Connaught Place. Randolph was offered the post of Secretary of State for India, by Lord Salisbury, and accepted it, but on the understanding that Sir Henry Wolff and Mr. Gorst, who had "borne the burden and heat of the day" with him, should be included. Lord Salisbury demurred, but finally gave way under pressure. Having joined the Government, Randolph was now obliged to seek reëlection at Woodstock. His new office giving him an enormous amount of work, he made up his mind not to contest it personally. I was therefore pressed into the service. Of nine elections in which I have taken a more or less active part (Woodstock twice, Birmingham three times, Paddington twice, Oldham and Manchester once each), if Birmingham was the most laborious, I think Woodstock was the one which left the pleasantest memories.

Accompanied by my sister-in-law, the late Lady Howe—then Lady Georgiana Curzon—we stayed at

Blenheim, but had our Committee rooms at the Bear Hotel in Woodstock. There we held daily confabulations with the friends and Members of Parliament who had come to help. We were most important, and felt that the eyes of the world were upon us. Reveling in the hustle and bustle of the Committee rooms, marshaling our forces, and hearing the hourly reports of how the campaign was progressing, I felt like a general holding a council-of-war with his staff in the heat of a battle. A. was doubtful, B. obdurate, while C.'s wife, a wicked, abominable Radical, was trying to influence her husband whom we thought secure, to vote the wrong way. At once they must be visited and our arsenal of arguments brought to bear on them. Sometimes with these simple country folk a pleading look, and an imploring "Oh, please vote for my husband; I shall be so unhappy if he does not get in," or "If you want to be on the winning side, vote for us; as of course we are going to win," would be as effective as the election agent's longest speeches on the iniquity of Mr. Chamberlain's unauthorized program or Mr. Gladstone's "disgraceful" attitude at the death of Gordon. In some ways the work was arduous enough.

The Primrose League was still in an embryonic state in Woodstock, and there was no Habitation to furnish us with the Primrose Dames, who for the last twenty years have taken a prominent part at every election. The distances to cover were great, and motors were not in existence. Luckily, Lady Georgiana Curzon, who was a beautiful driver, brought down her well-known tandem, and we scoured the country with our smart turnout, the horses gaily decorated with ribbons of pink and brown, Randolph's racing colors. Sometimes we would drive into the fields, and getting down, climb the hayricks, falling upon our unwary prey at his work. There was no escaping us. Many of the voters of those days went no further than their colors. "I votes red" or "blue," as the case might be, and no talking, however forcible or subtle could move them. Party feeling ran high, and in outlying districts we would frequently be pursued by our opponents, jeering and shouting at us; but this we rather enjoyed. We were treated to jingling rhymes, the following being a specimen:

But just as I was talking
With Neighbour Brown and walking
To take a mug of beer at the Unicorn and Lion,
(For there's somehow a connection
Between free beer and election)
Who should come but Lady Churchill, with a turnout that was
    fine.

And before me stopped her horses,
As she marshaled all her forces,
And before I knew what happened I had promised her my vote;
And before I quite recovered
From the vision that had hovered,
'T was much too late to rally, and I had changed my coat.

And over Woodstock darted
On their mission brave, whole-hearted,
The tandem and their driver and the ribbons pink and brown.
And a smile that twinkled over,
And that made a man most love her
Took the hearts and votes of all Liberals in the town.

READY FOR AN ELECTIONEERING TOUR

Lady Curzon (the late Countess Howe) is seen driving the tandem used in the election contest for Woodstock in 1885. Lady Randolph Churchill sits beside her and Lord Curzon (now Earl Howe) stands at his wife's side

Bless my soul! that Yankee lady,
Whether day was bright or shady,
Dashed about the district like an oriflamme of war.
When the voters saw her bonnet,
With the bright pink roses on it,
They followed as the soldiers did the Helmet of Navarre.

At the end of a tiring fortnight, Randolph was returned at the head of the poll. From the window of the Bear Hotel I made a little speech to the crowd, and thanked them "from the bottom of my heart" for returning my husband for the third time. I surpassed the fondest hopes of the Suffragettes, and thought I was duly elected, and I certainly experienced all the pleasure and gratification of being a successful candidate. I returned to London feeling that I had done a very big thing, and was surprised and astonished that the crowds in the streets looked at me with indifference. I often think that these must be the sensations of a newly made Member of Parliament when he first goes to the House of Commons, fresh from the hustings of his own meetings, where his dullest and silliest inanity is listened to and applauded. In the House he finds his level, alas! only too soon, and in a cold and inattentive audience realizes that perhaps he may not be the born orator he was led to believe.

The following letter from Lord James of Hereford, then Sir Henry James, alludes to the Woodstock election.

MY DEAR LADY RANDOLPH: NEW COURT, TEMPLE, 1885.

You must let me very sincerely and heartily congratulate you on the result of the election, especially as that result proceeded so very much from your personal exertions. Everybody is praising you very much.

But my gratification is slightly impaired by feeling I must introduce a new Corrupt Practices Act. Tandems must be put down, and certainly some alteration—a correspondent informs me—must be made in the means of ascent and descent therefrom; then arch looks have to be scheduled, and nothing must be said "from my heart." The graceful wave of a pocket handkerchief will have to be dealt with in committee.

Still, I am very glad.

Yours most truly,

HENRY JAMES.

Of a very different order from Woodstock was the contest for Birmingham at the General Election of 1885, when Randolph and Colonel Burnaby opposed Mr. John Bright and Mr. Chamberlain. During the election I had occasion to see a good deal of Colonel Burnaby, whose "Ride to Khiva" gave one an idea of his adventurous spirit. He was a gentle voiced, amiable man, notwithstanding an enormous frame and gigantic strength. I remember one night in Birmingham, that while walking back after a meeting to the hotel where we were staying, we encountered a crowd of opponents, who were inclined to be hostile, jostling us in such an alarming manner that I became nervous; but seemingly with the wave of his arm, Colonel Burnaby scattered them. Innumerable were the stories told about him. Once at Windsor Barracks, for a bet, he walked up a narrow staircase with a fair-sized pony under each arm. The dumb-bells he exercised with weighed two hundred pounds, and on one occasion, hearing a brother-officer (who, by the way, was six foot two) make some disparaging remark about him, he took him up and flung him across the room. Had it not been for the fact of landing on a sofa, the wretched man would have had his back broken. A few months after the election Colonel Burnaby was killed in action at Abu Klea. In one of his letters from India Randolph says: "Poor Fred Burnaby's death is a great blow to me, and it was so sad getting his letter inclosed in yours this morning. I wonder if he got my letter—I shall miss him greatly."

The Duchess of Marlborough, my mother-in-law, came down to help me. It was the first time that women had ever indulged in any personal canvassing in Birmingham, and we did it thoroughly. Every house in the constituency was visited. The Duchess would go in one direction, and I in another; the constituency was a large one, and the work arduous. The voters were much more enlightened than the agricultural laborers of Oxfordshire; the men particularly were very argumentative and were well up in the questions of the day. The wives of the Radicals were also admirably informed, and on more than one occasion routed me completely. Sometimes I invaded a factory addressing a few words to the men in their dinner-hour. On one occasion I was received in sullen silence; when I inquired why, one, speaking for the rest, said they did not like being asked for their vote. "But you have something I want," I cried; "how am I to get it if I do not ask for it?" This struck them as quite reasonable and when I left they cheered me. Whether or not I secured any votes I shall never know.

The excitements and amusing incidents repaid one for the fatigue. During the whole of the election I never encountered a disagreeable incident or any rudeness, however poor the slum into which I went. Only once did I come across a Philistine—a publican who was in the cellar when I called. "Lady Churchill wants to see you," said the wife through the trap-door. "Oh, does she?" came in guttural tones from behind the barrels of beer. "Well, tell Mrs. Churchill to go to ——," at which I beat a hasty retreat. On the other hand I had a great success with a butcher, with whom I exchanged flowers; he gave me his vote and some time after the election I was the proud recipient of half a sheep, sent by my useful admirer. The election, alas! was not won, but to have brought down the great Mr. Bright's majority to 400 was a virtual triumph. The Radical Caucus and Mr. Chamberlain's stronghold were shaken to their foundation. In spite of his defeat, Randolph did not give up hope of contesting Birmingham again. He kept in touch with the constituency, and often held meetings there.

Of political and electioneering anecdotes one can often say, *"si non è vero è ben trovato."* But among true experiences amusing or otherwise, I remember one in particular. Being asked to help canvass for Mr. Burdett-Coutts, I was pleading with a waverer for his vote. Waggishly and with a sly look he said, "If I could get the same price as was once paid by the Duchess of Devonshire for a vote, I think I could promise." "Thank you very much," I replied, "I 'll let the Baroness Burdett-Coutts know at once."

About this time Sir Henry James, of whom we saw a good deal, although politically he was of the "other way of thinking," being a Liberal, was instrumental in bringing about a reconciliation between the Prince of Wales and Randolph. Friendly messages had already been conveyed from his Royal Highness, and the matter finally culminated in our giving a dinner for the Prince and Princess of Wales. Lord Rosebery, Mr. and Mrs. Gladstone, Mr. Henry Chaplin, and Mr. and Mrs. Chauncey Depew were among the guests. The dinner was animated, Mr. Gladstone and Mr. Chauncey Depew keeping the ball rolling. This reconciliation, I am happy to say, was a lasting one, all old wounds being healed. A few days later the peacemaker, delighted with his success, went off with Randolph for a little jaunt abroad. I cannot refrain from giving the letter Sir Henry James wrote me, which proves what good company he was.

GRAND HOTEL, PARIS, Sunday.

MY DEAR LADY RANDOLPH:

A word of our journey. At Charing Cross Station (Friday morning) the Inspector informed me it was blowing roughly from the S. E. in the Channel. R. C. derided the idea. "Nonsense! What a weak creature you are! Beautiful day." Arrived at Folkestone, captain's cabin reserved for two. Randolph spurned it. "Beastly place! I shall go on the bridge."

I reclined and read, and saw no more of my companion until we arrived at Boulogne. At first I could not find him. At last a sailor came up to me and said, "The gentleman is very ill, but he is trying to come up-stairs now." Then I saw a figure crawling out of the forecastle. He had been on the bridge, but had been literally washed off it and for a time had lain on the deck with the sea pouring over him. It had been the roughest passage known, I believe, for years. I rushed to my altered friend. He really was very ill, and placed a fixed gaze on the ground,

175

still thinking of, and feeling, the horrors of that passage. A stout, red-haired man approached him. "Let me, as one of your most ardent admirers, shake hands with you." I much doubt if that man will ever make that request again. Propping himself up by means of my umbrella, tottering notwithstanding, sea water running away in large quantities from his great-coat, a new hat quite spoilt, Lord Randolph slightly inclined a fixed eye embedded in a ghastly countenance of a leaden yellow color upon that admirer, who fled. In the buffet old Baillie Cochrane quite cheerfully desired "to communicate something of great interest affecting the party." This time a slight groan was heard, so I knew my fellow-traveller was improving. At length he found his way into our carriage, reclining on cushions and covered with rugs. In two minutes he was asleep. Before Amiens he awoke, quite sprightly and with a good colour, and smoked two cigarettes, and abused Granville, so I knew he was quite well. We are enjoying ourselves very much—and behaving in a most exemplary manner.

If I had a decent pen and ink free from dust, I should have made this a most interesting letter.

Yours, dear Lady Randolph,

HENRY JAMES.

Among the many political meetings I attended with Randolph during those two years, I think the biggest and most imposing was that held in the Manchester Drill Hall. Eighteen thousand people filled the place to suffocation—no singer that ever lived can command the audience of a popular politician. If the building had held 40,000 or 50,000, it would still have been crowded. Most of the people had been standing for two hours before we arrived. Manchester gave Randolph a magnificent reception, thousands lined the streets and covered the roofs of the houses as we slowly drove through the town in a carriage drawn by four horses. Over 200,000 people were said to have turned out that day. I felt very proud. Randolph's speech lasted for over two hours. The heat was great, and on leaving the building the crowd pressed round the carriage to such an extent that two men were killed. I was also with Randolph at Sheffield, and heard the famous speech in which he asked Lord Hartington to abandon Gladstone and Home Rule and "come over and help us." This phrase led me later into trouble. Happening to meet Lord Hartington at dinner while he was still making up his mind as to whether he would join the Liberal Unionists or not, I asked him if he intended responding to Randolph's invitation. "I have not yet decided; but when I do, I suppose I shall be thought either a man or a mouse." "Or a rat," said I. Lord Hartington laughed, as the French say, *"d'un rire jaune."* Very pleased with what I considered my "bon-mot," I repeated it to Randolph, who, to my discomfiture, gave me a severe lecture on the iniquity of ill-timed jests. "Those are the sort of remarks which upset a coach," he said.

Many of our Liberal friends were in great trepidation at that time, torn between their hatred of Home Rule and their reluctance to leave the "Grand Old Man." The following letter from Sir Henry James is some indication of their feelings:

28, Wilton Place, Sunday.

My Dear Lady Randolph:

It is very kind of you and the Secretary of State to ask me to come to you on the 3d. Of course I will do so with the greatest pleasure. But unless the horizon clears I shall not, I warn you, be very lively.

I fear a ripple of scoffing laughter, but still I am really in very low spirits. I see no way out of the breakers—worse than breakers—which we have drifted into, and *where* is the Pilot?

I will regard No. 2 Connaught Place as a Lighthouse—but that fixed—forgive me for saying by way of correction—rotatory object will scarcely suffice.

Yours most truly,

HENRY JAMES.

And again later he writes:

BROOKS'S, ST. JAMES'S STREET.

MY DEAR LADY RANDOLPH:

Of course I will come with the greatest pleasure on Sunday week.

Thanks for *your* sympathy on account of my Tuesday night vote. I want somebody's for I am having a little rough usage from candid friends. I know I intended to do right and I think and hope I did so.

Yours most truly,

HENRY JAMES.

This refers to the division on Mr. Jesse Collings's amendment to the address which took place on Tuesday, January 26, 1886. By means of the amendment Mr. Gladstone sought to turn Lord Salisbury's Government out of office, in order that Home Rule might be brought forward. Knowing this, seventeen Liberals including Lord Hartington, Mr. Goschen, and Sir Henry James voted with the Government against Mr. Gladstone. Thus was laid the foundation of the Liberal Unionist Party.

While Randolph was at the India Office, I was told that the Order of the Crown of India would be given to me if he recommended me for it. This decoration, which was instituted by Queen Victoria and designed by the Duke of Albany, has a pretty pearl and turquoise cipher attached to a pale-blue ribbon edged with white. I admit I thought it would be very nice to have it, but Randolph demurred at the idea of recommending his own wife, and therefore I sorrowfully gave up the idea. A few months later, however, much to my delight, the following letter arrived:

WINDSOR CASTLE, November 30, 1885.

DEAR LORD RANDOLPH:

The Queen wishes to personally confer the Insignia of the Order of the Crown of India on Lady Randolph Churchill on Friday next the 4th of December at three o'clock.

Will she come back here to luncheon?

The 1:10 train from Paddington is the most convenient one, and if Lady Randolph will let me hear whether she comes by that or another train, I will send the carriage to meet her here.

Yours very truly,

HENRY PONSONBY.

On the appointed day I went to Windsor, having been duly apprised by a note received in the morning from a lady-in-waiting, as to what garments I should appear in.

LADY RANDOLPH CHURCHILL:

Bonnet and morning dress, gray gloves.

To kiss the Queen's hand after receiving the decoration, like the gentlemen to-day. A room will be prepared for her.

The Queen, with one of the Princesses and a lady-in-waiting, received me in a small room. She stood with her back to the window, wearing a long white veil which made an aureole round her against the light. Addressing a few kind words to me, to which in my embarrassment I made some inaudible answer, she proceeded to pin the order on my left shoulder. I remember that my black velvet dress was thickly embroidered with jet, so much so that the pin could find no hold, and unwittingly the Queen stuck it straight into me. Although like the Spartan boy I tried to hide what I felt, I suppose I gave a start, and the Queen realizing what she had done was much concerned. Eventually the pin was put right and I courtesied myself out of the Royal Presence. As I reached the door, her Majesty suddenly stepped forward saying with a smile, "Oh! you have forgotten the case," holding it out to me at the same time. This little touch of nature relieved an otherwise somewhat formal ceremony. Remarking afterward to the lady-in-waiting that I was afraid I had been awkward, and nervous, "You need not be troubled," she answered, "I know the Queen felt more shy than you did."

Shortly after this we were commanded to Windsor to dine and sleep. We dined in rather a small room, the walls of which were hung with family portraits by Winterhalter. Conversation was carried on in whispers, which I thought exceedingly oppressive and conducive to shyness. When the Queen spoke, even the whispers ceased. If she addressed a remark to you, the answer was given while the whole company listened.

There is a story (which I give for what it is worth) told of an officer who, being on guard at the Castle, was asked to dine. The whispered conversation and the stiffness of the proceedings beginning to weigh on him, he thought he would enliven them with a little joke. The Queen, hearing smothered laughter, asked what it was about. Scarlet and stammering, the poor man had to repeat his little tale, amid dead silence. Fixing a cold eye upon him, "We are not amused," was all the Queen said.

The night we were there, the household seemed slightly agitated, and the Queen retired earlier than usual; so they said. The next morning we understood the reason when we were told that a young Prince of Battenberg had been born that night in the Castle. Following the ancient custom which prescribes that a Cabinet Minister should be in attendance in the royal residence on such occasions, the Home Secretary, Mr. Henry Matthews, had been hastily sent for from London, in preference to Randolph, whom the Queen thought "too young," although he was a married man and the father of a family, as well as a Cabinet Minister at the time, besides being actually in the house.

India and things Indian loomed largely in my eyes that winter, and I acquired more knowledge of the country and its history than I had ever possessed before. The Far East, although I had never been there, always had a great fascination for me, and Randolph's graphic descriptions of his travels made me very envious.

While he was at the India Office I was called upon to help Lady Dufferin with the fund she was getting up in aid of the National Association for Supplying Female Medical Aid to the Women of India. This was the beginning of a remarkable institution which is flourishing to-day. Besides giving employment to numbers of English female doctors, it opened, as Lady Dufferin pointed out, a career for native women, and alleviated

9

some of the terrible sufferings of others. The Lord Mayor agreed to hold a meeting at the Mansion House in aid of the fund. Already I had collected a goodly sum. Randolph was delighted with my activity. He wrote to me from Scotland:

AUCHNASHELLACH,

. . . I have written twenty-one letters to-day, some of them long ones, so you won't be vexed if I only send you a short scrawl. I think your letter to Lady Dufferin admirable and all your plans with regard to her fund most excellent.

At the meeting at the Mansion House a handsome sum was subscribed. Among the many speeches, I remember thinking that Mrs. Fawcett's was by far the most eloquent, perhaps on account of its simplicity, free from any attempt at rhetorical effect. There is no doubt that a woman's high pitched voice carries very far in comparison with that of a man, and when in the matter of delivery the manner is slightly deprecatory, it becomes very effective, particularly to the male sex.

Lady Dufferin, who was watching the progress of her fund from afar, wrote me the following letter:

GOVERNMENT HOUSE,
CALCUTTA, January 4, 1886.

MY DEAR LADY RANDOLPH:

I had intended writing to you as soon as I should get to Calcutta, but I have let some time slip away without doing so. I hope Lord Randolph told you that I wished to congratulate you upon getting the Crown of India. I was so glad to see that you had it.

I am going to ask Sir Henry Ponsonby to pay the Queen's £100 into Coutts's, and you can have it acknowledged in the "Times" whenever you think it would be useful. My public meeting takes place on the 27th, and I will send you a report. When some notice of this appears in the English papers it might be a good time for a further effort. I heard from Sir Frederick Roberts that Lady Burdett-Coutts talked of subscribing. I particularly wish not to ask her myself, but I thought that I might mention the fact to you. We are getting on very well, and I am constantly hearing of little things being started in unexpected places.

The great Durbungha is going to build and keep up a dispensary, and has asked me to go down to lay the foundation-stone, and to-day a certain Sir Walter de Souza has promised an annual subscription of 2400 rupees for training women in Calcutta.

Another little place in Bengal has set up a dispensary—and so on throughout the country.

We are just entering upon the short and sharp labors of a season which is being cut up by visits to Delhi and Burmah; there are so very few English visitors here this winter, I suppose the election kept all travellers at home.

To-day Lord Dufferin has been employed in the unpleasant task of putting on an income tax, and so now we shall probably hear howls of execration on all sides.

I hope that Lord Randolph is quite rested after all his election fatigues and is quite strong and ready for the parliamentary encounter.

I remain, dear Lady Randolph,

Yours sincerely,

HARIOT DUFFERIN.

The political events which led to Lord Randolph Churchill's resignation of the post of Chancellor of the

Exchequer and Leader of the House of Commons, which he held in Lord Salisbury's second administration, have been so well described elsewhere[1] that it is not necessary for me to dilate on them in these reminiscences. Although the recipient of many confidences, so little did I realize the grave step Randolph was contemplating, that I was at that moment occupied with the details of a reception we were going to give at the Foreign Office, which was to be lent to us for the occasion. Already the cards had been printed. The night before his resignation we went to the play with Sir Henry Wolff. Questioning Randolph as to the list of guests for the party, I remember being puzzled at his saying: "Oh! I should n't worry about it if I were you; it probably will never take place." I could get no explanation of his meaning, and shortly after the first act he left us ostensibly to go to the club, but in reality to go to the "Times" office and give them the letter he had written at Windsor Castle three nights before. In it he resigned all he had worked for for years, and, if he had but known it, signed his political death warrant. When I came down to breakfast, the fatal paper in my hand, I found him calm and smiling. "Quite a surprise for you," he said. He went into no explanation, and I felt too utterly crushed and miserable to ask for any, or even to remonstrate. Mr. Moore (the permanent Under-Secretary at the Treasury), who was devoted to Randolph, rushed in, pale and anxious, and with a faltering voice said to me, "He has thrown himself from the top of the ladder, and will never reach it again!" Alas! he proved too true a prophet.

[1] Life of Lord Randolph Churchill by Winston Churchill.

SANDRINGHAM

CHAPTER IX

AFTER RESIGNATION—SANDRINGHAM

WHEN Lord Randolph Churchill resigned his position as Chancellor of the Exchequer and Leader of the House of Commons, the political world stood aghast. Friends bemoaned, and the toadies and sycophants fell away and vanished. His action aroused much censure, and every hand seemed against him; yet his only crime was to advocate economy. How well I remember my bitter feelings in those days! The political atmosphere round us seemed suddenly full of strife and treachery. It was gall and wormwood to me to hear Randolph abused in every quarter,—often, as I thought, by the very men who owed their success, if not their political existence, to him. On every side I heard of the defection of political allies, even of some whom we had every reason to believe would remain loyal. But I suppose the flowing tide was too much for them, and they drifted away with the rest. It was fated that the first political speech made after Randolph's resignation should be by Sir John Gorst, who criticized him in no measured terms. Well might Randolph have exclaimed with Zechariah, "I was wounded in the house of my friends." In speaking some years later of Sir John at a public meeting, Randolph referred to him as "my honorable friend." To me, who had resented what I rightly or wrongly considered an unfriendly act on the part of Sir John, this was too much, and I remonstrated warmly. "The fact is," said Randolph, laughing, "it slipped out; I forgot." I remember hearing Lord Salisbury say that a man who could not be vindictive was not a strong man. I often quoted this without effect to Randolph.

When I looked back at the few preceding months which seemed so triumphant and full of promise, the *débâcle* appeared all the greater. I had made sure that Randolph would enjoy the fruits of office for years to come, and apart from the honor and glory, I regretted those same "fruits." But on this subject he was adamant. "Politics and money do not go together," he would often say to me; "so put the thought away."

How dark those days seemed! In vain I tried to console myself with the thought that happiness does not depend so much on circumstances as on one's inner self. But I have always found in practice that theories are of little comfort. The vicissitudes of life resemble one of those gilded balls seen in a fountain. Thrown up by the force of the water, it flies up and down; now at the top, catching the rays of the sun, now cast into the depths, then again shooting up, sometimes so high that it escapes altogether, and falls to the ground.

It is with pleasure that I turn from these disagreeable reflections to the remembrance of a charming visit we had paid to Sandringham a month previous, in honor of the Prince of Wales's birthday. The Prince and Princess dispensed their hospitality with that remarkable

STUDY BY GEORGE FREDERICK WATTS FOR A PORTRAIT OF
KING EDWARD VII, WHEN PRINCE OF WALES

The original is in the Watts Collection at Guildford, Surrey

simplicity of which English royalty alone has the secret. One felt at home at once; indeed, the life was the same as at any pleasant country house. Breakfast, which began at nine o'clock, was served at small, round tables in a dining-room decorated with Spanish tapestries given by the late King of Spain. The men were in shooting get-up, and the ladies in any dress they chose to affect—short skirts and thick boots or elaborate day gowns. No one cared or noticed. None of the Royalties appeared before midday, although the Prince of Wales joined the shooters, who made an early start after breakfast. The feminine contingent, left to their own devices, generally congregated in the large hall, which contained writing-tables, a piano, and masses of books and newspapers.

The amount of scribbling which goes on in a country house, and in which Englishwomen in particular indulge, is always a source of astonishment and amusement to foreigners. I have heard them exclaim: "Mais qu'est-ce qu'elles écrivent toute la journée?" No foreigner, indeed, can understand the Englishwoman's busy life, full as it is of multitudinous occupations ranging from household duties to political gatherings, and all necessitating correspondence.

Just before luncheon we sallied forth to join the shooters: some driving and others walking to the rendezvous. The Princess of Wales, looking in her neat dress and small felt hat as young as her own daughters, would drive a pair of ponies. The luncheon in a big tent was always very animated and sometimes so prolonged that a gentle reminder was needed of the birds waiting to be shot. At this time the young princesses were unmarried.

191

If their manners in public were perhaps too diffident and shy compared with those of foreign royalties, in private they were full of gaiety and fun, dearly loving a joke, particularly if it was directed against some familiar friend who might be staying there.

The sport was exceedingly good and well-managed, owing to the Prince of Wales, who, an excellent shot himself, took a personal interest in the arrangements instead of leaving them all to the keepers. The ladies stayed out to see the sport, many forming a gallery around Lord de Grey, who was one of the guns on this occasion, and whose wonderful shooting has gained him world-wide reputation among sportsmen. I remember once at Panshanger, when I was staying with the late Lord Cowper, seeing Lord de Grey shoot in one stand fifty-two birds out of fifty-four, and for a bet this was done with one hand. He had two loaders and three guns.

Five o'clock tea was a feature at Sandringham. The simplicity of the day attire was discarded in favor of elaborate tea-gowns. After tea, Signor Tosti, who was a great favorite with the royal family, would be made to sing some of his charming songs. He would ramble on in his delightful impromptu manner for hours. Besides his musical gifts, he was a most amusing man, and kept us all laughing at his stories and witty sallies. Sometimes I played duets with the Princess, who was particularly fond of Brahms's Hungarian dances, which were just then in vogue. Or it might be that we would go to Princess Victoria's sitting-room, where there were two pianos, and struggle with a concerto of Schumann. The pace set was terrific, and I was rather glad there was no audience.

Although no uniforms were worn at dinner, this was a ceremonious affair, with every one in full dress and decorations. Rather unpunctual in those days, I was always on the verge of being late. The clocks were put half an hour in advance; but that did not help me, as I traded on the fact, forgetting that it made no difference. When every one was assembled, Their Royal Highnesses would be announced, each lady in turn having the privilege of being taken in by her royal host, who arranged the list himself, and was very particular that there should be no hitch as to people finding their places at once. An equerry with a plan of the dining-table would explain to each man who was to be his partner and where he was to sit. The dinner, which never lasted more than an hour, was excellent and admirably ordered, which is not always the case in royal households where indiscriminate profusion is often paramount. Conversation was fairly animated; there was none of that stiffness which pervaded Windsor and made one fear the sound of one's own voice. The evenings were not prolonged, for in those days there was no Gottlieb's band to listen to, as there invariably is now, or bridge to keep one up late. The Prince would have his rubber of whist, while the rest of the company sat about and talked until the Princess made a move to go to bed, when the ladies would troop off together, stopping to laugh and chatter in the passages, which seemed to amuse the young Princesses more than anything else. Sometimes the Princess would ask one into her dressing-room, which was crowded with objects and souvenirs of all kinds. The dressing-table was so littered with miniatures and photographs of children and friends, besides every conceivable bibelot, that there was no room for brushes or toilet things. On a perch in the center of the room was an old and somewhat ferocious white parrot, which I remember made disconcerting pecks if you happened to be within his radius. At other times the Princess might surprise you by coming to your room, ostensibly "to see if you had everything you wanted," but in reality to give a few words of advice, or to offer her sympathy if she thought you needed any. For without people realizing it, few things escaped her observant eyes. To those who have the privilege of coming into contact with her, Queen Alexandra has endeared herself by many such kind acts, as well as by her gentle and tactful sympathy.

Among those who were at Sandringham on that occasion was the Comtesse de Paris, of whom I saw a great deal later, and who was much liked, every one finding her *très bonne enfant*. She was most unlike a Frenchwoman. Tall and rather thin, with a pleasant smile and a desire to please, she affected sporting clothes and distinguished herself with a gun. Personally, although I see no harm in a woman shooting game, I cannot say I admire it as an accomplishment. The fact is, I love life so much that the unnecessary curtailing of any creature's existence is more than distasteful to me. Not long ago, while in Scotland, I saw a young and charming woman, who was surely not of a bloodthirsty nature, kill two stags in one morning. The first she shot through the heart. With the aid of a powerful pair of field-glasses, I watched her stalk the second. First she crawled on all fours up a long burn; emerging hot and panting, not to say wet and dirty, she then continued her scramble up a steep hill, taking advantage of any cover afforded by the ground,

ISABELLE, COMTESSE DE PARIS
Mother of the Queen of Portugal and the Duchess D'Aosta

or remaining in a petrified attitude if by chance a hind happened to look up. The stag, meanwhile, quite oblivious of the danger lurking at hand, was apparently enjoying himself. Surrounded by his hinds, he trusted to their vigilance, and lay in the bracken in the brilliant sunshine. I could just see his fine antlered head, when suddenly, realizing that all was not well, he bounded up, making a magnificent picture as he stood gazing round, his head thrown back in defiance. *Crash! bang!* and this glorious animal, became a maimed and tortured thing. Shot through both forelegs, he attempted to gallop down the hill, his poor broken limbs tumbling about him, while the affrighted hinds stood riveted to the spot, looking at their lord and master with horror, not unmixed with curiosity. I shall never forget the sight, or that of the dogs set on him, and the final scene, over which I draw a veil. If these things must be done, how can a woman bring herself to do them?

But this digression has taken me far from the Comtesse de Paris. She cherished ambitious schemes for the Comte de Paris, and at that time was confident that he would eventually become King of France.

We had long conversations about the Primrose League, which interested her vastly. So greatly did she admire its organization that she started a league in France on more or less the same lines. "La Ligue de la Rose," as it was called, had for its symbol "la Rose de France," and its object was the restoration of the monarchy. Unlike the Primrose League, I fear it did not make the stir or gain the recruits that she hoped. Nevertheless, for some years it flourished in a mild way. Her Royal Highness having meanwhile honored me with her friendship, we met frequently, and she constantly sought my advice as to the details of her scheme. An inspired article on the "Rose League" appeared in the "Primrose League Gazette," which gave her great satisfaction.

SHEEN HOUSE

EAST SHEEN, SURREY, 25 Juillet, 1888.

MA CHÈRE LADY RANDOLPH,[1]

Vous avez bien voulu vous intéresser un peu à nos essais de Ligue en France, et je me permets de vous envoyer les deux circulaires qui seront imprimées et distribuées dans quelques jours, j'espère que vous voudrez bien les lire avec indulgence et les garder pour que si plus tard nous arrivons à un beau résultat nous puissions en causer ensemble. Vous savez que c'est vous qui m'avez donné l'idée de faire quelque chose de resemblable en France, c'est donc à vous que je pense toujours en travaillant à cette grande entreprise, et je vous dois déjà avant de commencer la ferme foi de réussir en suivant votre exemple. La Rose n'égalera jamais la Primrose; mais peut-être plus tard elles se retrouveront souvent.

Si je ne parle pas du Primrose League dans les Circulaires c'est uniquement par modestie n'osant pas comparer l'immense succès de la première fleur avec les très modestes commencements de la seconde, mais dans toutes mes lettres particulières et à toutes les personnes qui avec moi veulent bien travailler j'en parle pour leur donner à tous la même idée; celle de réussir comme vous.

Pardonnez moi mon ambition et en attendant que j'aie le plaisir de vous revoir croyez moi toujours

Votre bien affectionée

ISABELLE, COMTESSE DE PARIS.

[1] See Appendix for translation of this and following letter.

A DISTINGUISHED GROUP AT SANDRINGHAM

From left to right: Prince of Wales, now King Edward VII.; Lady Randolph Churchill, Comtesse de Paris, Princess of Wales, Lady Salisbury, Comte de Paris, Lady de Grey, Lord de Grey, Mr. Christopher Sykes, Miss Charlotte Knollys, Princess Maud, now Queen of Norway (with dog); Princess Victoria, Princesse Hélène d'Orléans, now Duchesse d'Aosta; Princess Louise, now Princess Royal and Duchess of Fife; Mr. Henry Matthews, then Home Secretary and now Viscount Llandaff; Marquis of Salisbury, Lord Randolph Churchill, Mr. C. R. Spencer, now Lord Althorp, Lord Chamberlain.

LADY RANDOLPH CHURCHILL

East Sheen, Surrey, 7 Oct. 1888.

Ma chère Lady Randolph,

Je ne sais pas si vous êtes à Londres mais je vous écris un petit mot pour vous dire que j'ai reçu hier soir un numéro du Primrose League Gazette contenant un article des plus aimables sur La Rose Ligue; je viens vous remercier et de l'envoi et de l'article, car je suis bien sure que vous y êtes pour une bien grande part; si je me suis trompée je vous prie de transmettre mes remerciements à l'auteur. La Primrose League est vraiment bien aimable en faisant si bon accueil à sa sœur cadette La Rose Ligue.

Je vous ai envoyé avant hier un numéro du Soleil pour que vous puissiez voir en entier notre nouveau papier, vous y avez sans doute trouvé des phrases que vous connaissiez et j'espère que vous m'approuverez, j'ai je crois suivi vos conseils. Je reçois de tous côtés de très bon rapports, il parait que la Rose marche à merveille, j'espère que ce beau zèle durera longtemps, et c'est à vous la première que nous devrons notre succès.

J'espère avoir bientôt le plaisir de vous revoir, et en attendant je vous prie de me croire

Votre bien affectionée

Isabelle, Comtesse de Paris.

It is sad to think that so much energy and zeal came to nought. The "Ligue," as well as its object, is a thing of the past. But in France political movements are not furthered by the help of women: the existing form of government and the ridicule attached to their public appearance preclude them from airing their views or promoting a cause on a platform. Besides, the majority of Frenchwomen are too much occupied with the domestic affairs of their homes or with business matters to give much attention to anything outside. How different from the part Englishwomen play in politics, and particularly in London society, where they are more important agents than in any other capital of the world! This is owing to the happy blending of matters social and political which an established order of things has fostered for centuries.

Among the people at Sandringham were Lord and Lady Salisbury. I did not know Lady Salisbury well, but she impressed me as being a woman of great strength of character and full of common sense. One could not help liking her, notwithstanding a rather brusque manner. I fancy she detested affectations of any kind, and her masterly mind must have disdained the ordinary society twaddle to which she was often called upon to listen. I remember a heated argument on the duties incumbent on a politician's wife, which, according to her, were rather arduous, involving the necessity of making a study of the various political problems of the day. I confess I felt no desire to tackle either the Plan of Campaign or the Budget, which were the two prominent questions of the moment, and thought I could help Randolph in other ways.

In looking at the old photograph of the party, I see that Lord Salisbury and Randolph are standing side by side. How little did I or any one else there realize the great and irretrievable breach which was to come so soon and so suddenly between these two! In the midst of delightful people, occupations, and amusements, I was quite happy and far from imagining that the political horizon was not clear.

The celebration of Queen Victoria's Jubilee (1887) was the occasion of every sort of festivity. London was crowded to its utmost, and people came from all parts of the world to see the pageant and the crowning ceremony in Westminster Abbey. The day was blessed with the proverbial "Queen's weather." Rarely had I seen London look so festive—blue sky and bright sunshine, flags everywhere, and an excited yet patient crowd filling the thoroughfares and the route of the procession. As the wife of an ex-Cabinet Minister, I was given a good place in the Abbey. The magnificent sight impressed me greatly. Gorgeous uniforms and beautiful dresses were enhanced by the "dim religious light," pierced here and there by the rays of the summer sun as it streamed through the ancient stained-glass windows. The Queen, representing the glory and continuity of England's history, sat alone in the middle of the great nave, a small, pathetic figure surrounded by that vast assembly, whose gaze was riveted upon her. A wave of emotion passed over it as silent tears were seen to be dropping one by one upon the Queen's folded hands. Perhaps the fact that the Te Deum which was being played had been composed by the Prince Consort added yet another note of sadness to the burden of her memories.

Once again I had occasion to see Queen Victoria at a great function. This was at the opening of the Imperial Institute. The Queen, with a look of intense anxiety on her face, sat on a throne in the middle of the huge hall, which was filled to overflowing. She had to make a speech, which evidently was a great ordeal; but when she did so, her voice, soft and gentle as it was, never wavered for a moment, and every word could be heard by all.

Many were the public functions of all kinds to which we were bidden that year in honor of the Queen's Jubilee. Among them was an invitation from the White Star Company to cruise for a few days on board one of their ships, and to see the Naval Review, which was to take place in the Solent. In the middle of the London season, suffering from the heat and glare of a big city in the month of June, the prospect was a delightful one. The trip proved most enjoyable. The Duchess of Manchester (since Duchess of Devonshire), Mr. Chamberlain, Lord Hartington, and a host of well-known and agreeable people, were on board. Great were the political foregatherings; arguments and discussions never ceased. Although Mr. Chamberlain had left Gladstone and the Home-Rule Party, he was not yet prepared to join the Conservatives, notwithstanding the overtures made to him by Lord Salisbury. Tired of inactivity, he was revolving at that time, in conjunction with Randolph, a scheme for a new party which was to be called the National Party, and both were anxious that Lord Hartington should join it. The moment was thought propitious, and it was settled that Mr. Chamberlain should speak to Lord Hartington. That afternoon I was sitting on the deck with the latter when Mr. Chamberlain joined us. Drawing up a chair, he suddenly plunged into the matter without preliminaries and with his usual directness. Lord Hartington, taken *au dépourvu,* looked uncomfortable and answered very shortly. Mr. Chamberlain, full of his scheme, pressed the points home, taking no notice of the monosyllables he got in answer. But after a time the frozen attitude of Lord Hartington began to take effect, and the conversation languished and died. I believe the subject was never reopened. In any case, nothing came of it. I imagine that Lord Hartington was a difficult person to persuade against his will and most uncompromisingly definite in his likes and dislikes. I have always thought that there existed a gulf between him and Mr. Chamberlain that no political expediency could really bridge. But of course this is only my own opinion.

I have heard Randolph say that in most political questions he considered Lord Hartington's judgment infallible. He was slow, but sure. If an important paper, requiring an early answer, was sent to him to read, it might be pigeonholed for weeks. But when he *did* read it, he would at once discover any flaw or weakness, and his verdict generally carried the day. In private life no one was pleasanter or easier to get on with than the late Duke of Devonshire. His rather stern countenance belied a mirth-loving soul, and he thoroughly appreciated a joke.

He was rather careless about his clothes and once on his birthday his friends, as a joke, sent him every conceivable sort of head-gear from the ceremonious silk hat to the flannel cricketing cap. My contribution, I remember, was a pot hat. For hours they poured in; I believe he received over fifty. In old days before he succeeded to the dukedom we used to stay with him at Hardwick Hall for shooting-parties. It was a wonderful place, full of thrilling historical associations. I never tired of hearing about them, or of wandering through the beautiful rooms filled with memories of Mary, Queen of Scots, most ill-fated of Queens, and of her gaoler the great "Bess of Hardwick" (Countess of Shrewsbury), ances-

10

tress of our host. During our visit Randolph slept in "Queen Mary's Bedroom" which was of small dimensions, and had a window by the side of the door so that the unfortunate occupant could be spied upon at all times of the day or night. Two centuries later Marie Antoinette was put to the same indignity in the Conciergerie. Bess of Hardwick, when she pulled down the old Hall to build the present house (begun 1576, finished 1599) evidently intended this room for her prisoner, but Queen Mary did not live to occupy it. Beheaded in 1586, all her belongings were subsequently removed to it, including the original bed-hangings and coverlet worked by herself. Hence the name given to this room by tradition. My imagination ran riot as I gazed upon the screens and cushions worked by the Queen during the long years of her captivity. Who knows? On these very canvases her tears may have been as numerous as were the stitches with which she tried to find solace.

Close by was the Long Gallery which was supposed to be haunted by the restless spirit of the redoubtable Bess, not to speak of Queen Mary and Queen Elizabeth. There are some lines written *àpropos* of this Gallery by the beautiful and celebrated Georgiana, Duchess of Devonshire, who spent long periods after her marriage at Chatsworth and Hardwick, whence she writes in French to her mother, Countess Spencer:

Sept. 3, 1777.

"We set out for Hardwicke this morning. . . . Hardwicke looked extremely well. We walk'd all about the house, & paid our compliments to Queen Mary & Queen Elizabeth. I never look at the melancholy picture of Mary which was drawn in the 10th year of her imprisonment, and which has a countenance

THE MARQUIS OF HARTINGTON, THE LATE DUKE OF DEVONSHIRE

that looks worn by misfortune without pitying to the greatest degree the misery she must have liv'd in—for even the pomp she was treated with, those melancholy hangings and coffin like beds—must have added to the tristesse of her situation". . .

And again:

(Wednesday, the 14th of Feb. 1780.)

". . . Sachant comme vous le faites notre solitude ici, que nous avons pour toute société, les arbres du Parc, et Les portraits de La Gallerie et Les Ombres des bonnes gens qui y sont peints, ici . . .

> Où nous avons pour compagnie
> L'Ombre de La Reine Marie,
> Qui eut un nombre étonnant
> De maux, de soucis et d'amants.
> Ou bien par sa bonté extrême
> La Grande Elisabeth même
> Sort quelques fois du Canevas
> Pour demander comment l'on va,
> (Celle qui régnant sur la terre
> De sa Virginité fut fière
> Et si l'on croit en ces temps-là
> A tort la Reine s'en piqua)."

I remember having a large, tapestried room the door of which had a keyhole big enough to put one's hand through, and which gave on to the Presence Chamber. The first night I thought the arras seemed to move about, so arming myself with a poker, I thrust it here and there, when to my dismay I felt the tapestry give, and on looking behind, saw a small, winding stone staircase disappearing into unknown depths. This made me so nervous that I sat shivering for hours in an arm-chair,

(now Duchess of Devonshire); and Lady Cardigan, who would drive up in an old-fashioned, yellow tilbury, in which she sat all day. Lady Bradford and Lady Cadogan were always there; as were Lady Castlereagh (now Lady Londonderry), Lady Gerard, and a few others. It was the fashion to ride, those who did not appearing in ordinary country clothes. Nowadays velvets and feathers are worn by the mob which throngs the stands, many not knowing a horse from a cow, but coming because it is the fashion. I have heard amusing tales of the ignorance displayed on these occasions. One lady was overheard declaring that as she had not been to Newmarket for years, she had quite "forgotten the names of the horses," and another, that some one had told her the name of "the yearling which was going to win the Derby at the next Newmarket meeting." A charming duchess, who cares only to see her friends at the races, generally brings her needlework, and takes no heed of the strenuous efforts of the horses and jockeys as they race past her.

The shining light of our stable was the "Abbesse de Jouarre," for which Randolph gave £300 at the Doncaster sales, eventually selling her for £7000. I had been reading "L'Abbesse de Jouarre," written by Renan in order, so it is said, to disprove the assertions of his friends that he could not write something imaginative. I suggested the name as a fitting one for the beautiful black mare, which was by "Trappist" out of "Festive." She was a gallant little thing, with a heart bigger than her body, and her size made the public so sceptical that she invariably started at long odds. When she won the Oaks those who backed her got 20 to 1. Neither Randolph nor I witnessed her triumph. He was fishing in Norway, and I was with some friends who had a house on the Thames. On that day we happened to reach Boulter's Lock shortly after the hour of the race. Asking the lock-keeper which horse had won the big race, he replied, to my great delight and amusement, "The Abcess on the Jaw." The "Abbesse," after winning many races and producing numerous progeny, died in the breeding stables at Welbeck. It was with great satisfaction that I witnessed her grandson "Land League" win the Cambridgeshire in 1907.

CHAPTER X

RUSSIA

DURING the winter of 1881 we went to Russia, where we spent a most interesting and delightful month. The Marquis de Breteuil, whose ancestor had been French Ambassador to the court of the Great Catherine, and Mr. Trafford made up our party. Everything was new and attractive to us. The people were charming and hospitable, and seemed full of *bonhomie,* and we saw no signs of that grinding despotism and tyranny which is supposed to be synonymous with Russian life. My first impression of the scenery was one of disappointment, the country between Berlin and St. Petersburg, or rather the part beyond the Russian frontier, being flat and uninteresting. The waste and dreary expanse, when covered with snow, inspires a feeling of deep melancholy. To live for months every year buried in that cold, monotonous silence is quite enough, I should imagine, to account for the vein of sadness which seems to be the basis of the Russian character, and which betrays itself in all Russian music and painting. As our snow-laden train crawled into the station in St. Petersburg, and we stepped out joyfully and stretched our cramped and tired limbs, the broad streets, full of life and animation, and as bright as day with

214

electricity, seemed a delightful contrast. I do not know what I expected to see, but the city disappointed me with its modern appearance. Looking at the houses of rather mean exterior, with their small double windows and tiny doors, little did I dream of the splendor within. Space, however, seemed to be immaterial, and this struck me the more forcibly, accustomed as I was to London, with its narrow streets and considered inches.

The French system of apartments is common in St. Petersburg, although not so general as in Paris; but where it exists, the entrance and staircases are much more decorated and cared for than is usual where several families live under the same roof, and this gives the appearance of a private dwelling. In the great houses I was struck by the very large number of servants, and was told that in the cases of some rich noblemen whole families of useless dependents—mujiks, with their wives and children—were installed in the lower regions. If this was the case in town, what must it have been in the country? Such generosity, combined with the utter absence of real supervision in the financial management of the establishment, must have been a heavy tax on the largest fortune, and it is not surprising that the Russian nobility of to-day, with the added burden of the late war and the internal dissension of their unhappy country, are in an impoverished state.

However, we saw nothing of this, and all the entertainments and functions to which we went, whether private or public, were extremely well done. Russians dearly love light, and on these occasions made their houses as bright as day, with a profusion of candles as well as electric light. Masses of flowers, notwithstanding their rarity in such a rigorous climate, decorated every available place, and the staircases were lined with footmen in gorgeous liveries. Although many of the houses were very smartly furnished with all that money could buy and modern art suggest, they struck me as lacking in the real refinement and true artistic taste that one sees in Paris; but the French are born connoisseurs, and think of little else than artistic comfort.

In those days the average Russian drawing-room was superior to the ordinary English one. If there was a lack of imagination, there was also an absence of tawdriness, which contrasted favorably with the overcrowded London room, where, at that time, the esthetic and Japanese craze reigned supreme—where evenly balanced structures of paper fans, Liberty silks, and photographs were thought decorative, not to speak of labyrinths of tiny tables, chairs, and screens. I was prepared to suffer a great deal from the cold, but found, as in most Northern countries, that the houses were heated to suffocation, and the windows were rarely opened, a small ventilator being thought quite sufficient. Russians assert that all foreigners bring so much caloric with them that they do not feel the cold at first. This may be so, but there is no doubt that they feel the want of air and the stuffiness of the rooms, which dries up the skin and takes away the appetite.

On the other hand, I thoroughly enjoyed the outdoor life of sleighing and skating. Comfortably seated in a sleigh, behind a good, fat coachman to keep the wind off, I never wearied of driving about. The rapidity with which one dashes noiselessly along is most exhilarating, notwithstanding a biting wind or blinding snow. The ordinary Russian sleigh, smaller than the American cutter, barely holds two, but the thick fur rug, even in a common droshky, or cab, is so well fastened down that it helps to keep one from falling out, besides protecting from the cold. The troikas, wide sleighs with three horses, of which the middle one trots while the other two gallop, have become rather rare, and are used principally for traveling or for expeditions in the country. Nothing is prettier than a really smart sleigh with two horses, one trotting and the other galloping, covered with a large net of dark blue cord fastened to the front of the sleigh, to keep the snow from being kicked into the face of the occupant. The coachman, with his fur-lined coat gathered in at the waist, and his bright red or blue octagonal cap with gold braid, drives with his arms extended in order to preserve his circulation. I was much impressed with the fact that the coachmen hardly ever seemed to use their short, thick whips, which they kept carefully hidden. A footman stood on a small step behind, his tall hat and ordinary great coat looking a little incongruous, I confess, and marring an otherwise picturesque sight. The horses are so beautifully broken that a word will stop them. The whole time I was in Russia I never saw a horse ill-used. No need for a "Society for the Prevention of Cruelty to Animals" there. The *Isvoshnik* who owns his cab-horse looks upon him as his friend, and very often shares the animal's stall at night.

Among the many acquaintances we made were M. and Mme. Polovstow, who showed us a great deal of hospitality. He was President of the Council, a very important post, and was high in the favor of the Czar.

His early history was rather romantic. As private secretary to the millionaire Steiglitz, Polovstow won the affections and the hand of his adopted daughter, to whom Steiglitz left the whole of his fortune.

Among many institutions founded by her adopted father, Mme. Polovstow took us to see the "Steiglitz School of Art," which was kept up at her own expense. I was much interested to find in the museum a certain Italian cabinet which the late Duke of Marlborough had sold from Blenheim, and the destination of which had always been a mystery.

One night we went to the opera with them to hear "La vie pour le Czar" by Glinka, charming music, imprint with all the national characteristics of sadness and wild, boisterous gaiety; but the orchestration however seemed rather feeble. All the ladies wore high dresses, which took away from the brilliant appearance one is accustomed to in other opera-houses. Sometimes the performance was entirely ballet—no singing—and one night I had the opportunity of seeing the famous dancer Zucchi, in "Esmeralda." She was then in her prime, and she certainly was a marvelous dancer of the old school.

After the opera, enveloped in great fur coats and caps, we drove in troikas to the islands in the Neva, where the Polovstows had a charming pavilion. We were ushered into a large conservatory brilliantly lighted and full of orchids and rare flowers, a dazzling and wonderful contrast to the snow-clad scenery outside, on which "the cold, round moon shone deeply down," turning everything to silver. Hidden by palms, a band of Tziganes was playing inspiriting melodies, while in the dining-room an excellent supper was served on genuine Louis XV plate.

We did not get back to our hotel until the small hours of the morning. Russians, I found to my cost, love late hours and seem never to go to bed, the evening generally beginning for them at midnight.

On one occasion I was taken for a spin on the Neva with a fast trotter, which I did not enjoy quite so much, owing to the end of my nose being nearly frozen. When we returned, my host rushed up to me and rubbed it violently with snow, as it looked ominously white. So long as your nose keeps a glorious red, you are safe.

While in St. Petersburg I was able to indulge to my heart's content in my favorite pastime of skating, which I did on the lake of the Palais de la Tauride, a royal palace where Russian society congregated. But great was my disappointment to find that the Russians did not care for figure-skating, and, in fact, did not skate well. I was told that had it not been for the Czarina (Marie), who was an adept in the art, people would not have appreciated skating at all. As it was, they much preferred tobogganing down the ice-hills, half a dozen or more persons in a sleigh. It was in one of these that I had my first experience of this sport, and was duly "blooded" (if one may call it so) by being placed in the front seat of the sleigh and shot into a bank of snow. The ice-hills, which are built on the lake, are merely blocks of ice placed on a wooden path raised to a platform at a steep angle, which you ascend by a staircase. To go down one of these hills on skates for the first time gives the same delightful feeling of satisfaction and pleasure which in hunting is experienced in getting over a big fence, leaving the field a bit behind. It is not an easy matter, as the pace is terrific, and coming to the level again at the foot of the hill makes it difficult to keep one's feet; but if successful one shoots across the whole lake. Many were the accidents, and I saw one poor lady break her arm.

Sir Robert Morier, the British Ambassador, was away when we first arrived, but later he and his family showed us great kindness and hospitality. Meanwhile we were bidden to Gatchina to have an audience with the Czar and the Czarina. Gatchina, about an hour by train from St. Petersburg, is the Windsor of Russia. It is a curious mixture of splendor and unpretentiousness, and is approached from the station through a series of small parks, which must be lovely in summer. I was surprised to see so few sentries: to all appearances the Czar was not more guarded than the King at Windsor. The entrance to Gatchina on the public road had only one sentry.

The palace has no great architectural merits, but its six hundred rooms and endless corridors were filled with priceless Oriental china, and the walls were adorned with tapestries and treasures of art. *Coureurs* in black-and-orange liveries, their caps embellished by tossing black, white, and orange feathers, gave a slightly barbaric appearance to the scene, which was added to by the mass of bowing attendants, and by two Nubians dressed in white, with turbans and scimitars, standing outside the Czarina's audience chamber.

While waiting to be received, we were shown into an apartment which savored of the early Victorian style, with paintings of mediocre quality. Here a *déjeuner* was served, and afterward we went to our respective audiences. Randolph stayed quite an hour with the Czar, who discussed all the political questions of the day.

THE WINTER PALACE, ST. PETERSBURG

The Czarina, whom I had had the honor of knowing as Czarevna at Cowes some years before, was most gracious and charming, reminding me of her sister, Queen Alexandra, although not so beautiful. She asked endless questions about England and all that was going on politically and socially, and finally, having arrived *"au bout de notre Latin,"* and Randolph not appearing, I was taken to see the palace.

Among many rooms, I remember a large hall worthy of an old English country-house, full of comfortable arm-chairs and writing-tables, games, and toys. I even spied a swing. In that room their Majesties often dined, I was told, even when they had guests, and after dinner the table would be removed, and they would spend the remainder of the evening there. This seemed strange to me when I thought of the many hundred rooms in the enormous building. But their tastes were of the simplest, and the Czar particularly affected tiny rooms, though they were much at variance with his towering frame and majestic bearing. His manner impressed me with a conviction of sincerity and earnestness.

Before leaving St. Petersburg, we were invited once more to Gatchina. This time it was in the evening; a special train conveyed about one hundred and fifty guests. On arriving, we were met by a long stream of royal carriages, which took us to the palace, where we witnessed an entertainment consisting of three short plays in three languages, after which supper was served. I had been given a seat in the third row, but when the Royalties came in, I was bidden to sit behind the Empress, who every now and then would turn round and make some pleasant remark.

There are some curious customs at the Russian court which do not harmonize with one's idea of a despotic and autocratic sovereign. While we were sitting at small tables, the Czar walked about talking to his guests, all of whom, including officers, remained seated. It appears that that was the habit of Peter the Great, who disliked ceremony of any kind; and as tradition is everything in Russia, this custom was religiously kept. There is no doubt that the etiquette of the Russian court is much less rigid than it is in England or Germany. For instance, it is not the custom to treat the members of the Imperial Family with so much deference as in other European courts; I noticed that the ladies did not think of courtesying to a young Grand Duke, and would rise only when the Czarina did, or at the entrance of the Czar. So too, in making their obeisance, they bowed stiffly from the waist, which was even more ungraceful than the English bob, our apology for a courtesy. The men, on the other hand, were very deferential, particularly to the ladies. At private dinners, when we were announced, the host would rush forward, seize my hand, and kiss it, and then proceed to introduce all the men present. I then had to ask to be presented to every lady, and duly call on them personally the next day. This I found very irksome and wearying, as it stood in the way of my sight-seeing.

One of the most interesting sights we were privileged to see was the New Year's Reception at the Winter Palace. At eleven o'clock in the morning the whole court attended, and society paid its respects to the sovereign. The Czar, dressed on this particular occasion in the uniform of the Gardes du Corps, gave his arm to the Czarina, and was followed by the imperial family. The train of each Grand Duchess was carried by four young officers. I remember that that of the Grand Duchess Vladimir was of silver brocade, with a sable border half a yard in depth. These were followed by long files of ladies-in-waiting, dressed in green and gold, and maids-of-honor in red and gold. The procession ended when all the court officials, resplendent in gorgeous uniforms and covered with decorations, walked with measured steps through the long suite of rooms, and lined up on each side with officers in the red, white, or blue of their regiments. To these the Czar spoke as he passed, saying, "Good morning, my children," to which they replied in unison, "We are happy to salute you." In other rooms ladies were assembled, dressed in the national costume of every hue, and covered with jewels, mostly cabochon sapphires and emeralds. All wore that most becoming of head-dresses—the "Kakoshnik," made of various materials from diamonds to plain velvet. The Czarina, with her graceful figure and small head, looked very stately in a magnificent tiara, and a blue velvet and ermine train, as the cortège passed on to the chapel to hear mass. This lasted an hour, every one remaining standing—an art which Royalty alone seems to have the gift of practising without breaking down, and without apparent effort.

I cannot adequately describe the scene in the chapel, which, if it had been less perfect in detail, might have appeared somewhat theatrical. On the right, the dresses of the women formed a sea of warm color, the soft red and green velvets of the ladies-in-waiting predominating, their long, white tulle veils looking like halos round their heads, touched here and there by iridescent rays from the rich stained-glass windows. On the left, the men presented a scarcely less brilliant group, the dark velvet cassock of a Lutheran pastor standing out in effective contrast to the vivid red of a Cardinal close by. The royal choir, which follows the Czar wherever he goes, is the finest I have ever heard. Composed of male voices alone, without the aid of any instrument (none being allowed in the Greek Church), it was perfection. The character of the music I found rather monotonous, and thought to myself how they would have rendered one of Handel's grand anthems.

A story was told me of this celebrated choir. Clad originally in funereal black, they offended the eyes of a certain maid-of-honor, a favorite of the Czar, who, remonstrating with her for not attending mass, asked the reason. The lady pleaded that she was suffering from melancholy, and that the sight of the black choir would aggravate it. The next day her excuse was gone, for the choir appeared in crimson surplices braided with gold, and they have continued to do so ever since.

Mass over in the chapel, the procession reformed, a pause being made in the room reserved for the ambassadors and diplomatic corps. His Majesty entered into conversation with a favored few, who improved the shining hour, since, with the exception of some court balls, this was the only occasion they had of speaking to him during the year. Finally the ladies passed before the Czar and kissed hands, holding on to each other's trains, a sight which was more quaint than imposing. When all was over, we sat down to luncheon, reaching home about three o'clock. Not having any such sumptuous day gowns as I found were worn, I was reduced on this

GRAND DUKE SERGE
Brother of Alexander III, assassinated at Moscow in 1905

THE GRAND DUCHESS SERGE
Princess Elisabeth of Hesse, sister of the Czarina

occasion to a blue-and-gold tea-gown, which did quite well, although it seemed a strange garment in which to go to court. On our way out, I saw a sentry guarding a magnificent sable cape, which I was told belonged to the Czarina. It was nearly black, and it had taken years to collect the skins at a cost of £12,000.

Most Russian ladies smoke cigarettes, and at all the parties to which I went one of the reception-rooms was set apart for the purpose, which caused a continual movement to and fro,—taking off the stiffness of a formal party and enabling people to circulate more freely. This in itself would insure a pleasant evening; for who has not seen with despair the only chair at hand triumphantly seized by a bore, whom nothing but a final "Good night" will move?

Russians, as a rule, have enormous appetites, and are very fond of good living, eating—not to mention drinking—often to excess. Drinking in Russian society is not considered a heinous offense. The night we went to Gatchina, the officer in charge, the Colonel of the Preobejensky Guards, the smartest regiment in Russia, who was responsible that night for the safety of the Czar, was so drunk that he fell heavily on my shoulder when presented to me. Those near laughingly propped him up, evidently thinking nothing of it.

We lunched several times at the celebrated restaurant kept by Cubat, where our plates were piled with enormous helpings fit for a regiment of soldiers. Cubat was a most interesting person, late head chef to the Czar, whose service he had only just left. When asked the reason, he said that the supervision in the kitchen of the royal palace was so irksome and stringent,—dozens of

detectives watching his every gesture and pouncing on
every pinch of salt,—that the salary of £2000 a year
did not compensate him. He later bought the hotel
Païva in the Champs-Elysées and started the Cubat Restaurant; but the prices were so high that it soon came to
an end.

One night we dined with the Grand Duke and Duchess
Serge at the beautiful old "Beloselski" palace. It was
built in the reign of the great Catherine, whose hand
is found in everything of real taste in Russia. Decorated and furnished by the best French artists of the
day, to whom the Empress was a generous patron,—
with its lovely Bouchers and carved white panelings,—
I thought it quite the finest house we saw while in Russia.
We waited some time for a belated guest, Mme. X.,
who finally appeared, looking regal, with the most magnificent jewels I had ever seen on any private person;
but on her bare arm,.as distinct as possible, was the black-
and-blue imprint—fingers and thumb—of a brutal hand.
No one could help noticing it, and the Grand Duchess
pointed at it in dismay. "No, no," cried Mme. X.,
laughingly, "X. is at Moscow." *"Quelque jaloux!"* said
my neighbor. At dinner I sat between the Grand Duke
Serge, and the Grand Duke Paul, who was quite the
best-looking man I saw in Russia. I found an old friend
there in Count Schouwalow, who had been Ambassador
in London; also M. de Giers and his wife, at whose
house I afterward met the redoubtable Pobiedonostzeff,
Head of the Synod, with whom I had a long talk—a
tall, gaunt man, whose strange yellow teeth, seemingly
all in one, impressed me more than anything else. Other
interesting people dining there that evening were

Count and Countess Ignatieff, Prince and Princess Solytzkow, and Prince and Princess Worouzow.

No politics nor anything of that nature, whether internal or external, were discussed; reticence as regards public affairs in Russia is only equaled by discretion as regards the affairs of other nations of other countries.

Much to my chagrin, we did not stay in St. Petersburg for the court balls, but, time passing, went on to Moscow. Before leaving, however, we visited the Winter Palace, Prince Troubetsky, the Lord Chamberlain, being deputied to take us over it. He had evidently been asked to "do the civil," but was dreadfully bored, and hustled us smartly through the immense number of rooms and interminable corridors. Even then it took us two good hours to get round.

We also visited the School for Naval Cadets, the admiral and his staff receiving us with much ceremony. The cadets looked pale and rather hunted. I felt so sorry for them, penned in small rooms, with only a strip of yard, surrounded by tall brick walls, in which to exercise.

Our friend M. de Breteuil did not go to Moscow with us, as he was invited by the Grand Duke Vladimir to join an expedition to shoot bears. It was significant that on the day they started, the Czar, who was setting out on some journey at the same hour, had three trains kept in readiness, and not even the Grand Duke knew in which his brother was traveling!

For the tourist there is no comparison between St. Petersburg and Moscow, the latter is so much more striking and so full of local color. Everything was a source of interest, from the narrow streets filled with a motley crowd of fur-clad people, the markets with their frozen fish or blocks of milk, from which slabs would be chopped off, and carcasses of beasts propped up in rows against the stalls, to the Kremlin with its palaces and churches. *"La ville des marchands,"* as it is called, is full of riches and rich people. We visited the Trichiakoff picture-gallery, belonging to a retired merchant, where I was amazed to see depicted all the grimmest and most gruesome historical incidents of Russian tyranny and cruelty: Ivan the Terrible murdering his son, or receiving on the red staircase of the Kremlin a hapless envoy whose foot he transfixed to the floor with the spiked ferule of his walking-stick, while he read some unwelcome message; Siberian prisoners; horrible deeds perpetrated in the fortress of Peter and Paul; and many other atrocities.

Shortly after our arrival we received a visit from Prince Dolgorouki, the Governor General of Moscow. A charming old man of eighty, a *grand seigneur* of the old school, he looked very smart and upright in the uniform of the Chevalier Gardes. He told me that he had been twenty-two years Governor of Moscow, and had served fifty-six in the army, under three Czars. He showed us much civility during our stay, and did all he could to make it pleasant. His aide-de-camp, Prince Ourousow, went about with us, and as he spoke excellent French, we found him most agreeable. Every morning he came to inquire what places of interest we should like to visit, and expeditions of all kinds were arranged for us. One day we drove to the Sparrow Hills, the spot where Napoleon stood when he first looked upon the city which preferred destruction to his rule. The marble

GRAND DUKE ALEXANDER, AFTERWARD ALEXANDER III, AND THE
PRINCESS DAGMAR, NOW DOWAGER EMPRESS OF RUSSIA

statue of himself crowned with laurels which he brought with him, is carefully preserved in the Kremlin; but, by the irony of fate, it is a trophy of war—instead of representing, as Napoleon intended, the Conqueror of all the Russias. It stands there as a reproof to the overweening ambition and vanity of the greatest of men.

With the Kremlin we naturally were enchanted. The old Organaya Palace, and the church, with its mosaics and Byzantine decorations, mellowed by centuries to a wonderful hue, had a mysterious and haunting effect. Could those walls have spoken, I have no doubt I should have fled in terror. As it was, we were so interested and fascinated that we returned again, and this time without an escort. I was amazed to find the whole place full of beggars and cripples of every description, who pestered us for alms; on our previous visit we had not seen one. We heard afterwards that the Governor had issued an order bidding them all to leave the precincts, that we might not be annoyed by them. During our stay in Russia, the authorities were everywhere anxious that Randolph should have a good impression, and while in St. Petersburg we were followed about by two detectives, not, as we at first imagined, to spy upon us, but to see that as distinguished strangers we were not molested in any way.

Prince Dolgorouki was an absolute autocrat in Moscow. Upon our expressing a wish one night when we were dining with him to hear some Tziganes who were giving a performance some distance off, a messenger was despatched forthwith, and they were ordered to come to the Governor's house. They gave us a very good representation of wild national songs and dances. What happened to the spectators from whom their performers had been snatched we never heard.

Before leaving, we attended the "Bal de la Noblesse" in the Assembly Rooms. It was a fine sight, the floor excellent, and the music most inspiriting. There was a "Marshal of the Ceremonies," who reminded me of the descriptions of Beau Nash—strutting about, full of airs and graces, introducing people, arranging and ruling with great precision the intricacies of the various dances. Officers would be brought up to me, clicking their spurs together and saluting; then they would seize my waist without a word, and whisk me round the enormous room at a furious pace, my feet scarcely touching the ground. Before I had recovered, breathless and bewildered, I would be handed over to the next, until I had to stop from sheer exhaustion.

I believe when the Court goes to Moscow, which it does every four or five years, it is the occasion of the appearance of families, bearing the finest old names of the country, who generally live buried in the provinces—people who look upon society in St. Petersburg very much as the Faubourg St. Germain looked on the heterogeneous mass of which society in Paris was composed under the Empire; and who are so Russian that even the Mazurka, since it is Polish, must not be danced too well.

The day we left Moscow our friend the Governor came to see us off, and presented me with a lovely bouquet of orchids, which was produced from a band-box at the last moment. But before I had had time to sit down, the poor flowers were shriveled as though they had been scorched, one instant of the twenty-two degrees below zero proving too much for them. I left Moscow with

236

great regret, as, apart from the delights of the place, I met some charming women, whose society I found most agreeable. I gathered from them that Russian ladies, not indulging in any sport and taking little or no exercise, stay a great deal indoors, and in consequence have much time to educate themselves, to read, and to cultivate the fine arts. Speaking many languages, and reading widely, they form a most attractive society. It is said that Russians are not given to intimacy, and that foreigners never get to know them well. I think that this is so, but I see no reason to credit them with less warmth of heart and faculty for lasting friendship than other nations possess. It was, however, a matter of surprise to me that women so eminently fitted by nature and education to influence and help those struggling in the higher vocations of life, should have seemingly but one ambition—to efface themselves, to attract no attention, to arouse no jealousies. Yet I doubt not that their influence is felt, though it may not be open and fearless as in England or America. As a refutation of the supposed insincerity of Russian character, it is an undisputed fact that a *succès d'estime* is unknown, and the stranger or diplomatist, however well recommended, or however good his position, is not by any means invited to the fêtes as a matter of course. After the first introduction, he is asked only according to his host's appreciation of him. I am not speaking of official circles, where policy is the master of ceremonies. The same may be said of the London society of to-day. Although formerly all foreigners and the staff of the Embassies were *personæ gratæ,* nowadays English society has become too large, and a hostess has to pick and choose.

I cannot leave the subject of Russia and the Russians without speaking of the one it has been my privilege to know best; namely, the Dowager Duchess of Saxe-Coburg-Gotha, formerly Duchess of Edinburgh. We used to see her very often when she lived in England. A warm-hearted woman of rare intelligence and exceptional education, her early life as the only daughter of the Czar (Alexander II) was a most interesting one, as, quite apart from the exalted position she held, it was her duty for two hours daily to read her father's correspondence and the secret news of the world, in itself a liberal education. An excellent musician, Rubinstein once said of her, so she told me, *"Vous ne jouez pas si mal pour une Princesse."* We frequently played together duets on two pianos, or quartettes in which Lady Mary Fitzwilliam, my sister Mrs. Leslie, and Signor Albanesi would join. A fine linguist, speaking fluently several languages, the Duchess wrote them equally well.

FROM H. I. AND R. H. THE DUCHESS OF EDINBURGH,
NOW MARIE, DUCHESS OF SAXE-COBURG-GOTHA

STUTTGART, June 16, 1886.

DEAR LADY RANDOLPH:

I had no time to thank you from Coburg for your kind, long letter from Hatfield. How triumphant you must be, and how pleased Lord Randolph is! Please give him my *heartfelt* good wishes on this parliamentary success. And so the G. O. M. is done for, at least for the present moment, and you all think that you have saved England! But when the new elections have to begin again, what hard work for you, though you are so full of energy!

THE KREMLIN, MOSCOW

I hope you enjoyed Ascot and that the hideous climate did not spoil, as usual, all the enjoyments.

I have come to Stuttgart for a few days on a visit to my aunt, the Queen of Würtemberg. She is a very charming and amiable old lady, a real *grande dame* of the past generation. The Queen lives in a most charming villa outside the town, with lovely grounds, and such roses as I have never seen before anywhere. The country around is very pretty, and a short stay here is very enjoyable. . . .

We are dreadfully struck by the tragic death of the King of Bavaria. As a child, I used to know him well: he was a charming young man, *so* good-looking and so pleasant. I quite fell in love with him when I was ten years old. He had the finest eyes one could dream about, and which often haunt me now after more than twenty years. Can any novel or drama be more tragic than the life and death of this unfortunate mad King? I have never seen Munich, and want to go there from here; also perhaps to Augsburg, where there is an interesting exhibition.

I hope the Eastwell flowers are pretty good, but I wish I could send you some roses from here; they are too magnificent. My aunt has created the place, and looks after it with "devoted attention."

I wish you would come to Coburg in September; it would be a great pleasure for me.

Accept my best love and many wishes to hear often from you.

MARIE.

PETERHOF, August 2, 1886.

DEAR LADY RANDOLPH:

I was so pleased to receive your interesting letter only a few days after my arrival here, and I thank you for it a thousand times.

What an interesting time you are having now, and how excited you must all be! Now I hear the Cabinet is formed and

Lord Randolph is Minister so soon again. Please offer him my most sincere good wishes for his success in public life, and though I shed a tear or two over the fall of "my idol," I sincerely hope that the new Ministry will be more successful. I do not believe it, however, and slightly chuckle over the difficulties they will have to face.

Here we do not think much of politics at present, and enjoy life more simply by having lovely weather, pleasant company, and being out-of-doors from morning till night. Nowhere does one enjoy the summer more than in Russia, and I must say that it is really heavenly weather when the summer is fine, for we have the very long days and hardly any night.

Here we live in separate small villas in the park, and the big, fine, old rococo palace is only used for receptions or distinguished guests. I live with the children in one house, and the Majesties live in a cottage some five-minutes' walk from us. It is all very delightful in fine weather, but not so convenient during rainy days, as one keeps running from one house to the other. Nearly all of my relatives live in the neighborhood— dozens of cousins of every description, masculine and feminine, uncles, aunts, nephews, and nieces. You never saw such a family party. The Queen of Greece is here with nearly all her children, grown-up young men and babies, she herself looking younger than me, and dancing away merrily whilst I look on. I cannot make up my mind to dance in the same place which witnessed my début some sixteen years ago, a slim young lady then, a fat matron now. So I walk about, renew old acquaintances, have people presented, and try to make myself agreeable. All welcome me with joy and such cordiality that the task is an easy one. One dresses here immensely and is wonderfully smart and well got up; it is a real pleasure for me to see all the lovely toilettes, bonnets and cloaks—quite a study.

My uncles and cousins have beautiful country places all about Peterhof, and the other day one of them gave a very animated small dance. To-day there is a big ball at the palace, with ambassadors, etc., and we expect one or two more dances. On Monday was the Empress's nameday; also mine, and it is always a grand day for festivities and presents. We had in the evening a lovely ballet in the open air and grand illuminations in the park. There are beautiful fountains here, a copy of Versailles, which light up in a wonderful way. Every evening bands play in the park and quantities of people walk, ride, and drive about. It is a very animated sight, and we go about in big char-à-bancs with postilions *à la française*. My lovely *belle-sœur*, now the Grand Duchess Serge, lives in the same house, while three of my brothers are at the camp, serving with various regiments. We have also to go there from time to time to witness various military performances. It is a grand sight, as there are always about 30,000 troops assembled there. We are soon to spend a week there for the grand manœuvers. After my very quiet London life, I feel perfectly confused at this very animated existence; but it does me a great deal of good.

My children are very happy; ride about, bathe in the sea, and run wild nearly the whole day long.

We have an Austrian Archduke staying here with a very nice Archduchess, whom we try to amuse.

I must now finish this very disjointed letter, written during several days.

What will you do this autumn, dear Lady Randolph? London must be detestable now. I quite pity you, and wish you were here.

Au revoir, mais quand?

MARIE.

MALTA, January 13, 1888.

DEAR LADY RANDOLPH:

It is quite unpardonable of me not to have written to you before, but somehow, cruising about as we did the whole autumn and living on board ship, being very hot and lazy, all this did not predispose one to active correspondence. And now it is the slight boredom of the Malta life, its uninteresting course, and *mille autres excuses.* I am sincerely glad that you have both gone to Russia and have such pleasant impressions: your nice letters, from England first and next from Petersburg, gave me much pleasure. Many sincere thanks, and I feel quite touched that you found a moment's time to write from my native country amidst all the excitement.

I did very strongly recommend you to all my relations, but two of them you had already previously greatly impressed, the Grand Duchess Vladimir at Paris, and my brother Serge last summer in London. . . .

My countrymen and women are very lively and demonstrative; they have kind, warm hearts and are really fond of one. I feel that more and more when I go back to Russia.

Give many messages to Lord Randolph, and I also hope he will write me a few words. I am always thinking of his "escapade" last winter at Messina, and cannot help laughing at it very sincerely. How I should enjoy another good talk with him, because, you know, I have a *faible* for him. . . .

The Duke is hurrying me, as the post starts at once; it is most irregular here. I am so sorry I cannot write a more interesting letter; I have not half told my tale yet. *Au revoir,* dear Lady Randolph. Many more thanks, and do not forget a true friend.

MARIE.

The "escapade" to which the Duchess of Coburg refers, was an incident which happened in one of Lord Randolph's journeys abroad, which is described in the following letters:

LADY RANDOLPH CHURCHILL

Here we are, caught like rats in a trap. Just as we were packing up yesterday to leave for Naples it was announced that on account of cholera at Catania quarantine had been imposed in Sicily, and that we could not leave. This is a great blow, for we do not know how long we may be detained here. There is nothing to see or do, and the hotel is dirty and uncomfortable. We are in despair . . .

Naples, March 12, 1887.

I send you the enclosed under what the Foreign Office calls "Flying Seal," which means you are to read it and send it on; it will tell you of our proceedings. At last we have got here, but without either servants or luggage; goodness knows when they will come. Harry T. and I made up our minds we would not stand being detained prisoners indefinitely at Messina. We made a fruitless application to the Ambassador at Rome to be exempted from quarantine; all regular steamboats had been taken off, and even if we had got a passage we should have had to do five days' quarantine at Gaeta . . . a horrible prospect. So we went to the Consul . . . a character he is! He introduced us to a man who knew a man who knew some Sicilian fishermen who for a consideration would put us across the Straits. *Nous n'avons fait ni une ni deux*, but pursued the project. We embarked in an open boat at eight o'clock on Wednesday evening in Messina Harbour, with nothing but a tiny bag and a rug, with a dissolute sort of half-bred English-man and Sicilian, to act as interpreter and guide, and six wild, singing, chattering Sicilian fishermen. We reached the Cala-brian coast about 9.30; but the difficulty was to find a landing place where there were no gendarmes or coastguards or inhab-itants awake. The last danger was the greatest, for the peas-antry are awfully superstitious about cholera, and are a wild,

245

savage people; and we might have had rough treatment if any number of them happened to see us.

At last we found a little fishing village where all was quiet. In we ran, out we jumped, and off went the boat like lightning. After clambering up some precipitous rocks, fortunately without waking any one or breaking our necks, we found temporary shelter in a miserable inn, where we represented ourselves as having come by boat from Reggio, and being unable to get back on account of the strong Sirocco wind which was blowing. We had to wait about an hour here all alone, with two wild men and a wild woman, while our guide was quietly endeavouring to find a conveyance. At last he got a common cart, and about eleven o'clock we started for the house of an Englishman at San Giovanni who has a silk mill, and to whom we had a letter from the Consul. The inn-keeper and his companions asked a lot of tiresome questions and seemed very suspicious, but 'n the end let us go quietly. Just after starting we met two gendarmes, and afterwards two coastguards, but fortunately they asked no questions; so everything went well for some four or five miles, except for the awful jolting of the cart, which exceeded anything in the way of shaking you ever dreamt of. All of a sudden the peasant who was driving the mule ran the cart against a great stone, and sent us all flying into the road. I never saw such a sprawling spill. Fortunately we were only shaken and dirty, but the driver was much hurt, which served him right, and he groaned and moaned terribly for the remainder of the journey; being a big, fat man, he had fallen heavily, and I should not be surprised if he had since died.

At last at one in the morning we reached the house we were looking for, and had a great business to awaken the people; nor did we know how we should be received, arriving in so strange a manner. The Englishman, however, was very good, took us in, gave us supper, and we lay quiet till the evening of the following day, when we slipped into the direct train for this place,

246

which we reached without further trouble. But what a thing it is to have an evil conscience! I kept thinking that every station-master and gendarme on the road scrutinised us unnecessarily; and what a trouble and scandal it would have made if we had been arrested and put in prison! However all is well that ends well!

Before closing this chapter I must mention one more Russian friend I was fortunate enough to have in the late M. de Staal, for many years Russian Ambassador in London. His delightful personality, charm of conversation and kind heart, made him extremely popular; and his memory will live long in the thoughts of his many friends. I used to meet him at Eastwell, a fine place in Kent which the Duke of Edinburgh had for some years and where M. de Staal was the life and soul of the party. He sent me his photograph some time before his death with the following charming and characteristic note:

CHESHAM HOUSE

CHESHAM PLACE, S. W., le 31 Oct. 1902.

CHÈRE MADAME ET AMIE:

Voici la très vieille face d'un très vieux homme qu'est à demi-mort mais vous aime bien.

Ne l'accueillez pas trop mal.

Sincèrement à vous,

STAAL.

CHAPTER XI

ON our way back from Russia, in 1888, we stayed for ten days at the British Embassy in Berlin. Sir Edward Malet, who was the Ambassador, was very much in favor with the Imperial Family. A man of small stature, he has nevertheless a commanding presence, with a pleasant and open countenance and the most courteous of manners. He is very well informed, and talks agreeably on all subjects. Lady Ermyntrude, his wife, who was equally liked, is a daughter of the late Duke of Bedford, and an extremely cultivated woman. They both showed us the greatest hospitality, even giving a dinner in our honor.

After ultra-fashionable and brilliant St. Petersburg, Berlin society seemed a little quiet. But there were some exceptions, notably Princess Karl Egon Fürstenberg (now Comtesse Jean de Castellane), Princess Antoine Radziwill, and Countess von Hohenau. This lady was renowned for her beautiful figure, which I have seen equaled only by that of Lady Claud Hamilton. Princess Fürstenberg (who was a stepdaughter of the late Duc de Valançay and half-sister of the Prince de Sagan, already mentioned in these reminiscences) held

248

a unique position. To her own vivid personality she added her husband's great name and immense wealth. Well educated, and with a restless and ambitious mind, she has always taken a keen interest in politics. Had her life been spent in England instead of abroad, she would certainly have played a greater part. In Germany there is little scope in that line for a woman, and in France still less. Her dinners and her parties were the most successful entertainments given in Berlin. Prince Fürstenberg, who has since died, was a very independent man, and some years later he incurred the present Kaiser's wrath in a quarrel which made considerable stir at the time. William II issued an order to the effect that army officers should take precedence of the nobility. The Prince retired from the Court in high dudgeon, after writing a letter to the Kaiser in which, it is said, he expressed his views with more vigor than diplomacy; not hesitating to compare the Hohenzollerns to their detriment with his own high and mighty, not to say much older, family.

We spent our days pleasantly in visiting the palaces, galleries, and museums. At one of the galleries we were much interested to see three pictures which used to be at Blenheim, one of them being the famous "Bacchanalia" by Rubens, which had filled one side of the dining-room. Sans Souci I found enchanting, and could hardly tear myself away from its lovely rooms, with their Louis XV decorations and delicious Watteaus. How strange that those two grim men, Frederick the Great and Voltaire, should have lived in such incongruous surroundings! Visions of beautiful women in powder and patches could alone be associated with these boudoirs, where the panels, adorned with silver tracings, and the soft-colored silk curtains would have made a fitting background for their loveliness. The bedroom so long occupied by Voltaire, with its priceless Dresden china, and hangings of green damask, looked like a nest for a pink-and-white maid of honor. One note, however, gave an indication of the king's mind in respect to the guest whom he hated and feared as much as he admired him. A large, grinning china monkey did service for a chandelier, holding in its hands the candles which lighted up the sardonic features of its human counterpart. At the end of a *cul-de-sac* was a small, round room of which the only outlet was a window giving on to the garden. With books to the ceiling, and a huge writing-table in the center, this was Frederick the Great's sanctum. Perhaps it was on this very table that he wrote the verses he was so anxious Voltaire should admire, and which in the hands of the "Patriarch of Ferney" became the weapon with which he ridiculed the King at the time of their famous quarrel.

Among the many festivities to which we were bidden, was a gala performance at the opera. A gala night under the auspices of the German Court is a very different thing from the same function in London. In Berlin the boxes and seats are not sold, and only those who receive a royal invitation may attend, whereas in London it is a case of the longest purse and the highest bidder. In consequence, the audience is anything but representative of London society. I remember being very much struck by the wonderful ensemble and perfection of the orchestra, far surpassing any in London of those days. Sembrich sang in "Les Noces de Figaro," and the whole royal family were present, including the aged Emperor William I. The prospect of a state concert, preceded by an informal Drawing-room, at which we were to be presented, rather alarmed me, not knowing the rules and etiquette of a court so different from any I had yet seen. Also, not expecting to attend any such function, I had no court train with me, and this added to my embarrassment, for there is no doubt that to be well dressed gives confidence. In the end, however, it all proved quite simple.

Etiquette required that before appearing at court I should visit the Mistress of the Robes. I therefore called with Lady Ermyntrude Malet on Countess Perponcher, a rather formidable lady with an 1830 coiffure and a stiff, rustling silk gown. She received me with *force révérences,* which I duly returned. On the night of the concert, we were ushered into a small room where the Emperor William stood surrounded by the royal family, the officials of the court, and the diplomatic corps, and with others we were presented. The Emperor, looking most upright in his smart uniform, welcomed me in a few well-chosen words, also referring to our tea-party at Gastien and the jokes we had had with the children. Little did I or any one else present think that this was to be his last entertainment, and that in a few weeks the kind and noble old monarch would be no more. Suddenly a side door opened, and the Empress Augusta, sitting in a small bath-chair, was wheeled in. Dressed in pale-blue satin, with jewels to her waist, her venerable head crowned with a magnificent tiara, she made a brave, if somewhat pathetic figure. She asked me many questions in excellent English, addressing me as "Lady Churchill" and inquiring after the Czarina, "whom she understood I had just seen." She also asked so much after her "dear Queen Victoria" that I came to the conclusion she was mistaking me for Queen Victoria's lady-in-waiting, Jane, Lady Churchill. Her remarks were almost inaudible, and I had to answer in a very loud voice, as she did not hear well. I do not recollect ever having felt more embarrassed or uncomfortable than during this conversation at cross purposes, carried on before the whole court, which was listening in respectful silence.

Presently we all moved into an adjoining room, at the end of which was a small platform. Round tables were dotted about, the places being arranged beforehand. Randolph sat at the table of Princess William (the present Kaiserin), while I sat at Prince William's. After listening to an excellent concert, at which Sembrich sang, supper was served, the whole function being over by eleven o'clock. Much to my delight, in the course of the evening I made the acquaintance of the great Moltke, who, notwithstanding his stern and ascetic countenance, surprised me agreeably by his sunny smile and pleasant voice.

There is no doubt it would be difficult to find a greater contrast than the Russian and German courts presented at that time; the one, brilliant, imposing, lavish in its extravagance, barbaric in its splendor; the other, unpretentious and, perhaps, a little dull, but full of traditions and etiquette. In Berlin, and particularly at the court, signs of the all-conquering and victorious army were everywhere apparent; everything military was in the ascendant. I remember Prince William visiting me at the Embassy, and our having a great discussion on

COUNT VON MOLTKE

German and Russian uniforms, the gorgeousness of which had impressed me while in St. Petersburg.

If the Court of the Emperor William I was somewhat depressing, the magnificence of the existing régime is a great contrast. William II rightly wishes to maintain a proper standard, and while condemning extravagance, likes to see a dignified display. It has been reported that he once said, apropos of his court balls, that "men came for discipline, and women for deportment." Permission to dance is given only by royal order, and the privileged have for many days to rehearse the intricate steps of the stately minuets prescribed. Woe be it if they make any mistakes, for a dancing-master sits aloft in a gallery recording the *faux pas* of his pupils. This may sound arbitrary, but there is no doubt that if something similar could be introduced at the Court of St. James the proceedings would gain in dignity, as it is with difficulty that the majority of people can go through an ordinary quadrille.

Before leaving, we dined one night with Count Herbert Bismarck. At the end of the dinner he produced, as a *bonne bouche,* a sort of paste, made principally, as far as I could gather, of lard and garlic, of which he spoke with pride as having been made by his mother. Count Herbert was a kindly man, and although to English ideas he may perhaps have seemed a little rough and uncouth, he was really very popular in England, and left many friends to deplore his premature death. He was greatly interested in English politics, and I remember that at this dinner he had an argument on the subject of Mr. Gladstone, whom he cordially hated, remarking, much to our amusement, that his father always said "Gladstone would drag England to the lowest ground of hell."

Randolph and I were disappointed in not seeing Prince Bismarck, who was then in the country; but some years later, when at Kissengen, we were fortunate enough to make the "Iron Chancellor's" acquaintance. We dined with him at the old schloss where he was living, its picturesque red roof making a landmark in the flat Bavarian scenery. We were only a party of six: the Prince and Princess, Count Herbert Bismarck and his wife (who was of English origin), and ourselves. We dined in a large room which had a vaulted ceiling, and seemed to be used as a general living-room. At dinner I sat on one side of the Prince, and Randolph on the other, the huge boar hound, our host's constant companion, lying on the ground between us. Conversation was animated. Bismarck spoke excellent English, but very slowly; and if he could not find the word he wanted, he would pause and think until he did. His family looked up to him with awe and admiration, and listened with the greatest attention to every word he uttered. The old Princess, who seemed very feeble, did not take much part in the conversation. After dinner we adjourned to another part of the room, where we sat round a long table covered with books and newspapers. There were a great many illustrated papers, full of caricatures of Bismarck, which, in answer to a question, he assured me he did not mind in the least. Later, however, Count Herbert contradicted this, saying that his father was really very sensitive and disliked being caricatured.

Speaking of the country and the long walks he took

daily, Bismarck said he loved nature, but the amount of life he saw awed him, and that it took a great deal of faith to believe that an "all-seeing Eye" could notice every living atom when one realized what that meant. "Have you ever sat on the grass and examined it closely? There is enough life in one square yard to appal you," he said. When we were about to leave, his great dog fixed his fierce eyes on mine in so persistent a manner that I became alarmed and thought he was going to spring upon me; but the Prince reassured me, saying, "He is looking at your eyes, because he has not seen any like them." This was said in a grave voice and without a smile, leaving it doubtful if he intended to pay me a compliment.

Quitting Berlin with much regret and with gratitude to our kind hosts the Malets, we proceeded to Paris, where we remained for some time. Our friend the Marquis de Breteuil helped to make our visit delightful, for at his charming house, where we often dined, we met every one of note and interest. It was at one of these dinners that I saw General Boulanger for the first time. M. de Breteuil was a believer at that moment in Boulangism, and, in common with many Royalists, thought he saw in the General, *faute de mieux,* the preserver of the French monarchy, through a Restoration which was to follow a Republic under which all Frenchmen could rally. The Duchesse d'Uzès, the Comtesse Greffhule, the General, Randolph and I, made up the party. The duchess, who kept a pack of hounds in the vicinity of Paris, and hunted the stag with all the pomp and picturesqueness foreigners display in matters connected with the chase, had, it appears, been hunting that day,

and in consequence arrived late, breathless, and somewhat untidy, but covered with magnificent jewels.
Granddaughter of the Veuve Clicquot of champagne
fame, Mme. d'Uzès had inherited a large fortune,
and with this "fruit of the vine" was able to regild the
shield of the Duc d'Uzès, who bore one of the oldest
names of France. The Duchess, who was then a widow,
had espoused the cause of the *"brav' Général"* with all
the ardor of an energetic enthusiast, and she emphasized
her support by giving him three million francs. Mme.
Greffhule, who was a Belgian by birth and came of the
historic house of Chimay, had a European reputation
for grace, charm, and esthetic tastes. Although she was
very young, her salon had already acquired the name
for artistic and literary prominence which it bears to-
day, and people were eager to be counted among its
habitués.

Boulanger, notwithstanding a military bearing, a
fierce mustache, and, to French ideas, a handsome face,
gave one the impression of a man not quite sure of himself. At that moment his popularity was great, and
the eyes of France—not to say of Europe—were turned
upon him; yet he seemed unable to rise above his middle-
class origin and early surroundings. He talked little,
and preferred answering questions to putting them.
Later, when he came to London he dined with us several
times, but even on better acquaintance his diffidence did
not vanish. He was banal in conversation, and I cannot
recall anything of interest he said to me. As the General had no political mission in England, the Prince of
Wales honored us with his company on one of these
occasions. Among those who came, besides General

258

Bismarck

Kissingen, 15. August 1897

Boulanger and General Dillon who accompanied him, were the Duchess of Manchester (now the Dowager Duchess of Devonshire), Lady Norreys, Lord Hardwicke, Lord Hartington, Sir George Lewis, and Mr. and Mrs. Leopold de Rothschild, who got into great trouble with their French relatives for having been there. So confident of success were Boulanger and those about him at that time, that General Dillon, who sat next to Mrs. de Rothschild, invited her in the General's name to stay at the Tuileries—"where we shall be in a few months," quoth he.

There was in England a very strong opinion against Boulanger, and we were much taken to task for receiving and entertaining him; but Randolph was rather fond of exotic specimens of mankind, and liked to study them without regard to public opinion. Although undoubtedly a brave man morally, Boulanger was not sufficiently courageous to risk everything for a cause in which he undoubtedly was, as he perhaps suspected, a cat's-paw. The extraordinary rise and popularity of the man seems incredible, unless one takes into consideration not only the French character, which made such delirious enthusiasm possible, but also the state of France at that time.

Perhaps it will not come amiss here to recapitulate some of the salient points of this strange and eventful career. The malcontents of every shade of politics—Royalist and Bonapartist—each thought that Boulanger, having gained the confidence of the masses, would, once Dictator or President, pave the way to a Royalist or Bonapartist monarchy. Boulanger himself had vast ambitions, of which, it appears, he showed signs when a boy at college. Although a good officer, he had not attained his rank of general by prominence in the field, but, according to his enemies, by lobbying for many years in public offices and anterooms. Politically he coquetted with all parties, and it was probably for this reason that he was made Minister of War in the Freycinet Government of 1885, as he was on fairly good terms with both Radicals and Moderates.

It was while he was in the Government that he began to show his true colors, and some of his Royalist supporters fell away when they found him becoming more radical and voting with the advanced party for the exile of the Bourbon Princes. I was in Paris at the time of the publication of the Duc d'Aumale's letter from Boulanger, and well remember the great sensation it made. It revealed the fulsomeness of the court he paid to the Duke, to whom he owed his rank of general, and his ingratitude in joining those concerned in voting for a cruel and unnecessary law against harmless princes, not to say French citizens. Notwithstanding this revelation of his character, his prestige, shortly after the Fête Nationale on the 14th of July, seemed untarnished, and M. de Breteuil, in writing to me, said at that time, *"Son étoile est plus brillante que jamais."* Like a comet, Boulanger traversed the skies, "an empty-headed thing with a fiery tail," which, to continue the simile, fell to earth in the flash of a pistol report on the tomb of his one true friend, Marguerite Bonnemain.

Like Parnell, Boulanger, ambitious as some may have thought him, put the love of woman above that of power. All his thoughts were centered in and controlled by her who was the mainspring of his life. After the *plébiscite* of February, 1889, he had a majority of 70,000 votes in Paris alone, and his popularity rose to fever heat; but instead of going straight to the Elysée, where he might have challenged his fate and, who knows? been acclaimed President, he rushed off to Mme. Bonnemain's house, and could not be found. This was the turning-point in his career. He disgusted his followers and those who believed in him; and the opportunity never returned.

Randolph, writing to me from Paris, February 5, 1889, said:

> . . . Boulanger does not seem to me to have made as much out of his victory as he ought. If he does not do something soon, the effect of it will be forgotten.

And again in September:

> It is evidently all up with Boulanger. I suppose we shall have him now *en permanence* in London. People won't run after him quite so much.

Life in Paris was most attractive. I sought out all my old friends, and made many new ones. Society was then, as it is now, very cosmopolitan, but it was reinforced by a certain section of the "Noble Faubourg" who were not averse to being entertained by the foreign element. They did not feel it compromising to meet their own compatriots, were they Bonapartists or Republicans, on such neutral grounds. A number of Mexicans, Peruvians, Chilians, etc.—*"rastaquouères,"* as they were dubbed,—were much to the fore; and as they seemed to have millions, and entertained lavishly,

the gay young Parisians flocked to their houses *en masse.*
Exclusiveness is so much a thing of the past that one is
astonished nowadays to meet it, individual merit being
far more an open sesame to society than formerly.
Those who travel and mix perforce with their fellow-
creatures forget that people still exist in this world who
cannot understand or tolerate anything or anybody beyond their immediate entourage. Is it to be wondered
at that these people become narrow-minded, prejudiced,
and self-centered? Personally I feel my acquaintance
can never be too large. When I reflect that there are
thousands of delightful and interesting people one may
be missing, no opportunity ought to be lost of cultivat-
ing as many as possible. Friends are in another category. Time alone can prove friendships. The friends
who stand by you through all vicissitudes are more precious and rare than *"les amis des beaux jours."* To lose
one of them is indeed a calamity. To find a cold heart
where you were certain of a warm one, to find mistrust
and indifference where you hoped for trust and faith,
is the greatest of disillusions and the saddest. *"La
lampe de l'amitié a besoin d'huile,"* but if the lamp is
faulty, no amount of oil will keep it alight.

Speaking of exclusiveness, I am reminded of an
amusing illustration of it which I came across in Paris.
Having made the acquaintance of the Duchesse de la
Trémoille, we dined with her one night. The Duke, who
belongs to one of the oldest families in France, and owns
Serrant, a sixteenth-century château on the Loire, also
possesses a charming house in the Avenue Gabriel. Before leaving for England, I went to call on the Duchess
and asked if she was at home. Hearing that she was,

I walked through the courtyard to the front door, where, to my surprise, notwithstanding a bell announcing my arrival, no one came forward to meet me. I waited; still no one. There were two doors. I chose one, and found myself at the foot of a large staircase embellished with palms and statues. Making my way up, I saw a suite of three or four rooms. In vain I waited for a footman or some one to announce me. At last dimly perceiving a figure at the far end, I went toward it, and found the Duchess, who expressed her surprise that I had taken so long to appear. Presently the *timbre* sounded again; this time it was the Grand Duke Vladimir of Russia who arrived unannounced. It was amusing to see the man before whom Russia trembles dropping on one knee with mock solemnity, kissing the Duchess's hand, and thanking her in exaggerated language for some "divine turkeys" she had sent him. More visitors appearing, I departed, finding my way out as I had come. Having heard that the Duchess was supposed to be very exclusive, I confess I thought this a free-and-easy way of receiving, and said as much to a Frenchman. "You don't understand," he said. "During certain months of the year the Duchess receives her own particular coterie of intimate friends every day from four to six. They know they are sure to find her and be welcome. As habitués there is no need for them to be announced, and the appearance of servants would detract from the delightful *sans gêne* and intimacy of the visit." "But what about the casual caller, or possibly an unwelcome visitor?" "Oh," replied my friend, "none of these would dream of asking if Madame la Duchesse was at home unless they were on her particular list." This explanation somewhat disturbed me, and I felt myself, for the nonce, a trespasser.

M. de Breteuil would sometimes, for our delectation, invite strange people to meet us. Among them was a certain M. de Meyrenna, a young and good-looking man, who interested and amused us for a whole evening by relating the adventures of his extraordinary and thrilling life. He had a few months previously been proclaimed King of the Sedangs (a tribe somewhere in Indo-China) and called himself "Marie I." Although in a wild and distant country, his subjects *did* exist, which is more than can be said for the "Emperor of Sahara," a would-be monarch of the same type. Marie I invited me to pay him a visit. I was to be met by a caravan with elephants and camels and escorted to his capital, where he promised I should be treated royally. I believe he died a year or two later, an adventurer to the last.

Another eccentric person was King Milan, father of Alexander late King of Servia, who, with his wife Draga, was treacherously murdered by his subjects. When I first met Milan in Paris he had just abdicated in favor of his son after a fierce quarrel with his wife, Natalie, a Princess of Stourdza. He certainly was one of the most uncivilized beings I have ever encountered. A short, thick-set man with inky black hair and mustache, of little or no education save what his natural intelligence helped him to pick up, he was notwithstanding an agreeable personality. Later he came to London, where he was not *persona grata* either at the English Court or in general society, into which, however, he never attempted to penetrate. I remember once at a

M. DE BRETEUIL

GENERAL GEORGES-ERNEST-JEAN-MARIE BOULANGER

small dinner party he was induced to describe his early life before he became, in 1868, Prince of Servia on the assassination of his cousin Michael. Up to that time, barefoot and clad in rags, he had lived the life of a goatherd in the mountains, where he often went without food, sleeping in caverns. In relating these past experiences, his encounters with wild beasts, and narrow escapes from those who for their own ends wanted his life, he became so excited that, suddenly forgetting he was not in his native wilds, he began to eat with his fingers, tearing the meat on his plate. His life on the whole was a sad one, and he really deserved something better, although totally unfitted by his early bringing up to govern any country, far less a semibarbaric one like Servia. I dined with him again, this time at the Amphitryon, a restaurant which was half a club, and was much in vogue in London at the moment. We were a party of eight or ten. In a private room, the walls of which were entirely covered with orchids, we had a most fantastic repast. Although nightingales' tongues and peacocks' brains did not figure on the menu, I have no doubt the bill was equally extravagant, for Milan had absolutely no sense of the value of money. A few months later he went back to Servia, whether in the hope of helping his son or to intrigue against him I do not know. Disgusted at Alexander's marriage, which took place shortly after his arrival, with Mme. Draga Maschin, who had been lady-in-waiting to Queen Natalie, Milan left Servia in haste, never to return. Writing to me from some Austrian Baths, he poured forth his troubles in his impulsive manner:

13

Chère Madame :

Depuis longtemps j'ai voulu vous écrire. Cette lettre vous parviendra-t-elle? Je ne le saurai que si vous voulez bien me répondre deux mots pour me dire que vous l'avez reçue. Je n'ai rien de bon à vous dire sur mon compte. Après m'être dévoué corps et âme à mon fils, il m'a joué le tour d'épouser une personne plus qu' impossible et ayant quatorze ans de plus que lui au grand scandale du pays et de l'Europe entière.

Je n'ai pas voulu accepter cette situation, et me revoila de par les grands chemins sans savoir ce que je ferai. Pardon si je vous parle de ces choses, mais dans mes vieux jours, et avec mes cheveux plus que poivre et sel, c'est dur. J'ai mieux merité que cela.

MILAN.

One of the most interesting incidents in Paris in 1889 was the great Secrétan sale, which took place in July. Among the art collectors and connoisseurs who flocked to it was H. R. H. the Duc d'Aumale. His vast knowledge and exquisite taste made all who knew him desirous of obtaining his opinions. The catalogue, which consisted of two large volumes, was admirably got up, and so largely sought for that, much to my chagrin, I was unable to procure a copy. The Duc d'Aumale, hearing of this, presented me with one of his, writing in it a charming inscription. These books, beautifully bound, are among the treasures of my library.

The duke, with his military prestige and martial bearing, was besides a man of great culture, and fitly described as *"un gentilhomme au bout des ongles."* He was, moreover, an ardent sportsman, and the magnificent Château of Chantilly which he presented in 1886 to the Institut de France is filled with his hunting trophies.

LADY RANDOLPH CHURCHILL

During his exile in England, I remember dining with him at his house in Rutland Gate, and being impressed by his charming and gentle manner. He talked much about France, and his love for his country seemed in no way impaired by the cruel measure which had been passed against him by his own countrymen.

One of the houses I frequented in Paris was that of Mrs. Ferdinand Bischoffsheim, a clever and beautiful American who died a few years ago. She had a salon in Paris which was quite literary. It was there that I first met M. Bourget, then unmarried, and began a friendship which has lasted unimpaired to this day. He had just written "Mensonges," which added greatly to his reputation as a novelist, although it was freely criticized. An animated and amusing correspondence was being carried on in the press, mainly by the fair sex, who were irate at his description of a *mondaine,* his heroine. I recollect his being chaffed by a compatriot, who asked him why he did not depict a real woman of the world in his books? Bourget, who thought he had accurately done so, was naturally annoyed but, unlike most Frenchmen, he could stand chaff. Perhaps his long stay in England had inured him to it. Now, one of the Forty Immortals, wearing *"les palmes académiques,"* and happily married to a most attractive and talented woman, his books are more serious; but to me the delightful "Sensations d'Oxford," which he wrote years ago, and which for literary style and charm of description he has in my estimation never surpassed, is quite staid enough. We often discussed his literary projects, and I have many pleasant letters from him, from which I quote at random the following:

LADY RANDOLPH CHURCHILL

. . . Ma vie à moi est attristée par la difficulté d'écrire "Une Idylle Tragique." C'est un beau sujet sur lequel je devrais vous écrire vingt pages. Avec de la patience j'en viendrai à bout—mais c'est terriblement dur. Arrivé à un certain point de la vie, on en sait trop, on veut trop mettre, et on ne peut pas dire ce que l'on a à dire. . . . Savez vous que Tourguéniew a résumé le dernier mot de tout quand il a dit "La vie est une affaire brutale."

CHAPTER XII

A T this period (1889) Lord Randolph Churchill's interest in politics was as great as ever, although he was out of office, and he then made some of his best speeches. His followers in Birmingham had never ceased working on his behalf since he had stood for the constituency in 1885, and at the death of John Bright their greatest desire was that he should represent them in Parliament. Randolph himself was very keen about it, and would probably have won the seat in time had he not listened to the over-scrupulous advice of the Unionist Party. Great were the *pourparlers* and controversies in their councils as to whether he ought or ought not to stand. The decision was finally left in the hands of Lord Hartington and Mr. Chamberlain, who, very naturally from their point of view, persuaded him to withdraw his candidature.

It was a great blow to his friends and supporters in Birmingham, who felt that they had been offered up on the altar of Mr. Chamberlain's ambitions. Bearing in mind the political campaign of 1885, and the hard work in which I had taken part and which now seemed

273

a waste of time and energy, I felt very incensed. On the day when Randolph returned from the House of Commons and informed me of the pressure brought to bear on him, and how he had given in, I accused him of showing the white feather for the first time in his life. He had, he said, "made up his mind to abide by the opinion of the leaders of the 'Party.'" "But not when those leaders are your political enemies," I cried. Arguments, however, were useless. If he was right, he got no thanks for it, and a great opportunity was lost for him to show his strength and power.

After Randolph left the Government, our relations with Lord and Lady Salisbury became gradually more and more strained. Outward appearances were kept up, such as our still being invited to the political parties given in Arlington Street, but all real cordiality ceased. Mutual friends, indeed, tried to bring about a *rapprochement,* and eventually we were asked to dine. Much against his inclination Randolph was persuaded to accept. The dinner, which was a large one, was a fiasco so far as the object of our being there was concerned, for beyond a bare greeting neither Lord nor Lady Salisbury exchanged a word with Randolph. This he resented very much, and regretted having gone. I do not think this was intended as a slight, for shortly afterward I received the following letter from Lady Salisbury:

April 24, HATFIELD HOUSE,
HATFIELD.

MY DEAR LADY RANDOLPH:

Will you and Lord Randolph come here to dine and sleep on Sunday the 22d, and help us to receive the Irish delegates on

274

LADY DE GREY

Monday? We shall be much pleased if you will come. No Sunday trains are good, but the best leave Kings Cross at 1 P.M. or 6.30 P.M. We will meet either.

Yours very truly,

G. SALISBURY.

There was to be a garden party on the Monday at which political speeches were to be made, Mr. Chamberlain and Randolph being advertised as the principal speakers. Great was to be the gathering of Unionists, and a solid front was much desired. At the last moment, however, Randolph flatly refused to go. No arguments moved him; he insisted that I should keep the engagement alone. As I drove up to the historic Elizabethan house, an ideal residence for the Prime Minister of England, my feelings were anything but enviable. I shall never forget the look of blank dismay and the ominous silence with which my feeble excuses for Randolph's absence were greeted. That night at dinner in the splendid banqueting-hall, I sat next to Lord Salisbury. Courteous as ever, he talked pleasantly to me, but made no allusion to the subject uppermost in my mind. The next day was fine, and masses of people brought by special trains from London filled the beautiful gardens, crowding round the various speakers. Cries for Randolph were heard on every side, many had come expressly to hear him, and bitter was the disappointment when they realized that he was not there. No adequate reason could be given for his absence, and the "rift within the lute" was made more apparent than ever. I confess I was very glad when I could slip away,

277

for rarely had I felt so uncomfortable or experienced anything more disagreeable.

London rejoiced that year in Jubilee functions and was very animated. A diversion was created by the arrival of the Shah of Persia, Nasr-ed-din, whose vagaries kept society amused and interested. A real barbarian, it was with difficulty that he was induced to conform to Western habits. Many were the stories circulated about him. One night at a banquet at Buckingham Palace, he was asked to give his arm to the late Queen Victoria. He refused, having made up his mind to take in a lady whose voluminous proportions had attracted his attention. Much pressure had to be brought to bear before he was prevailed upon to change his mind. With reluctance and a cross face, he dragged the Queen along as he strode into the dining-room.

Another night at the opera he sat with a glum countenance, evidently much bored, to the despair of his suite, until the orchestra during the entr' acte began to tune their instruments. At these discordant sounds the Persian monarch brightened up, and asked for an encore, applauding vigorously. At one of the Court balls at which the Shah was present we were commanded, much to Randolph's and my embarrassment, and the annoyance of the Lord Chamberlain (as it was against all royal etiquette), to go to the dais and be presented to his Majesty. Sir Henry Wolff, who was then Ambassador at Teheran, had often spoken to him about Randolph; hence, I suppose, his desire to know him. Muttering something which sounded like "Lady Churchillias," he grasped my hand with terrific force, and then with a peremptory gesture, waved me away

278

to make room for Randolph, who no more than I understood one word uttered by the fierce old man. As I went down the two or three steps of the dais feeling miserably self-conscious, the Prince of Wales with his usual kindness came forward and shook hands, saying, "This presentation is contrary to all precedent, but the Shah insisted," and added laughingly, "You had better go quickly as I see you are getting black looks from the Duchesses' bench."

Strangers came to London in numbers that season, attracted by the unwonted sights and festivities. I met many at Lady de Grey's, she having always been one of the most cosmopolitan of hostesses. Her well-known artistic and musical appreciation made her house then, as now, the rendezvous of all the gifted artists and intellectual foreigners who come to London. She is indeed the Mecca they journey to, and many of the former owe their success to her timely aid and good counsels. Given, in addition to personal charm and beauty, a thorough knowledge of the world and of the difficult art of receiving, it is not surprising that invitations are highly prized to her small but delightful entertainments.

Taking into consideration the abnormal size of London society as it is at present, to be a popular hostess is no easy matter. As for "salons"—they were nearly extinct twenty years ago. It is obvious that none is possible without selection, and this naturally leads to the exclusion of all who do not possess wit or talent. The passport to the famous Parisian salons of the eighteenth century, those of Mme. du Deffand, Mme. Geoffrin, Mlle. de Lespinasse and others, consisted in brains; no other credential was necessary. If the rooms of these celebrated women were crowded, it was with the genius and talent of Europe, and the new-comer was only admitted after searching inquiry; to be elected was in itself a guarantee of excellence, and was as eagerly sought for as Academic honors. Con-versation roamed over a vast range of subjects, from framing a new policy for the Government to the latest sonnet or spiciest new scandal, and on the decision of these arbiters of merit success depended. How remote seem these brilliant *causeries* from the caravanserais of the "Mrs. Leo Hunters" of to-day, where crowds jostle each other on the staircase, often not getting any further, and where bridge replaces conversation. Hap-pily there are exceptions, and now as then it is possible to find people who like something better. At a particu-larly pleasant luncheon-party, given by Lady de Grey, I remember once meeting, among others, M. Jules Claretie of the Francais, Mlle. Bartet the gifted actress, Lord Ribblesdale and Mr. Oscar Wilde—than whom a more brilliant talker did not exist, that is when he was in the mood for it. An argument arose between him and Lord Ribblesdale on after-dinner speeches, Mr. Wilde declaring that there was no subject on which he could not speak at a moment's notice. Taking him at his word Lord Ribblesdale, holding up his glass, said "The Queen." "She is not a subject," answered Wilde, as quick as lightning. Once, having been accused of mis-quoting from "The Importance of Being Earnest," I appealed to Mr. Wilde, telling him I had made a bet on my accuracy, and that if I found I was right, he should receive from me a beautiful pen-holder. This was his answer:

BARON MAURICE VON HIRSCH

COLONEL NORTH

LADY RANDOLPH CHURCHILL

DEAR LADY RANDOLPH,

"The only difference between the saint and the sinner is that every saint has a past and that every sinner has a future." That, of course, is the quotation. How dull men are! They should listen to brilliant women, and look at beautiful ones— and when, as in the present case, a woman is both beautiful and brilliant they might have the ordinary common sense to admit that she is verbally inspired.

I trust your bet will be promptly paid, as I want to begin writing my new comedy, and have no pen!

Believe me,

Yours sincerely,

OSCAR WILDE.

As I had won, the pen was duly sent him.

It was about this time that I made the acquaintance of two financiers who had come prominently to the front. One was Colonel North, the "Nitrate King," as he was called, and the other Baron Hirsch, who ended by making many friends in England. Colonel North was what might be called a "rough diamond." He had a large place near London, which was furnished regardless of expense, where he kept open house and entertained in a most lavish manner the hordes of hangers-on and sycophants by whom—like all rich men of that type —he was invariably surrounded. Dining with us once I was much amused at the description he gave me of his picture gallery. That very day he had bought a "grand picture" for which he had given the large sum of £8000.

I asked who it was by; that he could not remember, nor even the subject. "But," he added, "it is twelve feet by eight!" He was a kindly man, and very charitable.

Baron Hirsch, whose generosity to his co-religionists will long preserve his name, was one of the few millionaires I have met who knew thoroughly how to enjoy himself. He had the real *"joie de vivre,"* and delighted in seeing people amusing themselves. His shooting-parties in England and in Austria were most pleasant. No mean sportsman himself, he had the knack of getting together congenial people and the best of shots. On one occasion at his place, St. Johann (in Hungary), when the Prince of Wales, Lord de Grey, Mr. H. Stoner and Lord Ashburton were of the party, the total bag of partridges for one day reached 3000. Life at St. Johann was simple and healthy. Shortly after breakfast eight or ten victorias would appear at the door, the horses in gay harness and the postilions in hussar-like blue jackets, Hessian boots and shiny, high-crowned hats. We would then drive to the rendezvous where an army of beaters—six hundred or more—were waiting. Drawn up in line, we started off at the sound of a bugle and the cry of *Vorwärts,* and then advancing, still in line, walked for miles over the sanded plains, dotted about with tufts of stubble which afforded cover for the enormous blue hares common in that part of the country. Now and then we came across woods in which roe-deer, blackcock and pheasants abounded. Luncheon took place out of doors, in all weather. Some days only part-ridges would be driven. I remember once laughing heartily at a shooter in whose butt I was. As the huge coveys flew over him seemingly from every point of the compass, he kept calling out to them in his excitement, "For Heaven's sake, stop! Oh, do wait one moment!"

On my way back from one of these parties I stopped in Vienna for a few days. The late Colonel Kodolitch, who was very well known in London, invited me to go and see his Hungarian regiment. He procured me a charger of sorts and on this prancing steed I galloped down the line with him, afterward witnessing the different manœuvers, and the charging *en masse* of hurdles and fences, a very pretty and unusual sight. As I was leaving, escorted to the station by Colonel Kodolitch and some of his officers, he said to me, "Please say *Ich danke sehr* to the officers." This I did, much to their amusement, as I found later it was the customary remark of a general after inspecting a regiment. I was much chaffed over the joke perpetrated on me.

Once in passing through Paris, I had a strange and unpleasant experience. I was going by the midday train, and happened to be standing in one of the archways in the Gare du Nord, which presented its usual busy and animated scene, when I suddenly heard a shot fired, followed by two or three more in rapid succession, and a man with his hand to his hip and an agonized expression on his face, ran, or rather hobbled, past me from behind one of the pillars of the archway. He was closely followed by another man who held a revolver, which he again fired off, this time so close to me that I fled in terror, seeing, as I ran, the victim fall to the ground, the murderer still firing at him. A large crowd, which had scattered in every direction at the first shots, now rushed to the spot. Meanwhile, fearing that the man was running amuck and that I might be the next recipient of his wild firing, I ran down the platform as fast as a heavy fur coat and various encumbrances permitted me. Unfortunately, I dropped my muff, which happened to be a sable one adorned with tails, containing my purse and ticket. Before I could pick it up a man pounced on it and made off at top speed toward the swinging glass doors leading out of the station. As I followed calling out, I saw him vanish through one of the doors and reappear by another like a clown in a pantomime. Calm and unconcerned he was swinging a cane and no muff was visible. While I stared at him in utter amazement I spied one of the tails of the muff sticking out from his coat, which he was endeavoring to keep closed. At that moment the bell which announced the departure of the train began to ring. There was no time for words; it was a case of "Do or die." I rushed at the thief, seized the tail of the muff and jumped into the train, which I just managed to catch, leaving the man with his mouth wide open, still staring as we crawled out of the station. As to the wretched victim of the shooting, I heard afterward that the assassin had shot him seven times before he was overpowered, and then tried to beat out his brains with the butt-end of the revolver, so great was his determination to kill him. A passenger received a stray shot in his leg, and altogether it was a scene of wild excitement and confusion. From the paper which gave an account of the fray it appeared that both men were Americans, the murderer having stalked his prey for more than a year and caught him as he was leaving France for America. It was proved at the trial that love and money were the motives of the crime. With

286

the usual procrastination of French justice, the case dragged on for so many months that I lost sight of it in the newspapers.

In 1891, I paid my first, to me a memorable, visit to Bayreuth. Wagner's music was not as popular then as it is now, at least in England. The "Ring des Niebe-lungs," which had been given for years with the greatest success in New York, had not as yet been produced in London. The ordinary opera-goer thought himself very advanced if he could sit through "Lohengrin"; as to "Die Meistersinger" or "Tristan and Isolde," to most people they were a concatenation of discordant sounds. Vast was the ignorance displayed by the public. I myself on one occasion when "Tristan" was being given, heard a couple who were sitting behind me, sympathize with Isolde for her "long wait" for Tristan in the third act. Van Dyck as Tristan had been singing for more than half an hour, and, although by a stretch of the imagina-tion, he might have been mistaken for a woman lying there covered with a rug, still they should have distin-guished between a tenor and a soprano. On the other hand, even would-be Wagnerians were sometimes led astray. A friend of mine, who is anything but musical, was persuaded by an embryo enthusiast to go with him to hear "Lohengrin." "But I don't think I care about music," said the poor martyr; "and I know I shall not understand a thing." "Nonsense, of course you will," replied the other, and so accordingly they went. As the violins attacked the long sustained note in A which marks the opening of the overture, the two friends looked un-easily at each other. "What is that noise?" asked the unmusical one. "I can't think," said the other, as the note was still being held, "unless it is the gas escaping."

My sister Mrs. Leslie, who intended to go with me to Bayreuth, had the happy idea of arranging some lectures on the "Ring" at her house in order to familiarize us with it. A German musician, a well-known exponent of Wagner, was pressed into the service, and he brought with him a lady who was to sing the different motifs. The lectures became a great success, and were attended by all our musical friends. The professor's knowledge of English was, at that time, as slight as his accent was strong, and this added a hilarity to the proceedings which was certainly not intended. As some young ladies were present, he was at times greatly exercised in explaining the story of the "Ring." "Siegfried" in particular worried him much. "Dee ladees mus not mind dis bad bisness of *Sigmund* und *Sieglinde;* it is *schrecklich,* but it is only zee lofs of zee gods, vich do not count. . . . Und here we have zee lofe motif illustrated by 'triolets' or triplets as you say in English." And amid smothered laughter, the lecturer would play the motif and the lady would warble.

A few years have increased Wagner's popularity in England to an astounding degree. Now no concert can be given without one or more Wagnerian selections, and at the Covent Garden Opera House, the "Cycle" which is performed two or three times every season, attracts huge crowds. Not content with this, the public largely supported a very creditable performance given in English by an English company in the winter of 1908. It must be added that Dr. Richter conducted, which may account in a large degree for its excellence. Contem-

THE WAGNER THEATER AT BAYREUTH

porary music seems imbued with a Wagnerian spirit, and no doubt orchestration has gained what in originality has been lost. This reminds me of a musical critic who had a place next to mine during the Leeds Festival of 1907. He was an ardent admirer of Elgar, whose "Kingdom" was being given. Observing that I was making some notes on my score, he asked at the end of the performance if he might inquire what I was recording. "Only my recollections of 'Tristan' and 'Parsifal' as they recur to my memory in this work," I mischievously answered. Looking at me with a rather dubious expression, "Oh, yes, quite so," he murmured; "I do not deny that Wagner came first, but," with a comprehensive wave of his hand, "Elgar has gone on." Such enthusiasm is refreshing.

Speaking of the Leeds Festival it is curious that these musical orgies flourish in this country better than in any other, considering that the English nation is not thought to be musical. Perhaps this is owing to the excellence of the Leeds, Birmingham, and Huddersfield choirs which, according to Dr. Richter, are the finest in the world. Be that as it may, it is only an English audience which will stand a week of oratorios.

The opera even is taken much more seriously than formerly. What with "all lights out" and "no talking," it is a solemn affair, not to be treated lightly. In Paris, the contrary prevails. You are invited to come to the opera to "see so-and-so dance," and it is generally treated as a place for social intercourse and conversation. One night, at a dinner in London, I sat next to the Duc de G——, who had just arrived from Paris. "Délicieuse soirée à l'Opéra hier," said he; "il y avait

14

foule." "What was given?" I asked. "Oh, je n'en sais rien—mais nous avons reçus cinquante-quatre visites dans notre loge!" This is one way of treating the opera, but the person who insists on explaining everything, or hums the melodies which are being sung is equally aggravating. A story is told of the late Lord L——, who was a frequenter of the opera, and had, it is said, this bad habit. One night in the omnibus box, he began whistling and humming as usual. "What a bore that Jean de Reszke is!" said a wag who was in the box. "Why?" asked Lord L—— in astonishment. "Because the fellow is preventing me from hearing you properly."

But this digression has led me far from Bayreuth. Our party consisted of Lady de Grey, my sister Mrs. Leslie, Mr. Evan Charteris and one or two others. Bayreuth was not as luxurious in those days as it has since become. It was only frequented by the real lovers of music, who were prepared for the sake of it to be as uncomfortable as German ideas of comfort could make them. We were all billeted on different people, who in some cases could have only one lodger. My sister and I were fortunate enough to secure rooms at a banker's, where we fared sumptuously compared to some. We gave ourselves up entirely to the object of the moment, and took it *au grand sérieux,* only thinking of what we were going to hear or had heard.

My first impression of "Parsifal" was, as the Teutons say, *"colossal."* The pilgrimage to Bayreuth, the "low living and high thinking," combined with the musical atmosphere we were living in, contributed no doubt to the rapture we felt, but that it existed was undeniable.

JEAN DE RESZKE

EDOUARD DE RESZKE

Our little party had settled to meet between the acts and exchange opinions, but so great were our emotions that we all fled in different directions, avoiding one another, until the performance was over, when we should be more calm. So serious was the audience that they were not even disturbed by the fact that Parsifal's wig came off in the third act, during the Flower Maidens' song. Not a titter was heard.

We spent a delightful week, although, personally, I was suffering agonies with toothache, until I found an unexpected Good Samaritan in the lady who sat behind me, and who produced cocaine. This lady was no less a person than Mrs. Sam Lewis, wife of the well-known money-lender; an excellent musician, she was a God-send to innumerable artists, and at her death left many legacies to them, besides £10,000 a year to a Consumptive Hospital, out of the huge fortune left her by her husband. Mr. Lewis, unlike his wife, was not artistic. It is told of him that, having once made a fortnight's stay in Rome, he was asked how he liked it. "You can 'ave Rome," was his laconic answer.

We varied our pleasures by excursions on the off days of the all-important performances, and by attending Frau Cosima Wagner's receptions, which were charming and unconventional.

Later in Paris and in London, I had occasion to meet her son, Siegfried Wagner. I remember at a dinner given in his honor that the question arose as to which composers one would choose if limited to two. We were twelve at the table and I was the only one who did not name Wagner. Partly out of contradiction and partly because I think so, I mentioned Bach and Beethoven.

"My father would also have chosen them," said Siegfried, to the confusion of the flatterers! I met him once or twice afterwards in Paris at Countess Wolkenstein's, the Austrian Ambassadress at that time. This distinguished lady, who as Countess Stieglitz had a salon in Berlin, was supposed to be the only woman whose influence was feared by Bismarck. A life-long friend and patron of Wagner, she stood by him in his dark days, and later assisted at his triumphs. Mme. Wolkenstein never misses her yearly visit to Bayreuth, where she generally stays with Mme. Wagner. When in Paris, we often went sight-seeing together, accompanied by Widor, the celebrated organist of St. Sulpice. A wonderful pianist, Mme. de Wolkenstein was rather hypercritical, and positively feared hearing indifferent music. I asked her to dine one night to meet a young and talented amateur, who was very amusing besides. *"Est-ce qu'il pratique?"* she inquired hesitatingly. On being assured that he would not play, she accepted. In the end, however, he did perform, much to my delight and her appreciation.

I was once asked to meet the Abbé Liszt at the Russian Embassy in London, when M. de Staal was Ambassador. I sat next the great man, whose strong and characteristic face, so often delineated both by brush and chisel, seemed strangely familiar. He was so blind that he ate his asparagus by the wrong end, until I pointed out his error. "Ah!" he exclaimed, "merci bien, il me semblait tout de même que cela n'était pas très bon!" After luncheon, notwithstanding his gouty fingers, he was prevailed upon to play. "Hélas," he said, "le moindre de mes élèves jouent mieux que moi maintenant." And it was pathetically true. I never heard him at his best. Rubinstein I well recollect with his long hair tossed about, the perspiration pouring down his face as his big hands tore up and down the piano. Full of tricks—to which so many artists become addicted—when he reached the culminating *fortissimo,* wild with excitement, he would hit with his palms or his forearm as many notes as he possibly could, until he seemed positively to get to the end of the instrument, making the strings snap and the wood sound. When I was in Russia, I was told that the head-teacher of a well-known ladies' school in St. Petersburg asked him how many hours a day her pupils should practise the piano. "None," said Rubinstein.

Many musicians have honored me by performing at my house, and apart from the pleasure they have brought me, I have always felt great sympathy for them in their arduous and precarious careers. "So many are called and so few chosen," and on what slender foundations their success rests! A cold, an illness and their voice and fortune may vanish; and think of the grinding slavery instruments mean! Planté the pianist, that pastmaster in technique, told me that if, for some reason or other, he was incapacitated from practising for three months he would never have the courage to take it up again. Then again the empty concert-rooms and the adverse criticism of the struggling days must try the hearts of the stoutest. Paderewski, when he first came to London, brought me a letter from a mutual friend. I invited to meet him a select few whom I knew to be capable of appreciating and judging him. Needless to say, their admiration and enthusiasm were unbounded.

A few days later he gave his first concert in St. James's Hall. The place was only half full and behind me were two musical critics taking notes for their papers. "There's not much in this fellow," said one. "He would be all right," said the other, "if he would leave Chopin alone, which he plays against all traditions." Stephen Heller, one of Chopin's friends and my first music professor, told me that the great composer never played his works twice in the same way—so much for the musical critics! The following year Paderewski, having had a gigantic success in Paris and elsewhere, returned to London, where he received an ovation from an excited and enthusiastic audience who stormed the platform to kiss his hands!

Personally I have never been able to surmount the nervousness one feels in playing before the public whether in concerted pieces or alone. What musical performers good, bad, or indifferent, have not at some time or other, felt their nerve giving way as they approached a difficult passage? Only to think of it is fatal! Once, at some concert for charity, I was playing a classical piece, the first movement of which had a few bars of some difficulty. The first time for the *da capo*, I got over it all right, but to lead to the next movement it had to be repeated with variations in another key. To my consternation, I found myself embarking on the same one, which, of course, led me to repeating the first movement. Again, as I came to the fatal passage, I trembled and did the same thing. Three times did I repeat that movement until the audience were becoming quite familiar with the tune. As for me, I felt in a hideous nightmare and was on the verge of jumping

FRANZ LISZT

IGNACE JAN PADEREWSKI

SIR ARTHUR SULLIVAN

up from the piano and rushing off the stage, when, oh! joy! the fourth time I mechanically played the right bars and was able eventually to bring the piece to its conclusion. Hans von Bülow is supposed to have done the same thing once with a sonata of Beethoven, until in desperation he had to send for the music.

On another occasion I was brought to confusion, but this time not through my own fault. It was at a concert in the city given at the Mansion House before a large audience. Mlle. —— and I were to play a Polonaise of Chopin on two pianos. As our turn came Mlle., who was a professional of some experience and execution, said hurriedly to me, "At the eleventh bar on the sixth page, when I make you a sign stop, as I mean to put in a little cadenza of my own." Before I could remonstrate or point out that it would be an unnecessary addition to one of Chopin's masterpieces, the lady had seated herself at the piano, and perforce I had to follow suit. When she arrived at the eleventh bar of the sixth page, she nodded violently to me, and then proceeded to dazzle the company with arpeggios, runs and trills, until I began to wonder if I should ever find the propitious moment to reënter. I finally did, and had the pleasure of hearing from the occupants of the front row as I went out, "Poor Lady Randolph, what a pity she lost her place for so long!"

To be able to read music well and to accompany is all that need be required of amateurs. It is an age of virtuosi and mechanical instruments, and the poorest judge is becoming hypercritical. There is no doubt that the day has passed when people will listen patiently after dinner to the playing of the "Moonlight Sonata" or the

"Prière d'une Vierge," executed by the daughter of the house. Formerly in England, every girl was taught to sing whether she had a voice or not, but the intelligent mother of to-day realizes that her daughters are better employed in listening to good music than in performing badly.

I think I may fitly end this chapter, which somehow has drifted into one on music, by speaking of the late Sir Arthur Sullivan, who was one of the kindest and most gentle of men and a great friend of mine. It was my good fortune to be present at most of the "first nights" of his productions and no one, who did not assist at them, can realize the unbounded enthusiasm with which they were received, or the excitement with which a new work was looked forward to by the public. It was quite a national event. Gilbert's delicate and subtle humor and Sullivan's melodies and exquisite orchestration make such a felicitous combination that I cannot think "Time will stale their infinite variety."

At the outbreak of the South African War, Sullivan wrote the music to Rudyard Kipling's "Absent-Minded Beggar." The sale of this song realized £75,000, which went to the war fund. Happening to visit Sir Arthur one day when he had just finished it, I begged him to play it—which he did. I confess I did not like it. "Well, what is your opinion?" he asked. I answered guardedly, "I 'm afraid I think the words are rather vulgar: 'Cook's son, duke's son, son of a belted earl!'"

"And so is the music," said he.

CHAPTER XIII

ON the morning of the 27th of June, 1894, I started with Lord Randolph Churchill from Euston Station for a tour round the world. Quite a number of friends besides our families came to see us off; among them were Lord and Lady Londonderry, Lady Jeune, Lord Rosebery, and Mr. Goschen. Randolph was very pleased and touched at his old friend Lord Rosebery coming, and frequently alluded to it afterward. At Liverpool Mr. Ismay met us on board the *Majestic;* he reminded me of the Jubilee trip on the *Teutonic,* which already seemed in the distant past. Rough seas and uninteresting passengers were not conducive to the time passing quickly. The only incidents I remember were the inevitable concert, in which I was pressed into the service, and the excitement another night of nearly running down a vessel. It was a strange sensation to awake finding our ship stopped, and to feel instead of the throbbing and noise of the machinery an unwonted calm, broken only by the incessant and irritating sound of fog-horns.

We remained only two days in New York as the thermometer recorded 81 degrees in the shade. Mr.

Chauncey Depew, who was one of the few people we saw, was good enough to place his private car at our disposal for the projected journey to Bar Harbor. I remember asking him if it was true that he had telegraphed to Lord Rosebery when "Ladas" won the Derby, "Nothing left but Heaven." He replied that it was.

This was my first experience of a private car, which proved to be as well appointed as a small yacht, and was a most enjoyable mode of traveling. The colored cook prepared an excellent dinner, and we slept as comfortably as we could have done in our own beds. After the dust and heat of New York, Bar Harbor seemed a haven of rest with its fresh sea-breezes, lovely drives, and mountain walks. As far as I could gather the life there was very much a second edition of Newport, and consisted in perpetual dressing, dinners, and dances, and that horror of horrors, the leaving of cards. It was very pleasant notwithstanding, and we indulged in all the amusements of the place. We were invited to a dance at the Kebo Valley Club, a charming house thoroughly suited to the country. It was a real joy to dance the "Boston," which only Americans know properly. There we met a number of pretty girls whom I often saw driving or playing lawn-tennis, and who, anticipating the "hatless brigade" of to-day, were invariably without hats. This I was told was to bleach their hair. I made the acquaintance of some delightful women with whom I found myself in that perfect sympathy which can only be felt among compatriots. Mr. George Vanderbilt— a very cultivated young man—was then unmarried; he had a steam-yacht in which he took us to see East Harbor, where we had a fine view and a sea below. Close to his house, which faced the sea, was a swimming-bath open to the sky, through which salt water was constantly flowing. Here he and his friends of both sexes disported themselves, bobbing up and down, diving and swimming, without shyness—and, I must say, without vanity; for it must be owned that women do not look their best under such circumstances. While in the water there was no hilarity or chaff, everything was conducted with the greatest decorum, not to say ceremony, which added to the ludicrous effect upon the spectators.

We dined one night with Mrs. Van Rensselaer Jones to meet Marion Crawford, who was staying with her. Mr. Marion Crawford was the best of company. Tall, dark, with piercing blue eyes, a decided chin and kind mouth adorned with a small mustache, I thought him the very best type of a good-looking American. He has a pleasant voice, modulated by his constant use of the Italian language, and talked most agreeably on all subjects. At that time he took a very gloomy view of the political outlook in America, and declared that the problem of socialism would be solved there. Some one accused him of being an idle man and loving the *dolce far' niente.* "Idle!" he exclaimed, and his eyes sparkled with indignation; "for sixteen years I have worked and made a living by my pen, and have produced twenty-five novels!"

At the same dinner I met for the first time Mr. Courtland Palmer, a young amateur pianist who was inspired with the real *feu sacré,* and was able then as now to hold his own with professionals. During my stay at Bar

Harbor we met frequently and played the piano together.

One of our many expeditions was a sail in the *Mayflower,* the yacht which won the International Yacht Race against the *Galatea.* There was a Bishop on board who was described to me as a "bully Bishop," but we thought his appearance somewhat disreputable, and did not cultivate him. Mr. C——, commonly called the "Greek god"—a name which suited him admirably—was also there. When I told Randolph his nickname, he declared he "could have nothing to do with a Greek god." But he did, and liked him. Before leaving Bar Harbor the *Nourmahal,* a big steam-yacht belonging to the John Jacob Astors came into the harbor. Mrs. Astor's beauty and grace, not to mention the charming simplicity of her nature, must always command admiration; but, had she been the Empress of Russia, her arrival could not have caused more commotion.

It was with regret that we left Bar Harbor and its bright and hospitable inhabitants, and started on our Canadian journey. With some difficulty we procured a private car from the Pullman Company, the president of the Canadian Pacific Railway, notwithstanding our letters to him, proving a broken reed. The officials were persuaded to place us at the end of the train in order that we might make use of the observation room with which our car, the "Iolanthe," was furnished, and which proved a great boon. We sat there all day, or on the platform, regardless of dust and cinders. The scenery at first was very disappointing—an endless straight track, bordered on either side by a small pink flower which never left us until we reached Vancouver. The names of the various stations seemed to represent all the nations of the world: Portage la Prairie, Winnipeg, MacGregor, Medicine Hat, and so on. At the latter place we stopped an hour and visited the hospital, where the superintendent with much pride showed us in the visiting-book the signatures of the Duke and Duchess of Connaught. On an average our train stopped every half hour, with much whistling, ringing of bells, and exchange of greetings between the engine-driver and the inhabitants. Every log-cabin was a station and every platform the club of these poor people, whose only excitement was the daily arrival of the train. After Winnipeg we had two days of prairies which I should have liked to ride over. Every now and then in the distance one caught sight of a ranch surrounded by trees, looking like an oasis in the desert. Before reaching the Rockies we saw some prairie-dogs, strange little animals like hairless squirrels with rat-tails. Life on one of these prairies, although probably monotonous, must have the compensations which come with peace and the close study of nature.

At Banff we had our car put into a siding, and passed two days there, which well repaid us. For the first time we saw the Rockies in all their grandeur. Unfortunately, a prairie-fire which we passed on our way some thirty or forty miles from Banff, had filled the air with smoke and made the mountains misty. Still, we could see enough to realize the magnificence of the scenery. The heat and the "skeeters" were rather drawbacks to expeditions, but we could not resist the "call of the wild," and drove about all day in uncomfortable buckboards and "cutunders." On one of those drives I insisted on getting down and touching some "Hoodoos" for luck. These curious natural monuments, half earth, half stone, are looked upon by the Indians with great superstition and awe, "hoodoo" being the Indian word for "spook." They certainly were uncanny objects. One over seventy feet high was exactly like the half-formed figure of a man seated on a pedestal. Our driver was a very intelligent, well-educated young man; I was amused at his telling me that the last Englishman he had driven thought "it was a mistake to plant the trees so close together"! The Vermilion Lakes (so called because the reeds with which they abound turn bright red in the autumn) enchanted us with their marvelous beauty. We were rowed the whole length of the two lakes—eight miles. The enormous snow-clad mountains made a vivid contrast to the fresh green vegetation around us, brilliant with mauve, pink, and yellow flowers, while the blue water was so clear that we could see the bottom of the lake, over which two eagles were circling.

On the journey to Vancouver we could not tear ourselves away from the observation room and the platform, so glorious was the scenery. Among those stupendous heights one expected to see the Valkyries rushing along from peak to peak and Wotan on the war-path. Again, however, we lost much of the view by the smoke which sometimes hung for miles between us and everything. Great forest fires seemed to be raging everywhere, and at times we would wend our way through burning trees on either side. It was a melancholy sight to see the miles of black stumps and

LADY RANDOLPH CHURCHILL

leafless skeletons, their twisted and tortured branches standing out against the background of snow, while the bright green ferns and variegated flowers made a carpet at their feet. I thought the destruction rather wanton, as in some places we saw trees burning down close to the stations on the railway track, but no one attempted to put the fires out.

Twenty-four hours of Vancouver was enough for us, and we left for Victoria in a small steamer filled with a motley crowd. The weather was so cold we could only gaze at the scenery through our cabin windows. We found Victoria far more attractive than Vancouver, even though it is possible that it is being "left behind," as is asserted by the rival city. I lunched one day with the Bishop of Columbia, and suddenly realized that I was in a British dependency when a bevy of healthy-looking girls came in from playing off a lawn-tennis tournament escorted by a couple of curates. While there we received a visit from Colonel Baker, a brother of Valentine Baker of Egyptian fame. Being in the British Columbian government, he was full of information. I was somewhat startled when he said, "Now that I am in the Cabinet." My ignorance was so great that I learned for the first time that British Columbia had a constitution and a Parliament of its own. Home Rule with a vengeance! Colonel Baker enlightened me. I gathered that their Parliament lasts for four years, and their Parties are not divided into Liberals and Conservatives, but are called the "Ins" and the "Outs." Their policy is merely that of Local Government Board or County Council, and interest in such foreign questions as may affect them. The "Ins" want to stay in, and the "Outs" strive to get in, which struck me as describing the feelings of politicians of all countries and parties.

At Victoria I had my first experience of a male Chinese housemaid whom I mistook (notwithstanding trousers) for a comfortable old woman. I found an excellent Steinway piano in the hotel, and played to my heart's content, to the evident delight of some old ladies who used to congregate to hear me. On one occasion, however, I scattered them like frightened wood-pigeons when, to the inquiry what was the "sweetly pretty" tune I was playing, I answered, *"Götterdämmerung!"* with an emphasis on the third syllable. With one look of pained surprise they gathered up their skirts and fled.

H. M. S. *Royal Arthur,* with Admiral Stephenson on board was lying off Esquimault (pronounced Squimalt by the inhabitants) ; we lunched with him one day and saw the sights, such as they were. It was very pleasant to meet an old friend again, and he took us back to Victoria on his barge. On the way we came across many canoes filled with Indians, whole families, the old squaws paddling away for dear life. A large log with two men astride it and a dog sitting solemnly between them, formed a strange-looking craft. They paddled with great skill as the slightest movement would have upset them. A tight rope was security compared to it. At a distance they looked as if they were sitting in the water.

Continuing our journey we started for the Golden Horn in a steamer which rejoiced in the name of *Walla Walla.* After three days of cold, comfortless sea, over which I draw a veil, we arrived at San Francisco to find the weather windy and sunless. Walking was unpleasant owing to the innumerable electric tramways which seemed to come upon one from every direction. We visited Chinatown with a detective. The joss-houses, opium dens, and gambling places were very stuffy and astonishingly small. The opium-smokers lie on bare boards and in such uncomfortable attitudes that it is a mystery to me how they can find enjoyment in the pernicious practice. I was looking with amazement at a fat old Chinaman who had screwed himself up into a true lover's knot, which ought to have caused agonizing cramps to anything human, when he half opened his eyes and with an expression of beatitude said, "It makee me feel good." The smell of the Chinaman and the opium mixed—half sour, half sweet—was revolting. I was anxious to see the theaters, but our guide thought it might be rash.

I received many baskets of flowers artistically arranged, white, pink, and mauve sweet peas, roses of all kinds with long stems, and magnolia blossoms in profusion. But the flowers in California although lovely, have little odor, and the fruit, which is gorgeous, lacks taste, like a beautiful woman devoid of brains. At a dinner at the University Club (in which there is a room prettily paneled in oak where ladies may dine), I was introduced to an "oyster cocktail" to which I took kindly, and to a "fancy roast" also made of oysters.

In despair at not seeing the sun we departed to Monterey. We had heard much of its beauty and were not disappointed; indeed, the gardens surpassed all I had imagined. I was never tired of walking about and admiring the splendid trees, shrubs, and plants of all kinds, while the flowers were in a profusion I have never

15

seen equaled anywhere. The Arizona Garden with its tropical plants was new to me. We indulged in what is known as the "Seventeen-mile Drive" along the coast. The charm of this road is in its variety. As we drove through Monterey, which is very like a small Spanish town, and which California looks upon as extremely ancient—being over one hundred years old—our driver pointed out several buildings, and gravely said they dated from 1830 or 1850! After several miles of forest the ocean suddenly came into view, and a quantity of seals were seen disporting themselves on the rocks, while an exciting fight was going on between two. We watched them for a long while—sometimes they would tumble off into the water, but quickly scrambled up again to have a few more rounds. I proposed to wait and see the end, but our driver informed us that they might go on for a couple of hours. On our way back we passed through the celebrated Cypress Grove, a very entrancing spot, full of mystery and charm. These ancient trees, so old that generations have lost count of them, twist their gnarled trunks away from the sea, their dark green heads embellished by long pale strands of the feathery moss which eventually strangles them.

The Del Monte Hotel at Monterey was alive with the most energetic young people I have ever seen. They swam in the early morning, rode, drove, played lawn-tennis, and danced all night. Looking on at a ball one evening, I happened to relate to a gentleman whose acquaintance I had just made the remark of a Frenchman with whom I was once dancing. *"C'est terrible,"* he said, as, panting and puffing, he tried to regain his breath. "Well, why do you dance if you hate it?" I inquired. *"C'est pour l'hygiène—Mon médecin me le recommande."* I was rather startled to see my story twenty-four hours afterward in a newspaper, wonderfully embellished under the heading "Lady Randolph tells Good Stories in the Porch of Del Monte!"

While in America we managed to evade reporters fairly successfully; at San Francisco, however, an enterprising journalist, having been denied an interview with Randolph, published an imaginary one which was so comical that I could not be angry. A woman reporter having pursued me without success, invaded my bedroom one morning as I was emerging from my bath, and when I gently but firmly pushed her out burst into tears. Her weeping mollified me, and I saw her later. Poor thing! I daresay, if the truth were known, she hated the interview as much as I did.

Leaving San Francisco in the *Umatilla,* we repeated our somewhat uncomfortable journey, returning to Victoria on our way to the Far East.

The *Empress of Japan,* in which we sailed for Yokohama, proved to be an ocean palace, clean and comfortable, and, much to my delight and appreciation, the saloons were decorated with quantities of Japanese plants and shrubs. The Chinese waiters, too, were a novelty. Dressed in their butcher-blue or white, they looked picturesque. Among the passengers were Baron Speck von Sternburg, late German Ambassador at Washington, and Mr. Villiers, the war correspondent of "The Graphic." We were greatly interested and excited at the thought that we should find Japan in a martial state, as the Chinese and Japanese war was then at its height; and, not knowing Japan, we anticipated stirring scenes and sights. Great were to be the doings of Mr. Villiers, who expected to go at once to the front.

On arriving, we found that the harbor of Yokohama was laid with torpedoes and submarines, and the captain had to get a government boat to pilot us in. I was glad to leave the ship, as the Pacific had been anything but peaceful. Rough seas, gray and leaden skies, constant rolling and pitching, besides the monotony, had begun to weary us.

On anchoring in the harbor, we immediately found ourselves surrounded by a shoal of craft of all sizes and shapes, from a steam-launch to a sampan, Japanese junks hovering on the outside of the crowd. I watched the motley crew for some time, their various costumes— or the want of them—amusing me much. On a government launch were some little military men, *dorés sur toutes les coutures,* coming to greet the Japanese officers we had on board. Much bowing and scraping took place. We were surrounded by sampans trying to get out of the way, manned by coolies dressed only in white cotton Eton jackets and a bright bit of blue stuff bound round their heads, a great contrast to the gorgeous uniforms. We were not sorry to get ashore and betake ourselves to the hotel.

There we found many war correspondents, who looked very dejected, as they were not allowed to join the army. Mr. Villiers managed later to get to the front, but with such restrictions that I imagine his reports could have been of little value, as he was denied the use of the telegraph, and everything he wrote had to be submitted to the minister of war for supervision.

TRAVELING IN A STRAW CHAIR

There had been a great Japanese victory the day before, and this made the war more popular than ever, although we could not see many signs of rejoicing. I gathered from the different people I met that the situation was being forced by the government, to create a diversion from internal troubles. I was told that the English in Japan rather sympathized with the Chinese, whereas, when later we went to China, we found the situation there just the reverse. Although the Chinese had the men and the money, they hated fighting, as was proved by the result of the campaign. I have always thought that the Japanese were very badly treated by Europe in general and England in particular in not being allowed to reap the fruits of their victory. Even in the recent Russian war, although conquerors, they were not allowed a free hand.

After the cold of the Pacific, the damp heat of Yokohama was very trying, and we stayed only a few days before going up to Myanoshita, in the hills.

Before leaving Yokohama, I went to the theater, which certainly was unlike anything I had ever seen before. We sat on the floor of our so-called box, and had tea like the crowd. And such a crowd! It was an endless source of interest and amusement to watch them, whole families—mothers-in-law and daughters-in-law, children of all ages, and parents of different generations, fathers, sons, and grandsons. All had their dinners with them. Little trays were produced—tiny boxes full of rice, bowls containing weird food-stuffs, pink, white, and green, seaweed on rice cakes, raw fish, and nameless yellow condiments, tea in microscopic cups, of course, with no milk or sugar. The Japanese cannot understand

Europeans putting milk in their tea, as, according to them, it has a strong smell. The children were dressed and undressed during the entr'actes, and people smoked, slept, ate, talked, and fanned themselves. It was certainly a great contrast to see a little "musmé" such as Pierre Loti describes, daintily dressed in the gayest of kimonos and smartest of obis, sitting between a coolie wearing nothing but a loose cotton jacket and an old hag nursing a baby. Although it was true that most of the men had little on, and the thermometer was 85 degrees, the atmosphere was not impossible, as I am sure would have been the case in a European theater under similar circumstances. The plays have usually fourteen or fifteen acts, and last all day, and sometimes two. This particular one not having an actress such as Sadi Yacco to interpret it, was quite unintelligible to me; but I admired the grace of the actresses, their easy movements when dancing, and the way they managed their tight clothes. Imagine my surprise when I found out afterward that they were all men! Up to a few years ago men and women did not act together in Japan, the theatrical companies being composed of either one sex or the other. But a change has come over them, and there are now mixed companies.

One afternoon I visited the nursery gardens of Böhmer, where I saw quantities of the stunted shrubs and trees so dear to the Japanese heart, and with which they love to decorate their miniature gardens. I bought several, including a century-old maple about ten or twelve inches high, the tiny leaves of which were at that moment bright red. On my return to England I gave this little tree to the Princess of Wales, who was delighted with it;

for all I know it may still be alive. The whole place was perfumed by the gold and white "moxa," and I longed to bring some away, as well as the huge gardenia and daphne plants, which were as large as ordinary lilac bushes. Baron Sternburg, who was with me, proposed that we should walk back from the gardens, but we soon lost ourselves, and, hot and dusty, took refuge in an inviting-looking tea-house while we sent for a jinrikisha. The place was evidently not frequented by Europeans, as the little maids who waited on us hovered about me with the greatest curiosity, and before I could stop them, one had put on my gloves, another had seized my hat, which I had taken off, placing it on her greasy, black locks, and a third was strutting about with my parasol. At last they became quite obstreperous, and it was only when my companion promised them sake that they left us in peace.

On leaving Yokohama, we said good-by to our steamer friends, and started by train for Myanoshita.

At the station there was a great crowd: naked coolies; tradesmen in flowing kimonos, carrying Mrs. Gamp umbrellas and topped by monstrous pot-hats; artisans in blue cotton tunics, with the description and badge of their trade printed on their backs in white, or inclosed in a circle of black on a red ground; to say nothing of masses of women. The married ones were easily recognized by their shaved eyebrows and blackened teeth, in which hideous custom they indulge in order to remain faithful to their husbands, but which conceivably might produce the reverse effect on the husbands themselves. Among them were a number of girls, their shiny hair stiff with camelia oil, and adorned with combs, tiny chrysanthemums, and coral beads, their painted faces breaking into a smile if you looked at them. The motley crowd, which was reinforced at every station, walked, stumped, and toddled into the train, which consisted of a few diminutive carriages more like a glorified toy than anything else. Most of these people were mounted on clogs, making a loud and curious noise.

After two hours of slow winding between soft-green hills covered with feathery vegetation, we arrived at Kodga, where we got into a tramway (made in Birmingham), and rattled for an hour through one long street, which comprised endless villages. The weather being hot, the inhabitants, including the babies, were carrying on their various vocations in front of their open houses, minus their clothes. All seemed hard at work and good-humored. The Japanese are proverbially fond of children, who, for fear they should be lost, are each made to wear a little metal ticket with name and address attached. Attractive as they undoubtedly are, it is a mistake to say that they never cry; and it is equally untrue to say that smells do not exist in Japan. Defective drainage and stale fish do not, as a rule, remind one of the "perfumes of Araby." We stopped occasionally to change the wretched horses. Japanese horses have no quarters, and are sorry-looking quadrupeds; Chinese horses, on the other hand, have no shoulders. At Yumoto we all got into jinrikishas, each with two men, one to pull and the other to push, and we proceeded at a trot up the stoniest road I have ever traveled. Once we stopped at a tea-house, where the landlady, with much in-drawing of breath (to show her civility by not breathing in one's face) and with much bowing and rubbing of knees, gave us Japanese tea in the usual cups without handles, and the pink-and-white cakes one sees everywhere, impossible, dry, musty horrors. Our jinrikisha-men, the perspiration pouring from their brown bodies, took off their white jackets (the one garment) and proceeded to wash and dash water over themselves from the pump near by. The pump was pretty and picturesque, consisting as it did of two bamboos, one brown, the other dark green; in one of which there was a large bunch of wild flowers, while from the other the clear mountain stream poured into one of those delightful big Japanese tubs. The face of my maid (a prim, highly respectable person) was a study as the men resumed their mushroom hats and girded up their loins afresh. In consequence of my having treated them to sake at the tea-house, we were trotted briskly up to the Fujiyya Hotel.

The place looked pretty and quaint, and the calm and peace were welcome, but it was disappointing to find the hotel full of Europeans, mostly pale, jaded people from Hong-Kong, Shanghai, and even Singapore, come to recruit in the fresh air of Myanoshita, which is 3000 feet above the level of the sea.

We passed a pleasant fortnight there. I never tired of the mountains, with their changing shadows, deep gorges, and rushing streams and cascades, with here and there to rejoice the eye a peep of the sea in the distance. The vegetation was a great source of interest and pleasure, it was all so new and so attractive: on our journey up I counted fifty-five different kinds of agricultural products and shrubs. The number of little villages and houses dotted about everywhere afforded a good glimpse of Japanese peasant life. All seemed hard-working, contented, and good-humored. One day we went to the Lake of Hakone, carried thither in straw chairs supported on bamboo sticks by four men, not a very comfortable mode of progression. They had a wonderful way of changing places with one another to relieve the load on their shoulders, and doing so without shaking one in the least.

At a bend of the mountain path we suddenly came upon a large Buddha carved in the side of the rock. In-numerable prayers in the shape of bits of paper stuck on sticks were planted before him; his legs were crossed, and the soles of the foot turned up to show that he never sullied them by contact with things earthly. The look of eternal peace which characterizes all the effigies of Buddha is due, I think, to the closed eyes being so far apart, the serene and slightly smiling mouth adding to the unfathomable expression.

Japanese photographers are such excellent artists that they always manage to find the most picturesque point of view. If, in visiting some place, one does not follow in their footsteps, one is apt to be disappointed and think they must have idealized. These were my feelings at Lake Hakone, although I realized its beauty. We crossed the lake in two sampans, our noses in the air, gazing at the clouds for the *point de mire* of all Japan, Fuji-yama, the great, the sacred. But as usual she had veiled herself in a cloud of mist, and not having as yet seen her, I was fain to be content with her presentment on my new kimono, which I found on returning to the hotel. We walked back part of the way over very rough ground steaming with sulphurous springs.

Mr. Le Poer Trench, the English Minister, had arrived, and we were delighted to make his acquaintance; and also that of Professor Basil Hall Chamberlain, whose book, "Things Japanese," over which I had been poring with enthusiasm, is a standard work for all English-speaking people. They brought us the news of the great battle of Pyong-yang, where the Japanese claimed to have killed 20,000 Chinamen; and of a naval engagement where six Chinese and three Japanese ships were sunk and blown up. Mr. Trench, who was unmarried, had not at that time been very long in Japan. His health was not of the best, as the climate of Mexico, his previous diplomatic post, had not suited him. A thin, pleasant man of about forty-five, I found him a great acquisition. We used to take long walks together, climbing the most precipitous hills.

The three weeks of absolute rest at Myanoshita did Randolph much good, everything was so reposeful, from the quiet Japanese landscape, with its soft grays and greens, to the bevy of little "musmés" who waited upon us, moving silently and swiftly about in their stocking-feet, always smiling and gentle.

Intending to go to Tokio, we were obliged to retrace our steps to Yokohama, where we stayed two nights. There we found considerable excitement in the harbor over the arrival of four large German ironclads on their way to Korea to "watch" the progress of the war. We could not but think it a pity that the British seemed so apathetic and unrepresented. The Japanese were getting very much "above themselves," and the English government had rather given in to them over the last commercial treaty. So at least thought the English residents and merchants. The war was the one topic in the town. I went to a popular theater to see a play representing the battle of Pyong-yang. It was densely crowded, and with difficulty we got places in the gallery. In the last act the Chinese troops, represented by three Chinamen, were perpetually being killed by twenty Japs, who rushed about bugling incessantly, brandishing swords, letting off rifles, and enjoying it madly. In the center of the revolving stage was a cardboard town which was presently lighted up with red lights, the climax being reached when a small, yellow general in a smart European uniform rushed out from the smoke, and in a piping treble made a speech to the army of twenty, all there to a man. At this a paroxysm seized the audience, and they became so excited that we fled. Wata, my jinrikisha-man, asked me if it was not "good big play."

Although the distance to Tokio was only eighteen miles, we took nearly two hours to get there. We met a train full of soldiers going to the front; there was much cheering, and many *sayonaras* were exchanged. Fuji-yama, or "Fuji," as they affectionately call her, showed herself for the first time. The top alone was visible, and that only for a few moments, the "Peerless One" retiring again behind the clouds. The expedition to the top is, I believe, very tiring, but most thrilling. Descending, one "toboggans" on one's feet through the ashes. This was done by Sir Harry Parkes and his wife forty years ago, they being the first Europeans allowed to ascend the mountain, which up to that time had been held sacred from the foot of the Western stranger.

I was astonished to find Tokio such a vast place; it covers an area as large as that of London. The dis-

LORD CURZON OF KEDLESTON

tances are enormous, and I pitied the poor jinrikisha-boys, who often trotted for miles for a very small remuneration. We went to the Shiba Temples and saw the tombs of the shoguns. The inner temple is full of large stone-and-bronze lanterns, which are the offerings and tributes to the dead from their royal relatives. To go into the temple we had to take off our boots, while an apathetic priest looked on, his shaven head shaped like an emu's egg, and his somewhat tawdry kimono making him appear anything but prepossessing. We duly visited the shrines, admired the beautiful frescoes and lacquered ceilings; the gold-lacquered doors of great value; the carvings, ten or twelve inches deep, representing flowers and birds marvelously true to nature; and, last but not least, the plain stone urn over the grave of each shogun, the only ornament being the three gold asarum leaves, the crest of the Tokugawa royal family. Next we went to the tombs of the forty-seven Ronins, the brave and wonderful men, who, having revenged their ruined and murdered master by killing his powerful enemy, all performed hara-kiri, and have been worshiped ever since. The tomb of the chief Ronin, O-ishi-Kura Nosuke, was covered with flowers and paper prayers, and there was a large basket of cards hanging on the door, to which of course we contributed ours. Mr. Trench invited us to luncheon at the British legation, where we met, among others, Captain Brinkley and Professor Chamberlain. The legation showed signs of the last earthquake, which must have been a severe one, as evidences of it were everywhere. Although more than two months had passed, repairs were still being made.

Another day we lunched with Captain Brinkley, to see his wonderful collection of china and bronzes. He had been a resident in Japan for over forty years, was the editor or proprietor of "The Japan Mail." A man of great influence and vast information, he was most pleasant to meet. Every notable person who came to Japan, or wished to write about the country, consulted him as a walking encyclopedia. He told me that of all the searching inquisitions to which he had ever been subjected the severest was that of Lord Curzon of Kedleston (then George Nathaniel Curzon). For four hours he plied him with questions, which, notwithstanding Captain Brinkley's knowledge of the country, were often difficult to answer. He spoke of him with unbounded admiration as being the cleverest man he had ever met. Captain Brinkley's wife, a Japanese lady who had been married to him some years, did the honors of his house with that wonderful grace and gentleness of which Japanese women alone seem to have the secret. The extraordinary refinement and high-bred look of a well-born Japanese is most attractive. Dressed in a kimono of neutral-tinted silk, with a discreet *obi,* and a soft, pale-pink *eri,* or collar, a beautiful, old gold-lacquered comb in her shiny-black hair, this lady presented a very different appearance to the bedizened geisha, with the rainbow-colored garments, which is the accepted European idea of Japanese women. The late Mrs. Bishop, writing about Japan, says that to one who has lived there for some time, European women, however ladylike, appear in comparison loud and vulgar in their voices and manners. Through an interpreter, an English lady who seemed a sort of *dame de compagnie,*

Mrs. Brinkley and I were able to carry on a conversation. In speaking of their education, obedience, I was told, played the greatest part. "There are the three obediences," said my hostess, "the child's obedience to its parents, the wife's to the husband, and the mother's to the eldest son." Presently we plunged into the mysteries of "Peach bloom," "Sang de bœuf," and "Famille verte" as bit by bit the celebrated collection was brought in from a godown, or fireproof house, next door. In this custom, Captain Brinkley copied the Japanese, who always keep everything of value in such a place, each house having one of its own. A few objects are particularly selected according to the season of the year, and are placed in an alcove in the principal room. After being admired for a fortnight or so, these are sent back, and others are brought in their place. In this way the treasures can be properly appreciated, and each time appear as fresh revelations. The Japanese consider, not perhaps without reason, that Europeans crowd their houses in an absurd manner, and make them look like shops.

We ended our pleasant day by being taken to see the houses and gardens of Mr. Iwasaki, a magnate of Tokio, our host having arranged the visit beforehand. After a long drive in a landau, which was driven by a Japanese coachman garbed in a dark-blue kimono and mushroom hat, with a "belto," or groom, dressed in the same way, on the box, we came to the two houses. One was European, full of fine things, while the other, in which the owner lived, was Japanese. Having removed our shoes, we were taken over it. I wish I could describe its fascinations; but where there were no ornaments, no furniture, no pictures save a kakemono here and there, no curtains, no color anywhere, it is difficult to say wherein lay the charm. And yet it was charming. The fineness of the matting, the beauty and workmanship of the woodwork, the lacquer frames of the screens, which were so adjusted that they parted at a touch without a sound, the extraordinary cleanliness everywhere, and, above all, the different little courts on which the rooms looked, were delightful. The bath-room particularly pleased me. Made of some light-colored wood, it shone like satin and felt like it. A delicate carving round the base of the wall, representing flights of birds, formed a dado; two large wooden tubs of the same wood stood at the end of the room, encircled by brass bands beautifully polished, and half a dozen tubs of different sizes stood on a low table; the window looked out upon a small court with one large magnolia-tree and a very old gray-stone lantern. Another room, a *sanctum sanctorum,* where the "tea ceremonies" were held, gave upon a wild scene ten feet square, where jagged rocks, prickly bushes, and rushing torrents spanned by stone bridges, appeared in pleasant contrast to the urbanities and rigid etiquette of these ceremonies. The smoking-room, made by opening and closing a screen, looked out upon a lake artificially and cleverly planned, with beautiful trees and shrubs on its banks, and rocks of strange and varied colors. These rocks alone cost a fabulous sum, and had been brought from a great distance. The lake was fed from the sea, and as the sun was setting we watched the fish jumping high in the air. Walking round the gardens until it was nearly dark, every turn of the path presented an absolutely new aspect, the variety being marvelous. The gardens and houses covered twenty-four acres, and seemed four times that size. On our return to the European house, we found rows of servants and tables set out, with all manner of cakes, sandwiches, and tea, waiting for us. As Mr. Iwasaki did not live there, I remembered being astonished at the elaborate preparations. Captain Brinkley told me he thought it was a delicate Japanese hint to him not to bring strangers too often. Japanese, unlike their European brethren, do not care to be thought rich, and although hospitable, are not fond of showing their houses.

One night I went out for a walk in the main street after dinner, escorted by our guide. The Imperial Hotel at Tokio, although magnificent, was rather stuffy, and every sort of insect came in at the windows, from mosquitos to green grasshoppers three inches long. In the streets, people and vendors were selling their wares on the pavement. The open screens of the private houses permitted us to look through them; at one the sound of a samisen attracted me, and I could not resist stopping and looking in. Beyond two rooms, by a not over-bright light, I saw a little Japanese woman sitting on a mat singing softly in a minor key, accompanying herself on the samisen. I asked Matsuda if the women minded publicity. Looking very shy and uncomfortable, he said, "Oh, Japanese no look in—not good manners." I felt fearfully crushed.

Shopping expeditions were always amusing. On one occasion a Japanese woman who spoke English, the wife of Mr. Trench's valet, accompanied me, and I invested in some fascinating *obis*, Mrs. Tetsu helping me with her

16

excellent taste. Next we went to a curio-dealer. There seemed to be no shop, but we walked into a tiny garden, where, seated on the floor of a small house, was a smiling old man, who received us with many bows, placing cushions for us. Tea and shiny, brown cakes were brought in; he then produced a few little boxes, and, with much undoing of pale blue-and-green tapes and unfolding of silk handkerchiefs, showed us lovely old bits of lacquer, china, and bronze. The more I admired, the more he smiled and brought forth treasures, handling the things tenderly as though he loved them, which was altogether enticing. I could not help comparing this curio-dealer with those of Yokohama, where they try to please foreign taste by forcing themselves to forget all that is best in Japanese art, producing vulgar atrocities to catch the eye, such as gold-lacquered vases overladen with cloisonné placques. There is a form of Japanese art which seems to consist in the beauty of blemish; a vase to which no historical interest is attached, to our eyes without beauty of form or color, is of the highest value to the Japanese for the sake of certain blotches or imperfections. I believe they will give any price for what they consider such a curiosity, and no one has ever been able to explain to the most inquisitive mind the reason why.

Pierre Loti, in one of his charming descriptions of Japan, mentions the "Impératrice Printemps" in such glowing terms that I was very desirous of seeing her. Mr. Trench arranged an audience, but unfortunately it never came off, owing to the Empress's illness, and my being obliged to leave Tokio. I give the Lord Chamberlain's letters on the subject, as they are amusing:

LADY RANDOLPH CHURCHILL

IMPERIAL PALACE,

September 21, 1894.

MY DEAR MINISTER:

I am glad your Excellency came back here so soon, I sent telegraph to Myanoshita this morning.

I think Lady Randolph Churchill and you will be received by her Majesty the Empress on the 26th, however I shall not fail communicate to you *at once* when the day and hour of the audience is fixed.

I think Mr. Ito told you this morning about lady's dress was mistake, the rule of our Court being that a lady, at such audience time, wears long dress and high neck without a bonnet.

If a lady being a traveler, has not got the said costume I remember she appeared in morning dress having permission of the Empress beforehand.

I remain,

Yours faithfully,

S. SANNOMIYA.

IMPERIAL PALACE,

September 24, 1894.

MY DEAR MINISTER:

I am sorry to inform you that her Majesty the Empress, as I informed you on Saturday by Mr. Ito, will not be able to receive any one at least till the end of this month, for doctor advised to so do this morning.

I think Lady Randolph Churchill may make a short trip during the time, it would be better for her.

I remain,

Yours very truly,

S. SANNOMIYA.

335

REMINISCENCES OF

October 5, 1894.

My dear Minister:

I have at once informed to her Majesty the Empress that Lady Randolph Churchill is going to leave Tokio, she says she feels much sorry for not being able to receive the Lady owing to her indisposition.

I enclose you a letter of permission for the old Palace, Nijio castel, and other two small palaces.

Yours very truly,

S. SANNOMIYA.

Following beaten tracks, we went to Nikko, where the first thing to attract my eyes was the "Sacred Bridge," which is very beautiful, the big, red-lacquered arch spanning the white, turbulent waters of the rushing Daya-Gawa standing out in picturesque contrast to the dark-green avenue of magnificent cryptomerias. The public is not allowed to cross it, and the Emperor does so only once a year. A garish electric light at one end was rather an eyesore, but reminded one of Japan's "go-aheadness," which places pot-hats on its men and telegraph-poles in sight of its gods.

It was about eight or ten degrees colder at Nikko than at Tokio, and we shivered in our little summer rooms, notwithstanding attempts at a charcoal fire. We made many expeditions, one day to the falls of Kiri-furi-notaki, and on another we walked to see the stone images at Kamman-sa-fuchi, said to be the offerings to the gods of Nikko of Shodo Shonun, the "Opener of the Mountains," who lived somewhere about the seventh century, and was supposed to be a very holy man. We counted the figures, and each made out a different number, which

From a stereograph, copyright, 1904, by Underwood & Underwood, New York

THE YOMEIMON GATE AT NIKKO

was quite the correct thing to do; for, according to the legend, no two people are able to count them alike. Close by an inaccessible stone in mid-stream, with the Sanskrit word "Hamman," carved on it, was pointed out to us. Kobe Daishi, a saint, is supposed to have thrown his pen at the stone, and marked it forever.

Armed with a special permit which Mr. Trench had obtained for us, we were able to visit the inner shrines of the two finest temples, Iye-yasu and Iye-mitsu. Great expectations generally mean disappointments, but the realities and beauties of the former temple far surpassed my imagination. The surroundings of the shrines were most beautiful: the grand, solemn approach of huge cryptomerias; the imposing flights of stone steps covered with the moss of ages; the splendid granite *Torii* standing out in solitary grandeur against the sky, making a fine picture; and half-hidden in the dark-green foliage a quaint five-storied pagoda, its color giving the touch of warmth needed. The temple has been so often described that I cannot venture on it; indeed, one might visit it every day for a week and not master its beauties. The marvelous carvings, the frescoed ceilings, the gold lacquer, the bronzes, and the lovely old brocades, were entrancing. With our special permit we were treated with much respect, being received by the chief priest in person, supported by six minor priests. After passing the Yomeimon Gate, which is truly wonderful, with its hundreds of dragons and carved flowers, we passed under another, Karamon by name, and so into the temple, where the two priests knelt at the entrance of the inner shrine, one in bright green, with a conical black cap, the other in a transparent white garment. Inside this holy of holies the chief priest also knelt. The light was so dim I could not make out what he had on, and I confess, what with the solemnity of the priests, the gorgeousness of the surroundings, the dim religious light, and the air heavy with incense, I felt my curiosity must be kept under, and did not like to gaze about too much. Here Matsuda, our guide, prostrated himself, beating his head so many times that I wondered it did not ache. The shrine consisted of a rather small but beautifully decorated room, with a lacquered ceiling, containing only a few glass cases on the floor, with the swords and armor of Iye-yasu, the deified shogun. A fourth door of beautiful gold lacquer opened into the last shrine, which is shown only to the Mikado and the chief priest, and which contains the effigy of Iye-yasu. Through Matsuda we conveyed our thanks to the chief priest, a venerable old man with a pleasant smile, who was dressed in a pale-blue net garment over white, and a conical black hat with two cords passed under his chin.

The inner shrine of the Iye-mitsu, which we also went to see, was much larger, and had gold columns all round the room; on a low table in the center were some sacred missals, incense-burners, and vases with gold lotus flowers; a very fine canopy was suspended over it. This, being a Buddhist temple, contained more things than that of Iye-yasu, which was Shinto, and therefore simpler. Near by the sacred white pony "Jimme" was kept "for the use of the god" in a sumptuous stable in one of the courts. On our way back we met a family party of three struggling up the steps in a torrent of rain, the inconvenience of their dress being thoroughly demonstrated. Monsieur, in a brown kimono with a *soupçon* of white petticoat showing over his socks and high wooden pattens, a huge square pot-hat, a pair of spectacles, and a voluminous Japanese umbrella completing the costume. Madame, not a hair out of place, a sham camelia sticking up straight in front of the shiny black *pouf,* a mauve tassel hanging in the vicinity of her left ear, something in the nature of a green cord, a coral bead or two, and a couple of combs making up her coiffure. She wore a light-gray kimono, on the sleeves of which her crest was embroidered in coral; her *eri* was of pale mauve; a black satin *obi,* with some gold characters on it, and an extra high pair of pattens, made up a very effective dress; but, oh! the blackened teeth, which proclaimed her respectability! Why must virtue be so ugly? I must not leave out "Bébé," strapped on its mother's back, fast asleep; his head, with its tiny tuft falling backward as though it would drop off, and the bright red crape kimono, with green flowers, made him look exactly like a Japanese doll.

Deluges of rain drove us away from weird, mystical Nikko. It was not possible to resist the elements, and after changing our clothes and boots three times in one day, we succumbed.

We fitly ended our visit to Japan by staying at the best place last, Kioto, the ancient capital, which is considered the art center of Japan. We were enchanted with its quaintness and local color. The view from our rooms at Yaami's Hotel was most pleasing, and the first evening of our arrival I gazed for a long time at the thousand twinkling lights of the city lying in the valley at our feet, the mountains forming a background in the twilight.

We saw all the sights of Kioto in ten days, visiting many curiosity-shops, which were most enticing, and spending many hours at the cloisonné, satsuma, and silk factories. Here I was shown beautiful modern productions which quite equal any ancient Chinese or Japanese. Although it is said that all the really fine objects of art have left Japan and China, and are to be found in America or in London, there were many very attractive things.

The streets at night were a most attractive sight, particularly Theater Street, in which no jinrikishas were allowed. It was crowded with people and lighted up with Chinese lanterns. Outside each theater wonderful paintings were exhibited, representing the different blood-curdling dramas going on within. We went into a playhouse of actresses, and saw two acts of the usual impossible-to-comprehend Japanese play: wonderful clothes, *daimyos* in full war-costume, females in distress, tears and sobs, which were echoed by the audience, and of course hara-kiri, performed in detail and at much length.

The Mikado's palace, which we visited, had endless reception-rooms, with the usual screens and fine matting. The Emperor squats when receiving Japanese, but sits in a chair when giving audience to Europeans. Some of the ceilings were highly decorated. His private study was a pleasantly situated room looking south upon a garden and small artificial lake; its absolute quiet and peacefulness seemed very reposeful. The castle being older, and having belonged to the shoguns, was more decorated, everywhere the golden Tokugawa crest, gorgeous ceilings, and highly lacquered screens. In the two or three audience-chambers the Mikado's chrysanthemum replaced the three lotus leaves. One room was particularly nice, with a small raised platform, where the Emperor, arriving from a side room, would sit when he received. On the left was a recess in which were a few lacquered shelves ornamented with bits of old cloisonné, but of a lovely blue they seem unable to produce nowadays. A few curious screens completed the rooms. After Nikko I was too *blasé* of temples to go and see many in Kioto; but I did visit one with thirteen hundred and thirty-three gold-lacquered life-size images of Kwannon, the Goddess of Mercy; also the new, unfinished, colossal temple of Shokonsha, where one saw great stacks of rope made of human hair, offerings from the women of Japan. Near by was a hideous great mound, which made us shudder, containing, as it did, Korean ears and noses, trophies of war!

The Governor of Kioto, Nakai by name, died while we were there. He formed part of the escort to Sir Harry Parkes when the latter, on his way to have an audience with the Mikado, was attacked by some two-sworded men, which made a great stir in Japan at the time. We saw the funeral procession from a curio-dealer's shop in one of the principal streets, which was lined by a quiet throng, all dressed in blue (the mourning color). Masses of flowers in big baskets were carried before the hearse, which had the appearance of a Noah's ark borne on men's shoulders; through the sliding panels, which were open, one caught sight of a cocked hat and feathers. Immediately behind came a jinrikisha, with the daughter of the deceased entirely in white, with her face enameled to match. An enormous crowd followed, dressed in kimonos, and all wearing pot-hats of every conceivable shape, many with white cotton gloves. The effect was ludicrous. If people wonder what becomes of all the old hats, they have but to go to Japan.

One of our last expeditions was to the Lake of Biwa. It was a long and dusty road, and I found the jinrikisha very tiring; the sights on the way, too, were unpleasant. It was pitiful to see a mass of toiling peasants doing the work of beasts, dragging and pushing carts with huge loads up hill and down dale. All looked exhausted, and in most cases a woman was harnessed in front with a rope across her chest. I noticed one poor creature spitting blood when she reached the top of the hill. The lake was splendid, and we had a fine view from a temple. The street where the Cesarewitch (the present Emperor) was attacked was pointed out to us. The two jinrikisha-boys who saved his life were pensioned, and, it is said, given so much money that they lead an idle life, and are ruined by drink. The biggest pine-tree in Japan grows at Biwa, which, although curious, with its innumerable gnarled roots and branches growing into the ground, is so propped up with poles that one can hardly tell which is the tree, and in consequence its symmetry is lost.

We also saw the rapids of Katsuregawa, being skilfully forced up them in a sampan. The hills on each side looked lovely, with every sort of autumnal tint, the red maple leaves just turning. The monotony of our long drive back was relieved by a most beautiful sunset, the moon rising while the sky was still of the brightest pink with glimpses of turquoise blue, the trees and quaint cottages standing out in deep brown against it.

We rejoined our ship, the *Ancona,* at Kobe, on our way to China, more than sorry to leave Japan, restful country of enchantment, land of courteous men and soft-voiced women. For months my ears still listened for the two most characteristic sounds in Japan—the *tap-tap* of the little pipe as it is emptied before being refilled, and the mournful notes of the reed lute which the blind *masseur* plays as he walks through the village street.

On board the *Ancona* we found Mr. de Bunsen, the present English Ambassador to Spain; also a young officer who was returning to India having wasted all his leave in trying to see something of the war, but without success, the Japanese authorities proving too much for him. Mr. de Bunsen, an old friend of mine, whom I had known in Paris when he was in the embassy there, was at that time military attaché at Bangkok. It was a great pleasure to see him again. He told me many interesting things about Siam and his life there, and tried to persuade us to pay him a visit.

Three days exhausted the sights of Hong-Kong, the magnificent view being the principal attraction. My amusement consisted in going up and down the steep tramway to the peak two or three times a day. Many of the houses were in a dilapidated condition, owing to the last typhoon. We made a flying visit to Canton, going up the Pearl River in a large steamer which had an English captain. As I entered the ship, I caught sight of stacks of rifles in the saloon, with printed instructions to the passengers to use them if necessary. This did not make me feel at all safe, these river steamers having

REMINISCENCES OF

been known to be attacked by pirates. At Hong-Kong we were advised not to go to Canton, since, owing to the war and their defeat, the Chinese were in rather a turbulent state. We thought, however, as we meant to spend only the day there, we should be safe enough. The steamer was obliged to anchor at the mouth of the river, as there were torpedoes laid across it, and the Chinese pilots were rather vague as to their locality. It was a lovely moonlight night, and I remember the ghostly effect of a search-light from a fort near by, which was constantly being turned on us, lighting up strange crafts and great, lumbering Chinese junks with square sails which hovered near.

At Canton we were at once surrounded by a flotilla of sampans and junks. Our guide, A. Cum by name, had arranged everything for us, and we found a row of palanquins, each with three men, waiting. Mine was bright-green, lined with pale-blue, and supplied with transparent blinds. Not being a Chinese lady, I insisted on having them all pulled up. Our carriers went at a swinging pace through the labyrinth of narrow, crowded streets, uttering loud cries to the people, whom we were scattering right and left, to get out of the way. The streets were full of open shops, banners, Chinese lanterns, and gaudy signs. A continuous stream of people hurrying along made it a most animated scene. They scowled and glared at us as we passed, calling us "Frankwei" ("foreign devils"), and they spat at one of our party and hit another, who luckily did not retaliate, otherwise we might have been made into mincemeat. The shops were very attractive, and Randolph bought me one of the green jade bangles which have since be-

346

SCHWE DAGON PAGODA, SINGAPORE

GOVERNMENT HOUSE, SINGAPORE

come fashionable. It is supposed to keep the devil away, and I still wear it.

A visit to the execution-ground was not so attractive. Eight men had been decapitated a few days before, and the blood was still on the ground. We were asked if we would like to see the heads, which had been placed in jars, an offer declined with thanks. Some of our party, having been told by the captain and officers of the boat that our expedition was rather a dangerous undertaking unless we were prepared to "turn the other cheek" at any insult, persuaded us to get back to the ship as quickly as we could. So after luncheon at an old palace called "The Garden of Flowers," we started on our return journey, being rushed through more streets, sometimes meeting a "towkee," or mandarin, surrounded with many attendants. It was then a case as to whose criers could make the most noise.

We returned to Hong-Kong, and left the next day for Singapore, Mr. de Bunsen going with us. Sir John and Lady Mitchell invited us to Government House, where we stayed a week. I found the heat for the first time nearly unbearable; it was like a vapor bath, and so enervating that one felt absolutely incapable of doing anything. However, I was delighted with the beauty of the tropical plants, especially the traveler's palm, its height and symmetry being a revelation.

The Malay villages perched on poles were very picturesque, particularly those in the cocoanut plantations near the sea. In the town every nationality seemed to be represented in the streets—Malays, Chinese, Hindus, Klings, Japanese, and Europeans of all countries, the Chinese, who own all the best houses, predominating.

The late Sultan of Johore gave us a sumptuous luncheon at his palace which lasted as long as a lord mayor's feast. The house was a curious mixture of good and bad taste; a few real objects of art, such as old lacquered cabinets and boxes and fine Satsuma vases, were lost in a sea of tawdriness and vulgarity. In one room the tables and chairs were made of cut-glass, upholstered in bright-blue velvet, with glass buttons! After luncheon the Sultan, who was a charming and courteous old man, sent for his Sultana to come and see us. She was a very pretty Circassian of about twenty-five, a present from the Sultan of Turkey. Enormously fat, we were told that she was fed every two hours, the Sultan admiring large proportions. Her costume was most peculiar, to say the least—a Malay sarong of silk; a blouse with huge diamond buttons; round her neck a rivière of diamonds, and one of sapphires; and on her short, black curls, cocked over one ear, a velvet glengarry cap with an eagle's feather and a diamond aigret. The Sultan, thinking, I suppose, that she had been seen enough, suddenly pointed with a stern gesture to the door. Casting a frightened glance at him, she fled as fast as her fat little feet could take her.

At the end of the week we started for Rangoon in company with Sir Frank Swettenham, Resident of Perak and later Governor of Singapore. Mr. Swettenham, as he then was, went only as far as Penang with us, which we regretted, as he proved a very entertaining companion. A man of exceptional intelligence, he was virtually the ruler of the Straits Settlements, and certainly no one better understood the natives, and how to treat them. His books "Malay Sketches" and "Unad-

dressed Letters" are deservedly popular. Rangoon was
an agreeable disappointment, for although the heat was
great, it was dry, and therefore bearable.

The Governor, Sir Charles Mackenzie, and Lady
Mackenzie were away, but they had placed Government
House at our disposal. I found, to my surprise, a pleasant company of English people, who entertained us
most hospitably, and amused themselves playing golf
and polo, which, considering the heat, was most energetic.

I was taken to see the Royal Lakes, which are gorgeous and beautifully kept, with a wealth of tropical
plants and variegated flowers, great bushes of alaman-
ders growing in wild profusion at the edge of the lakes,
bougainvilleas climbing everywhere, and a tree of which
I did not find out the name with dark-green foliage and
large bunches of red flowers like grapes. As we drove
by, I saw half a dozen priests in their yellow "tamains"
or robes, worn like a toga, standing on some marble steps
leading down to the lake. Behind them in the setting
sun the great golden dome of the Schwe Dagon Pagoda
shone in the distance, the whole forming a superb picture. The pagoda was an endless source of interest,
and we spent pleasant hours among its many shrines. The
two huge white stone dragons guarding the entrance
stood out against the deep-blue sky, the waving palms
and tall cocoanut-trees in the background forming an
Eastern picture full of light and color. The lepers and
beggars infesting the steps were the only drawback. Inside, everything glittered; temples inlaid with colored
glass and bits of mirror shone like jewels in the sun, their
graceful minarets and domes marvelously carved. Piled

up before every shrine were the offerings of the Faithful,
conspicuous among them gaudy umbrellas with fringes
of gold or beads. I revisited the pagoda by moonlight,
and was well repaid, as it had lost the garishness and
tawdriness apparent in the glare of day. The spell of
silence was over the whole scene, broken only by the not
unmelodious voice of a fanatic reciting verses as he
walked solemnly round and round his favorite shrine.
I was rather amused one day at receiving a visit from
some relatives of the late King Thebaw. These were
three princesses; two of them were young and pretty,—
that is, according to Burmese taste,—and were swathed
in wraps, even their hands being hidden, whereas the
third, who was old and ugly, wore hardly any garments, as is the custom of the country. They presented me with some artificial flowers made by themselves, also some cheroots they "hoped I would smoke,"
and departed in a cart drawn by bullocks, for thousands
of years the unchanged mode of conveyance in Burmah.
Poor things! Perhaps they would not have been so
gracious had they realized that it was my husband who
had been instrumental in destroying their dynasty and
annexing their country.

Cholera was raging at Mandalay, which, much to our
chagrin, prevented our going there. Randolph naturally wanted to see as much of the country as possible,
he being very proud of the part he had played in the
annexing of Burmah when at the India Office.

Crossing the Bay of Bengal to Madras, we stayed a
few days with Lord and Lady Wenlock at Government
House, where we were treated with the greatest kindness.

It had been our intention to travel for several months in India, but Randolph's health, which up to then had been good enough to allow of his enjoying the tour, suddenly gave way. We were obliged to curtail our further travels, and proceeding to Bombay, we embarked for England.

CHAPTER XIV

IT was on one of the many visits I paid to Bradford between 1884 and 1886, when Lord Randolph Churchill was holding political meetings there, that I remember for the first time hearing Lord Curzon of Kedleston (then Mr. George Nathaniel Curzon) make a speech. Called upon unexpectedly to second a resolution, he spoke with natural eloquence and an astonishing choice of words. Randolph predicted to me then that he would go very far. We knew him well while he was still at Oxford when he used to come over to Blenheim, a distance of only eight miles.

When he was made Viceroy of India, his many friends gave a farewell dinner to him and Lady Curzon. The speeches were most amusing, notwithstanding the note of sadness which prevailed at the prospect of losing for several years so delightful a couple. Mr. George Wyndham contributed the following verses, which were received with great applause:

"Eight years ago we sat at your table:
  We were the guests and you were the host.
You were young, said the World, but we knew you were able
  To justify more than your friends dared boast.
We knew you would win all wreaths in the end,
And we knew you would still be the same dear friend:
  And that's what we cared for most.

354

FAREWELL DINNER TO LORD AND LADY CURZON, ON THEIR DEPARTURE FOR INDIA

LADY RANDOLPH CHURCHILL

"You wrote us some rhymes wherein friendship and laughter
    Played in a blaze of affection and jest
Round the name of each one for whom no years thereafter
    Could blunt the sharp edge of that festival's zest.
For we knew that your motto—'Let Curzon hold
What Curzon held'—was no whit too bold
    For its vaunt of your claim on each guest.

"Nor was it. We 're here, though eight years have rolled o'er us,
    All fond of you, proud of you, sorry to part;
And we ought, one and all, to give in one chorus
    The send-off you 've earned from our love for your start.
But the Brave men and Fair ones, sealed of the tribe
Of Nathaniel, have told one incompetent scribe
    To sing what each feels in his heart.

"He obeys: and he bids you recall all you chanted
    Of each man and each woman who sat at your board,
And, then, to believe that the tributes you granted
    Too kindly are now, and more justly, restored
To you and the Lady whom none of us knew
Eight years ago; but whom now, thanks to you,
    We have all of us known and adored.

"So 'Go in and win!' What 's five years but a lustre
    To shine round a name that already shines bright?
Then come back, and we 'll greet you and go such a 'buster'
    As never was seen—no, not even to-night!
Come back in five years with your sheaves of new Fame:
You 'll find your old Friends, and you 'll find them the same
    As now when you gladden their sight."

The few brilliant years the Curzons spent in India
are too recent and too familiar in people's minds for me

to dwell on that time or the tragedy which was so soon to follow their departure. To her great beauty Mary Curzon added grace of manner and kindness of heart, and her extraordinary and unselfish devotion to her husband made her a paragon among wives. I recall one other remarkable woman who was equally devoted and absorbed in her husband's career, and whose life was one of sacrifice to duty and care for others. This was my sister-in-law Fanny, Lady Tweedmouth, without exception the noblest character I have ever met. Apart from her brilliant gifts, which made her one of the most popular and influential political hostesses in England, her sympathy and advice were a tower of strength to all who came in contact with her. Indeed, it may be said with truth that society in general and the Liberal party in particular sustained an irreparable loss when her too short life ended.

It will always be a regret to me that I was unable to accept the Viceroy's invitation to attend the great Durbar, that crowning function of a most memorable viceregal reign. I often corresponded with Lady Curzon, and in one of her letters she says:

VICEROY'S CAMP,

May 18, 1903.

. . . The result of the Durbar for Empire more than justifies the expenditure of £200,000 (the cost). The mere bringing together of people from the Chinese frontier of Thibet and Siam, Burmah, Bootea, Nepal, Gilgit, Chitral-Swat, Beluchistan, Travancore, and Kathiawar has been the most marvelous object lesson. Chiefs from the outer fringes of civilization who for years had been turbulent, gasped, "Had we known we were

LADY CURZON OF KEDLESTON

fighting *this* we should have remained in peace!" There is no doubt it was the most surprising gathering the world has ever seen or will ever see again and the "lucky hand" of George's organization amazed every human soul there. . . . Forgive this dull scrawl. I am sticking to the sides of the Himalayas like a barnacle with only a three weeks' old copy of the "Times" to make me gay or witty. Do write. You are the only person who lives on the crest of the wave and is always full of vitality and success.

Yours ever affectionately,

Mary.

On the eve of their departure from England, the Curzons paid a visit to the Duke and Duchess of Portland at Welbeck. I was of the party, and sitting next to Lord Curzon at dinner one night, we approached a subject which, without my knowing it at the time, was fraught with great importance for me. In a despondent mood I bemoaned the empty life I was leading at that moment. Lord Curzon tried to console me by saying that a woman alone was a godsend in society, and that I might look forward to a long vista of country-house parties, dinners, and balls. Thinking over our conversation later, I found myself wondering if this indeed was all that the remainder of my life held for me. I determined to do something, and cogitating for some time over what it should be, decided finally to start a review. My ideas were of the vaguest, but they soon shaped themselves. I consulted my friend Mrs. Craigie ("John Oliver Hobbes"), whose acquaintance I had made some years before at the Curzons'. At her house I met various people who helped me with their good counsels, notably Mr. Sidney Low, who became much interested in the scheme and assisted me greatly, editing and bringing out two numbers during my subsequent absence in South Africa. Mr. John Lane, who published the first numbers of the Review, was full of ideas, and originated that of having a new cover for each issue. Mr. Cyril Davenport of the British Museum joined the staff and helped in the selection of the bindings, which were to be facsimiles of celebrated books of the sixteenth, seventeenth, and eighteenth centuries. They were mostly chosen from examples in the British Museum. He also contributed a short article descriptive of each cover. These essays were excellent, and form a liberal education in bookbinding. Mr. Lionel Cust of the National Portrait Gallery undertook to supervise the illustrations, which were reproduced as photogravures, and was indefatigable in finding original and interesting subjects. The late Mr. Arthur Strong, librarian of the House of Lords, and at Chatsworth, was responsible for the historical matter. A delightful and enthralling period began, which absorbed me from morning till night in the most interesting of occupations. I left no stone unturned to make the Review a success, and my friends helped me *con amore*. Sometimes I became a little bewildered at the conflicting advice and suggestions that I received. "Why don't you have articles in three languages?" said one. "That would damn it at once," said another. "Mind you have something startling in the first number, 'New Ideas on Free Love,' or 'Sidelights on Royal Courts.'" "Be lofty in your ambitions; set up a poetical standard to the literary world." "Why not get a poem from the Poet Laureate?" "Or an essay on bimetalism from Mr. Henry Chaplin." "Aim at a glorified 'Yellow Book'; that 's the thing!" How amusing it all was! Then the title. Many were offered, from "The New Anthology" to "The Mentor of Mayfair." Sir Edgar Vincent, whose classical and literary education is backed by the most admirable common sense suggested "Anglo-Saxon." I thought the name most apt, and was enchanted. "The Anglo-Saxon"—how simple! It sounded strong, sensible, and solid. Of course the moment I had settled on the name, some obscure man claimed it as being registered for his still more obscure paper or magazine. It seemed as difficult to find an unappropriated title as though I were naming a race-horse instead of a book. However, I found that adding the word "Review" made it quite safe. I had endless consultations with my literary friends, and received valuable information from Mr. John Morley and the late Mr. Knowles of "The Nineteenth Century" as to the financial part of the undertaking. I gave a luncheon party to introduce "Maggie," as the Review was affectionately called by some of my friends. The book in its gorgeous cover, the replica of Thevet's *Vie des Hommes Illustres,*" which was executed about 1604 for James I, presented a brave appearance. If I could only insure that its *"ramage se rapporta à son plumage"* I felt I might indeed claim to have produced a Phœnix.

The same night I dined with the Asquiths, taking the volume with me, where it was received with acclamation. I have the book still, with all the signatures of those present written on the fly-leaf.

In explanation of my venture I permit myself to quote here the preface to the first number, in which I tried to set forth my aims and objects:

REMINISCENCES OF

The explanation of the production of another Review will be found in the number of those already in flourishing existence: the excuse must be looked for in these pages. Yet a few words of introduction are needed by this new-comer who comes into the crowded world thus late in the day, lest, in spite of his fine coat, he be thought an unmannerly intruder. I desire to say something of his purpose, of his aspirations, of his nature, in the hope that, if these seem admirable, good friends instead of jostling will help him through the press, and aid him somewhat in his journey toward the golden temple of literary excellence.

The first object of every publication is commercial. "No one but a blockhead," says Dr. Johnson, "ever wrote except for money"; and "The Anglo-Saxon" is not disposed to think lightly of his wares, or set low value on his effort—for otherwise his green-and-gold brocade would soon be threadbare. But after the vulgar necessities of life are thus provided for, reviews, and sometimes reviewers, look to other and perhaps higher ideals. It is of those that I would write, for are they not the credentials which must carry the ambitious stranger on his way?

Formerly little was written, but much of that little was preserved. The pamphlets, the satires, the lampoons, the disquisitions—above all the private letters—of the eighteenth century have been carefully stored for the delight of succeeding generations. Now the daily production of printed words is incalculably vast. Miles of newspapers, tons of magazine articles, mountains of periodicals are distributed daily between sunrise and sunset. They are printed; they are read, they are forgotten. Little remains. And yet there is no reason why the best products of an age of universal education should not be as worthy of preservation as those of a less cultivated era. The literary excellence of the modern Review is high. How many articles, full of solid thought and acute criticism, of wit and learning, are born for a purely ephemeral existence, to be read one day and cast into the waste-paper basket the next! The most

364

miserable lampoons of the reign of Queen Anne are still extant. Some of the finest and cleverest productions of the reign of Queen Victoria are almost as difficult to find as ancient manuscripts. The newspapers of to-day light the fires of to-morrow. The magazine may have a little longer life. It rests on the writing table for perhaps a month; and thereafter shares the fate of much that is good in an age that, at least in art and literature, takes little thought for the future. The sure knowledge that their work will perish must exert a demoralizing effect on the writers of the present day. Newspapers and periodicals become cheaper and cheaper. To satisfy the loud demand of the enormous and growing reading public, with the minimum of effort, is the modern temptation.

I do not imagine that "The Anglo-Saxon Review" will arrest these tendencies. But its influence may have some useful effect. This book is published at a price which will insure its respectful treatment at the hands of those who buy it. It will not be cast aside after a hurried perusal. It appears, too, in a guise which fits it for a better fate. After a brief, though not perchance unhonored stay on the writing table, it may be taken up into that Valhalla of printed things—the library. More than this, that it may have company, another of similar character, but different design will follow at an interval of three months, until a long row of volumes—similar but not alike—may not only adorn the bookshelves, and recall the elegant bindings of former times, but may also preserve in a permanent form something of the transient brilliancy of the age.

It is with such hopes that I send the first volume out into the world—an adventurous pioneer. Yet he bears a name which may sustain him even in the hardest of struggles, and of which he will at all times endeavor to be worthy, a name under which just laws, high purpose, civilizing influence, and a fine language, have been spread to the remotest regions.

Lastly, I would in this brief note express my sincere thanks to all who have helped to fit "The Anglo-Saxon" for the battle of life—not only to those who have, as subscribers, furnished him with his costly habit, but also to those who—like the fairy godmother in the child's story—have given him something of their energy, their wisdom and their brains.

Among my most valued contributors was Lord Rosebery, who, on account of his great friendship with Randolph and out of kindness to me, wrote for the first number a short essay on Sir Robert Peel. Later, in one of the subsequent volumes an article appeared which, to my regret, criticized his political opinions. I had gone to Scotland thinking the number was completed as I had seen it, but owing to the exigencies of time and space, the offending article had been substituted at the last moment. I was very much annoyed, but it could not be helped. Writing to Lord Rosebery, I told him how grieved I was that anything even approaching criticism of him should have appeared in my review, and received the following characteristic answer:

DALMENY HOUSE,

EDINBURGH, September 28, 1901.

. . . It is very good of you to write to me about ——'s article. But I had not even heard of it. Frankly, I ceased to be a subscriber after the previous number, in which I perceived the cloven hoof of politics. Frankly, also, I think the introduction of politics into "The Anglo-Saxon" a great mistake. But you are a better judge of this than I am.

As to Mr. ——'s article, I think it very unlikely that I shall ever see it, and am quite sure that, if I do, it will not trouble me. But I tender my humble and hearty thanks to the Editress.

On looking back at the early period of the Review, I often wonder how I should have succeeded without Pearl Craigie's intelligent help and advice. A woman of great sympathies, her unselfishness was realized by all who ever came in contact with her, and her valuable time was always at the disposal of any one she could help. It is not for me here to dwell on her literary gifts, her works speak for themselves. A brilliant and clever conversationalist, she could hold her own with all manner of men, and yet, in the more frivolous company which she often frequented and thoroughly enjoyed, she never talked over people's heads. She had the art of drawing every one out and making them appear at their best, so different to some clever women writers I have met. I recall a luncheon party being wrecked owing to the presence of a well-known authoress, who persistently directed the conversation on her own subjects, which were as erudite and pedantic as they were uncongenial to the rest of the company.

I always made it a point to go to Mrs. Craigie's plays, and we had many discussions about them. In reference to "A Repentance," which she asked me to see and give my candid opinion upon, she wrote me the following letter:—

56 *Lancaster Gate, W.,* Wednesday, 1899.

MY DEAREST JENNIE:

I shall *love* to hear your honest criticism. The play of course is about Spanish Catholics: the man is not meant to be a hero, but he is a typical Carlist. The gist of his speeches show the political "talk," as it were, of the Period. My object was not to display *inhuman* excellence, but a psychological diagram of the Carlist question! Perhaps this is too daring an experiment for the stage. All the same, the experiment was worth trying. Browning, in his dramatic romances, always made a soul's crisis (lasting but a few moments) the test of a life. I thought this might be done on the stage. Some people love the play: others don't like it at all. So long as they admit that it is, at all events, *carefully* composed, I mind nothing else. You are quite right—*too* right, my dear, about the squalid side of literary life. Sometimes I get so sick of it that I long to retire to some lonely hilltop and meditate on the Four Last Things! But— after all—we cannot make terms with existence: we must culti- vate our garden and a sense of humor: and for the rest, Al- mighty God and the devil can deal with *that*.

Yours ever affectionately,

PEARL MARY TERESA C.

I thought the play most interesting, but too con- densed. There was tragedy enough in the one act to make a substantial play of three. The critics were not overkind, and I wrote telling her that the general public were much better judges than the ordinary theater critic, who was under the delusion that he could make or mar any unfortunate playwright with a wave of his pen.

To this she replied:

I love your letter. You recognize humanity when it is drawn. *Des Escas* is a man: the Countess is a real Spanish Catholic of the devout type. I dared not give the English public two acts about "foreigners." They all like "A Repentance," but it is against their will. They have no instinctive interest, such as we feel, in foreign politics or other races. All the same, the play has held its own, and it is well received at every perform- ance. Alexander is the one manager in London who will try experiments, and he always responds to good art, good music,

MRS. CRAIGIE (JOHN OLIVER HOBBES)

and the like. Remember what the English stage is: the dramatic critics are not all educated men like William Archer and Walkley, the public are patient, the actors mostly amateurs.

To-morrow I will send you my *proposed* contribution to your Quarterly. Say just what you think of it: the length is under 9000 words. This ought not to be too long for those pages. Poor Stephen Phillips—it is hard indeed for him to have his magnificent tragedy *published* before it is *acted*. What an outrage it would be if these uneducated pressmen had the *first* fling at work of such quality!

Yours ever affectionately,

PEARL MARY TERESA C.

Again she writes:

. . . As for criticism, if one gives work to the general public, one has to accept the fate of an "Aunt Sally" so far as the journalists are in question. These detest every educated influence, particularly on platforms and on the stage. They fear the brightening of the average intelligence, for, in the imbecility of the mob (well-dressed and otherwise) is the hack journalist's strength. But the times are changing rapidly. The mob—as a mob—is becoming well read, even philosophical. The press in England has less power, and the *country* more power, every day. Mistakes are certainly made in the House of Commons (where the average intelligence is not startling) because it is assumed that electors and others are mentally afflicted! I see much of the laboring classes and the Nonconformist classes; the *individuality* and independence of each unit in these forces is extraordinary. I hold that *nothing* (either in good sense or high art) is really beyond them. Where they don't wholly comprehend, they are slow in forming judgments. They reject nothing hastily. The discipline of their daily lives is the best of educations, and, where the so-called lower classes of England are concerned, I am full of hope. Our trouble lies with the sham-educated—the Bounderbys and lampooners of the press,—the "better vulgar" in middle-class life. There's a jaw for poor Jennie with a big Quarterly in tow! But you will pull it along in splendid style.

Yours ever affectionately,

P. M. T. C.

One letter more to show how strenuous her work was. Having sent her an allegorical war medal, she replies:

I am delighted with the Medal, and shall regard it as a treasure. Few things are so hard to design. The artist has to deal in allegory and semi-divine creations at a time when allegory means something inexorably dull and every one is exclaiming, "Les dieux s'en vont!" Forgive this scribble. I worked for nearly fourteen hours straight off at an article for the "Times" people —their new edition of the Encyclopædia, and as a result I have a cramped hand. The theme was George Eliot—fortunately an interesting one. This vile weather affects me, and I am rather furious with myself for giving up the trip to Egypt. But actors and actresses need constant encouragement. I wish they would remember the words of the immortal Mrs. Chick to Florence Dombey: "If any misanthrope were to put in my presence the question, 'Why were we born?' I should reply, 'To make an effort.'"

I am working now at my play (for the Haymarket) and a new novel. I propose to take my time over both. . . .

Ever yours affectionately,

PEARL MARY TERESA CRAIGIE.

To her many gifts Mrs. Craigie added that of being a very good musician, and her nimble fingers could discourse very effectively. We sometimes played together

372

at concerts, and on one occasion, at the Queen's Hall, she and I and Mademoiselle Janotha played Bach's Concerto in D Minor for three pianos, with an orchestra from the Royal College of Music, which was conducted by Sir Walter Parratt. This was the only time I can remember enjoying playing in public.

In the preface to Mrs. Craigie's last book, Mr. Choate says: "In her brief day and generation she contributed much by her charming intellectual productions to the entertainment and enjoyment of hosts of English and American readers, who deeply lament her early death, and in whose affections she will hold a permanent place." When one remembers that George Eliot *began* to make a great name for herself only at the age at which my poor friend's short life came to a close, it is possible to prophesy that, had she lived, she would have achieved a still greater name and fame for herself. It would have been a pity if the "John Oliver Hobbes" generation had allowed posterity to forget her brilliant gifts as a writer and her noble qualities as a woman and a friend. I am glad to think I have been instrumental, with others of her friends, in getting up a fitting memorial to her. A portrait medallion is now placed in University College in London, where she studied, and a scholarship is to be given annually in England. The same scheme has been adopted in the United States.

It is curious how sometimes *"les beaux esprits se rencontrent."* Mrs. W. K. Clifford sent me her play "The Likeness of the Night" for publication in "The Anglo-Saxon Review" before it was put on the stage. Shortly after the appearance of the number containing it, Mr. Sidney Grundy's play "A Debt of Honor" was given.

There was no doubt a great similarity between the two, and this led to an animated correspondence in the press between Mrs. Clifford and Mr. Grundy. Both parties were interviewed, and the literary and dramatic world were much interested in the controversy, the details of which it is unnecessary for me to dwell on. Mrs. Clifford, however, having in her first letter said that her play was published in "The Anglo-Saxon Review" "for all who run and pay a guinea to read," Mr. Grundy retorted: "I do not run, and I did not pay a guinea; *nor have I met any one who did.*" This was too much! Was it possible that a literary man existed who had not read my review? And worse, did not even know of its existence? I at once wrote to Mr. Grundy, regretting that such should be the case, and sent him the volume containing Mrs. Clifford's play. To this he replied that I "must perceive that his own ignorance of Mrs. Clifford's play would have mattered nothing, if he had met others who had told him its story. As a matter of fact, he had not."

The battle ended in peace, and the two plays were given with marked success.

The choice and study of my bindings afforded me the greatest pleasure; there was nothing tentative about them. I knew they would be a success and please all bibliophiles, for most book-lovers are particular about the appearance of their books. I remember once lending Pierre Loti's "Madame Chrysanthème" to Mr. John Morley (now Lord Morley of Blackburn). In one of his letters about it he alludes to people's fancies as to bindings.

The first ran:

LADY RANDOLPH CHURCHILL

Dear Lady Randolph:

Thank you very much for sending me the book; I will take it in such doses as you prescribe, unless I find it too attractive to lay down.

Yours sincerely,

J. Morley.

The doses must have been microscopic, for he kept the book so long that I wrote to remind him that he still had it, and received the following answer:

95 Elm Park Gardens,

South Kensington, S. W.

Dear Lady Randolph:

It cuts me to the heart that I should have given you cause to suspect me of being a book-stealer. I have suffered too much from that evil tribe. But I have kept the book so long that I am almost as worthy of reprobation as if I had lost it. The truth is, that I knew you were away from home, and so I kept it. I am shocked to find the dilapidated condition of the poor lady. I think, however, she was rather ragged when she reached me. I had half a mind to send her to be bound, but I thought you might have fancies of your own about bindings, as I have. The book will reach you to-morrow. It has amused me very much indeed, and I am most grateful to you.

I am devoted to French literature, but the modern French novel is rather too horrid for me, who was reared on George Sand.

Yours sincerely,

J. Morley.

In making up each quarterly volume of "The Anglo-Saxon Review," I did not find the difficulty I had an-

18

375

ticipated in procuring fitting contributors. The first number had established its reputation, and although critics were not wanting, it could rightly claim, on the whole, to be keeping up its standard of excellence. I aspired high; sometimes too high, as the following letter shows:

WALMER CASTLE,

WALMER, KENT, July 2, 1899.

DEAR LADY RANDOLPH:

It would give me great pleasure if I could aid you in any way; but I am not capable of complying with your flattering invitation. My allowance of time and energy are only just enough to enable me to keep up with my necessary work. I do not feel it possible for me to do any literary work.

Winston made a splendid fight—but the Borough[1] bears a bad name for fickleness.

Believe me,

Yours very truly,

SALISBURY.

I could hardly expect the Prime Minister, with the affairs of the nation weighing on him, to put them on one side to please me. "Mais qui ne risque rien n'a rien," and one must aim high, even if one falls short. I was also disappointed at not getting an article from Mr. Cecil Rhodes, who, although not a literary man, could speak clearly and with great authority on his own particular subjects.

I first met him in London in the early eighties. He was then a handsome young man, but with a delicate chest, and was just starting for South Africa, where he

---

[1] Oldham.

376

THE RIGHT HON. CECIL RHODES

HIS HOUSE AT CAPE TOWN

hoped the wonderful air would cure him. This it did, for although he died at a comparatively early age, it was not from consumption. I remember once having a most interesting conversation with him over his aims and ambitions. His whole soul was bound up in the future and progress of South Africa, and although he was not a self-seeker in any way, he was justly proud of having the immense province of Rhodesia named after him. In his heart of hearts he wanted his name to be handed down to posterity in this indelible manner, and he would have been bitterly disappointed had any other been chosen. When I questioned him as to this, he admitted it quite frankly. He was, I think, a very happy man, for he never allowed small things to worry him, and his mind was not encumbered with the subtleties with which so many are hampered. A man of big ideas, he knew what he wanted, and made for the goal. He was singularly outspoken. On one occasion, discussing a sculptor, he said:

"Why don't you let the fellow do you? You 've got a good square face." These two letters are characteristic:

VIENNA, February, 1899.

DEAR LADY RANDOLPH:

You must think I am very rude, but I only got your letter just before starting. It was not the secretary's fault, but it got mislaid; the excuse is that I get about one hundred a day— a telegram to me is always the surest.

I will come and see you if you will let me on my return in about three weeks.

We are getting through to Egypt fairly well. Maguire finds that he has to look after and attend to his servants as well as himself. I believe that is the usual thing with English servants; they simply collapse and do nothing.

I am learning the mysteries of bridge, and even with shilling points am only 30/—to the bad. I quite see that it is an assured income to a thinking player. Of course the annoyance—I would say amusement—is playing badly and seeing your partner's face; it sometimes changes their manners.

Yours,

C. J. RHODES.

I have been treated with great urbanity, in spite of some slight mistakes such as revoking, etc.

BURLINGTON HOTEL, W.

DEAR LADY RANDOLPH:

I think you will see me on your return from Paris. I will try to write something for you on board ship, but do not announce it. I shall try to do something to help you and my cause, perhaps my cause first and you second, but I shall see you again.

Yours,

C. J. RHODES.

You will have lots of bother, some pleasure, and you will be doing something, which is best of all.

After all, women, remember, have great imagination and a much more delicate instinct than my sex, who are rough and brutal. I think you should have a fair chance.

Among many interesting contributions, it was with much satisfaction that I received an article from Bernard Shaw, "A Word more about Verdi," beginning: "I have read most of the articles on Verdi elicited by his death, and I have blushed—blushed for my species. By this I mean the music-critic species." He ends the article (which is one to prove that Verdi was not influenced by Wagner) in this wise: "Certainly, where you come to a strong Italian like Verdi, you may be quite sure that if you cannot explain him without dragging in the great Germans, you cannot explain him at all."

I venture to disagree with him, as in "Falstaff" I think the orchestration is decidedly Wagnerian, compared to Verdi's other operas, and I remember at the time of its appearance it was thought extraordinary that a man of seventy could so alter his style. I had met Mr. Shaw a few times. He was tall, pale, thin and ascetic-looking, with wonderful, transparent eyes; his conversation was unconventional. Some correspondence passed between us apropos of a luncheon party to which I invited him, and which he, to my chagrin, refused; his refusal being couched in such Shavian terms that I felt justified in answering in the same spirit.

(Telegram:)

Certainly not; what have I done to provoke such an attack on my well-known habit?

To which I replied in another telegram:

Know nothing of your habits; hope they are not as bad as your manners.

I then received the following letter:

Be reasonable: what can I do? If I refuse an invitation in conventional terms, I am understood as repudiating the acquaintance of my hostess. If I make the usual excuses, and convince her that I am desolated by some other engagement, she will ask me again. And when I have excused myself six times running, she will conclude that I personally dislike her. Of course there is the alternative of accepting; but then I shall endure acute discomfort and starvation. I shall not have the pleasure of really meeting her and talking to her any more than if we happened to lunch at the Savoy on the same day by chance. I shall get no lunch, because I do not eat the unfortunate dead animals and things which she has to provide for the other people. Of those other people, half will abuse the occasion to ask me to luncheons and dinners, and the other half, having already spread that net for me in vain, will be offended because I have done for you what I would not do for them. I shall have to dress myself carefully and behave properly, both of which are contrary to my nature.

Therefore I am compelled to do the simple thing, and when you say, "Come to lunch with a lot of people," reply flatly, "I won't." If you propose anything pleasant to me, I shall reply with equal flatness, "I will." But lunching with a lot of people —carnivorous people—is not pleasant. Besides, it cuts down my morning's work. I won't lunch with you; I won't dine with you; I won't call on you; I won't take the smallest part in your social routine; and I won't ever know you except on the most special and privileged terms, to the utter exclusion of that "lot of other people" whose appetites you offered me as an entertainment. Only, if I can be of any real service at any time, that is what I exist for; so you may command me. To which you will no doubt reply, "Thank you for nothing; you would say the same to anybody." So I would, but it is a great concession to write it at such length to a lady who has bludgeoned me with an invitation to lunch. So there!

Yours sincerely,

G. BERNARD SHAW.

LADY RANDOLPH CHURCHILL

Among the many criticisms of "The Anglo-Saxon" the one which amused me the most appeared in "The Saturday Review,"—a slating article saying among other things that it was a swindle to ask people to pay a guinea for a book which, however magnificent in appearance, was not tooled by hand. This was too much for my proprietary pride, and I posted off to the British Museum to see my friend Mr. Davenport. "Look at this for honest criticism," I cried, flourishing the offending journal under his eyes. "What would be the cost if it were real leather and tooled by hand?" In view of the elaborate binding of that particular volume, he thought about £100, if not more. Delighted with my information, I then wrote to the late Lord Hardwicke, who was interested in "The Saturday Review," inclosing the criticism, and begging him to put my facts under the nose of his "ignorant reviewer."

One of the American notices ran:

It has been given out that no one but the upper ten are to put a pen in it. However, Lady Randolph is too shrewd to run a periodical for the amusement of the incapables!

Again some of the newspapers used me as a form of advertisement.

You pay five dollars for this magazine. It may be good, but you can buy "The World" for a cent.

Then there were some verses which appeared in "Books of To-day," from the pen of E. V. Lucas.

Have you heard of the wonderful magazine
Lady Randolph 's to edit, with help from the Queen?

It 's a guinea a number, too little by half,
For the Crowned Heads of Europe are all on the staff;
And every one writing verse, fiction, or views,
The best blue blood ink must exclusively use;
While (paper so little distinction achieves)
'T will wholly be printed on strawberry leaves;
And lest the effusions, so dazzlingly bright,
And brilliantly witty, should injure the sight,
A pair of smoked glasses (of ducal design)
Will go with each copy to shelter the eyne.
The articles promised already, or written,
Suggest what a treat is preparing for Britain.
The Princess of . . . will describe a new bonnet;
The Spanish Queen Mother has offered a sonnet,
Provided that all whom its scansion may beat,
Will refrain from indelicate mention of feet.
And the Duchess of . . . has accepted the section
Devoted to "Babies, their Tricks and Correction."
The Czar will contribute a fable for geese
On "Breaking up China and Keeping the Peace";
The Porte sends a batch of seraglio tales,
And our Prince will review "Mr. Bullen on Whales,"
Mr. Primrose who also has thoughts of the sea,
Addresses to Captains of every degree,
A treatise profound, yet delectable too,
On "How to be Father-in-law to a Crewe";
While William the Second, the ablest of men,
Will fill every gap with one stroke of his pen,
And, lest art be slighted 'midst hurry and rush
Will illustrate all with one flirt of his brush.

. . . .

Such, such is a hint of a new magazine
Lady Randolph will edit, with help from the Queen.

It was with the greatest regret that I ceased publishing "The Anglo-Saxon Review." But circumstances over which I had no control obliged me to bring its career to an end. No one can be responsible for a publication of that kind without having many anxious and annoying moments, but I shall always look back with pleasure and pride to that period, and to the ten volumes it produced. My heart will never forget the gratitude I owe to those who worked so efficiently for me and with me.

CHAPTER XV

RARELY has the London social world been so stirred as by the fancy-dress ball given at Devonshire House, on the 2nd of July, 1897. For weeks, not to say months, beforehand, it seemed the principal topic of conversation. The absorbing question was what characters our friends and ourselves were going to represent. Great were the confabulations and mysteries. With bated breath and solemn mien a fair dame would whisper to some few dozen or more that she was going to represent the Queen of Cyprus or Aspasia, Frédégonde or Petrarch's Laura, but the secret *must* be kept. Historical books were ransacked for inspirations, old pictures and engravings were studied, and people became learned in respect to past celebrities of whom they had never before heard. The less well-known the characters, the more eagerly were they sought after. "Never heard of Simonetta? How curious? but surely you remember Botticelli's picture of her—one of the beauties of the Florentine court? No? How strange!"

"My dress is to be 'old Venetian' pink velvet, with gold embroideries—one of those medieval women. I can't remember her name; but that 's of no consequence. Masses of jewelry, of course."

The men, oddly enough, were even more excited over their costumes than the women, and many paid extravagant sums for them. There is no doubt that when a man begins to think about his appearance, he competes with women to some purpose, money, time, and thought being of no account to him. On the night of the ball, the excitement rose to fever heat. Every coiffeur in London and Paris was requisitioned, and so busy were they that some of the poor victims actually had their locks tortured early in the morning, sitting all day in a rigid attitude, or, like Agag, "walking delicately."

Devonshire House, with its marble staircase and glorious pictures, was a fitting frame for the distinguished company which thronged its beautiful rooms. Every one of note and interest was there, representing the intellect, beauty, and fashion of the day, from the present King and Queen (then Prince and Princess of Wales) dressed respectively as the Grand Prior of the Order of St. John of Jerusalem and Marguerite de Valois, to the newest Radical member of Parliament, gorgeously attired as the Great Mogul. The Duchess of Devonshire, who looked exceedingly well as Zenobia Queen of Palmyra, and the Duke as the Emperor Charles V received on a raised daïs at the end of the ball-room the endless procession who passed by, bowing, courtesying, or salaaming, according to the characters they represented. Princess Pless, lovely as Cleopatra, was surrounded by a retinue in Oriental garb, some of whom so far sacrificed their appearance as to darken their faces. A number of the ladies were more becomingly than comfortably attired. A charming Hebe, with an enormous eagle poised on her shoulder and a gold cup in her hand, made a perfect picture, but, alas! in one attitude only, which she vainly tried to preserve throughout the evening, while the late hereditary Prince of Saxe-Coburg (Prince Alfred of Edinburgh), as the Duke of Normandy, A.D. 1060, in casque and chain armor, kept his vizor down until heat and hunger forced him to sacrifice his martial appearance. A beautiful and fascinating duchess, famous for her jewels, elected to appear as Charlotte Corday in cotton skirt and mob-cap, whereas Lady ———, trembling on the verge of bankruptcy, was covered with gems of priceless value. The late Lady Tweedmouth was a striking figure as Queen Elizabeth, with eight gigantic guardsmen surrounding her, all dressed as yeoman of the guard. Many people copied the portraits of their ancestors, and Sir John Kaye, in chain mail, represented Sir Kaye of the "Morte d'Arthur." Many, too, were the heart-burnings over failures or doubles. In one case a well-known baronet had been perfecting himself for weeks in the rôle of Napoleon, his face and figure lending themselves to the impersonation. But what was his dismay at finding in the vestibule a second victor of Austerlitz even more lifelike and correct than himself. It was indeed a Waterloo for both of them.

Few danced, as in a raree-show of that kind people are too much occupied in gazing at one another or in struggling to play up to their assumed parts. Sometimes this was carried further than was intended. Toward the close of the ball, two young men disputed over a certain fair lady. Both losing their tempers, they decided to settle the matter in the garden, and pulling out their weap-

LADY RANDOLPH CHURCHILL, AS THE BYZANTINE EMPRESS THEODORA,
AT THE DEVONSHIRE HOUSE FANCY-DRESS BALL

ons, they began making passes. But the combatants were unequally armed, one being a crusader, with a double-handed sword, the other a Louis XV courtier, armed with his rapier only. He, as might be expected, got the worst of it, receiving a nasty cut on his pink silk stocking. Where so many magnificent and exquisite dresses were worn, it is invidious to mention names, but I remember thinking that the Duchess of Somerset's was the most correct and beautiful, with every detail carefully carried out, the result being absolutely perfect.

On the Saturday following this great entertainment I went to Kimbolton to stay with the Duchess of Manchester, where most of the company were persuaded to don their fancy dress once more. Of course the ball was discussed *ad nauseam*. Many were the divergent opinions as to who looked the best, the majority giving the palm to Lady Westmorland.

In the winter of 1898, persistent rumors of war with South Africa were prevalent, although few realized how soon England was to be plunged into its grim realities. At a shooting party at Chatsworth, I remember meeting Mr. Chamberlain, then Secretary of State for the Colonies. One night at dinner we discussed the situation, and he frankly told me he considered it inevitable. A few months later, hostilities were declared, and great was the excitement. But not even the most gloomy of pessimists could have foreseen or imagined the proportions the war was going to take, or the length of time it was to last. As is well known, it was very unpopular with many people, particularly with those who knew South Africa well and had lived there; but in the growing enthusiasm their voices were as of "one crying in the

wilderness," and before long they were dubbed "Pro-
Boers," or even traitors.

Mr. Selous,[1] writing to me November 5, 1899, said:

I am terribly depressed about this war. I believe it to be unjust and impolitic, and fraught with the gravest danger to the
British Empire in the not distant future. By our attitude at
the time of the Jameson raid, and ever since, we gave the Transvaal every excuse for arming to resist an attack on their independence. The country was practically unarmed for war with
an European nation before the Jameson raid; but we now say
that the Transvaal Government has been arming for many years
past, with the idea of driving the British out of South Africa.
What your husband wrote some years ago as to what would have
happened had we carried on the war and crushed the Transvaal
Boers in 1881, is singularly applicable to the present situation.
You know the passage of course, but I will quote it: "Better
and more precise information combined with cool reflection leads
me to the conclusion that had the British Government of that
day taken advantage of its strong military position, and anni-
hilated, as it could easily have done, the Boer forces, it would
indeed have regained the Transvaal, but it might have lost Cape
Colony. The Dutch sentiment in the Colony has been so exas-
perated by what it considered to be the unjust, faithless, and
arbitrary policy pursued towards the free Dutchmen of the
Transvaal that the final triumph of the British arms, mainly by
brute force, would have permanently and hopelessly alienated it
from Great Britain." As this war has been entered upon, I
trust it will soon be brought to a victorious conclusion. That
is the only chance of peace in the immediate future, and there is
a possibility that by good government and a conciliatory and
sympathetic attitude towards the conquered Boers, we may

[1] Mr. Frederick Courtney Selous, author of several books on travel
and hunting adventures in South Africa.

Sir G. Tayner Welkpinx

W. Whitefoteulg. s.

The Duchess of Somerset
as "Jane Queene of Englande wyfe to Kynge
Henry the Eight and mother to
Kinge Edward the Sixt".

gradually wear away any ideas they may have of another war of independence a generation hence. But I have little hopes for the future. My views are of course very unpopular in this country just now, and I am freely called a traitor, etc., and have lost many old friends.

A few days later he wrote again:

. . . Now that the war has broken out in South Africa, no Englishman, I think, can wish for anything else than complete and absolute victory for our arms. I hope and I believe that soon after all our forces now on their way to South Africa have arrived there, Sir Redvers Buller will be able to overcome all opposition, so that our Government can dictate its own terms of peace. Should those terms of peace bear out Lord Salisbury's statement that the British Government seeks to gain neither gold-fields nor territory by this war, then every honest Englishman will support the Government, but not otherwise. I wish I could persuade myself that this war was just and necessary, and would bring honor to England and lasting benefit to the Empire, but I cannot believe any of these things. The Jameson raid was, though a seeming failure, in reality a magnificent success; for the Jameson raid caused the Transvaal and the Orange Free State to arm, and the arming of these States— the menace to British supremacy in South Africa, as it was called—is what has really brought about this war. . . . I long to go out to South Africa and offer my services to Lord Methuen, whom I know well; but yet cannot do so because of the views I hold as to the real causes of the war, and because I don't see how, holding the views I do, I could bring myself to raise my rifle against men from whom I have received nothing but kindness, and the vast majority of whom are patriots fighting for the independence of their country, which they believe to have been unjustly assailed by Mr. Chamberlain.

That Mr. Selous' pessimistic views as regards the Transvaal have not been fulfilled must be a great joy to him, as it is to all those who have the welfare of South Africa at heart. There is no doubt that the policy which he advocated of "a good Government and a conciliatory and sympathetic attitude towards the conquered Boers," which has been followed by the present Liberal Administration, has brought about the existing happy state of affairs. One sometimes wonders what would now be the condition of South Africa had the late Conservative government remained in power and carried out their proposed measures. But this is by the way.

In moments of great stress and struggle, inactivity becomes a positive pain. The people who were the most to be pitied during the war were, as a friend wrote to me at the time, those who had to remain at home. "It is like being in a country house, and seeing day after day other guests going out to hunt, while compelled oneself to remain indoors. I know nothing so depressing." People feeling this, every sort of movement was soon set on foot for raising funds to alleviate the miseries of the sick and wounded. Every one became interested and occupied in some scheme.

One day in October I received a visit from Mrs. Blow, an American lady who had lived for some time in Australia. The object of her visit was to suggest the idea of an American hospital-ship to be sent out to South Africa. I confess the project did not strike me as practical, and for some days I gave it no thought. Happening, however, to meet Sir William Garstin (of Egyptian fame), I discussed it with him, and he strongly advised me to take it up. "Believe me," he said, "you will be

EXECUTIVE COMMITTEE OF THE HOSPITAL-SHIP *MAINE*

From left to right: Lady Essex, Mrs. Griffiths, Mrs. Van Duzer, Mrs. Van André, Mrs. Ronalds, Mrs. Leslie,
Lady Randolph Churchill, Mrs. Arthur Paget, Mrs. Blow, Mrs. Moreton Frewen, Mrs. Haldeman, Mrs. Field.

making history apart from the excellence of the work."
Then and there I made up my mind to do it.

On October 25, 1899, the first committee meeting was held at my house, at which a number of my compatriots attended. Mrs. Blow was made honorary secretary, Mrs. Ronalds treasurer, and I was elected chairman, and subsequently Mrs. Adair was made vice-chairman. A large and influential general committee was formed.[1] All worked with zeal and enthusiasm, and soon the whole thing was well in train. There was a general impression that the war would be short and sharp. Hospitals of all kinds were greatly needed, and we hurried with feverish activity. Funds and a ship—those were our two great and immediate occupations. No stone was left unturned to procure money—much money, and it had to be all American money. It would be useless to deny here the fact that the war was viewed with disfavor by my countrymen. They had a fellow-feeling for the Boer, fighting, as they thought, for his independence. But the plea of humanity overran their political opinions, and the fund once started, money poured in. A resolution carried at the meeting of the executive committee was embodied in our appeal to the public:

That whereas Great Britain is now involved in a war affecting the rights and liberties of the Anglo-Saxon people in South

[1] Executive Committee of the American Hospital Ship *Maine:* Lady Randolph Churchill (Chairman); Mrs. Adair (Vice-Chairman); Mrs. Blow (Hon. Secretary); Mrs. Ronalds (Hon. Treasurer); The Duchess of Marlborough; Lily, Duchess of Marlborough; The Countess of Essex; Mrs. Bradley-Martin; Mrs. Joseph Chamberlain; Mrs. Earle; Mrs. Field; Mrs. Moreton Frewen; Mrs. Hugh Reid Griffin; Mrs. Haldeman; Mrs. Leslie; Mrs. Arthur Paget; Mrs. Taylor; Mrs. Van Duzer; Mrs. Ralph Vivian; Madame Von Andre.

19

Africa, and has under arms 70,000 troops to maintain such rights and liberties,

And whereas the people of Great Britain have, by their sympathy and moral support, materially aided the people of the United States of America in the war in Cuba and the Philippine Islands ; *it is therefore resolved:*

That the American women in Great Britain, whilst deploring the necessity for war, shall endeavor to raise, among their compatriots, here and in America, a fund for the relief of the sick and wounded soldiers and refugees in South Africa. It is proposed to despatch immediately a suitable hospital ship, fully equipped with medical stores and provisions, to accommodate 200 people, with a staff of four doctors, five nurses, and forty non-commissioned officers and orderlies.

To carry the above resolution into effect, the sum of $150,000 (£30,000) will be required.

Concerts, matinées, and entertainments of all sorts and kinds were organized. Large firms of many nations contributed their specialties, until the amount of medical comforts became so great that we found some difficulty in storing them.

Checks and gifts from two shillings to £1000 were given to us by private persons, whose generosity seemed to know no bounds. On the other hand, we sometimes met with rebuffs, notably in the case of an American multimillionaire to whom I cabled, asking for a subscription for the hospital. He replied that he had "no knowledge of the scheme." The press by that time both in England and the United States was full of our enterprise. I cabled back, "Read the papers," but this, alas! did not untie his purse-strings. Another, whose generosity in the shape of libraries we thought a good omen, also refused. Some of his workmen, however, subscribed £500.

We had asked for £30,000 but eventually received £41,597, which, it must be admitted, was a noble sum to raise in two months, particularly under the circumstances.

Our researches and inquiries respecting a suitable vessel were not at first crowned with success. We were particularly anxious to secure an American ship if possible, and cabled to Mr. Roosevelt, then Governor of New York, to know if he could help us in the matter. Unfortunately, he could not suggest anything. Had we but known it, owing to the large sum collected, a good liner might have been hired, which would have served our purpose admirably. As it was we were in a quandary, when the offer came through the chairman of the Atlantic Transport Company to lend us the *Maine*.

At the outbreak of the South African War this company offered the *Maine* to the English Government for service as a hospital ship; the captain and crew were to be maintained at the company's expense during such time as the ship was in use. The Government accepted the offer; but the ship being a cattle boat, and the expense of fitting her out as a hospital ship being very great, the Admiralty had taken no steps to alter her up to the time when the American Ladies' Committee was formed. Mr. Bernard Baker, President of the company, hearing of our committee and its aims, generously proposed to the Admiralty to hand over the *Maine* to us to fit out. The Admiralty agreed. The committee took over the ship from the Government on the same terms. This arrangement pleased all parties.

Our chief difficulty was ignorance of the requirements of such a hospital. Compared with it, the many field hospitals which were being organized were easy matters to arrange, for every detail was already laid down by the Army Medical Department. It is true that four or five other ships were being equipped for the same purpose, but I imagine they found themselves equally embarrassed. There was no precedent that one could go upon in England of a properly constituted floating hospital for war-times.

In vain I haunted the precincts of the Army and Red Cross Medical departments, they were of little help in the way of advice. Taken *au dépourvu,* they themselves did not know which way to turn, their resources being strained to the utmost limit. However, they supplied us with a certain number of men from the St. John Ambulance Brigade, who, owing to their training and military discipline, were of the greatest use and comfort on board.

The Atlantic Transport Company luckily proved more helpful, as, having already, during the Cuban war, equipped and given the twin-ship of the *Maine,* the *Missouri,* to the American Government, they had a certain amount of experience. We were determined that the staff of doctors and nurses should be American. Mrs. Whitelaw Reid was communicated with in New York, and with her knowledge of nursing and her connection with the Mills School, which her father, Mr. D. O. Mills, had founded, was able to send us out a most efficient staff of doctors, nurses, and orderlies.

During October and November the committee met almost daily. I shall always look back to that time as per-

402

haps the most absorbing of my life. The gloom and terrible depression which had settled on London at the unexpected reverses to the British arms did not affect us, and the daily accounts of horrors and sufferings only doubled our activity. We had no time for tears. All our thoughts were centered in that small cattle boat which was to be converted by our efforts and the generosity of our compatriots into a haven of rest and comfort where some of the terrible suffering could be alleviated.

The *Maine* Committee worked with such will and fire that they carried all before them. The War Office and the Admiralty were badgered and heckled: Would they supply us with this? Would they guarantee us that? We would not take "No" as an answer. Our cause was a righteous one, and we did not mind being importunate.

Nothing could exceed the kindness of Lord Lansdowne, then Minister of War. He helped us in every possible manner, waiving aside all red-tape, as he realized how anxious we were to get our ship under way. Indeed, it was greatly owing to him and the late Lord Goschen, the First Lord of the Admiralty, that our efforts were crowned with success.

On the 12th of November, we held our first general committee. It was with conscious pride that I was able to point out that although the scheme had been in existence only a little more than a fortnight, we already had a ship, a magnificent staff, hundreds of gifts, sympathizers working for us in every part of the globe, and, what was even more important, £15,000. I confess that I had a suspicion that some of those present criticized the policy which necessitated the sending of so many gallant soldiers to the front. But with this policy *we* had nothing to do. My friend Mrs. Craigie (John Oliver Hobbes), writing to me at the time, said: "The wounded are the wounded, irrespective of creed or nationality." This I quoted with much effect to the meeting; also the trite saying that "deeds were better than words," adding that the *Maine* would probably do more to cement the friendship between England and America than any amount of flag-waving and pleasant amenities.

Although the *Maine* was an American hospital-ship, it was very important for its welfare that we should have it under the ægis of the British Government. There were many privileges which they alone could give us. It was also absolutely necessary for our proper status that we should be recognized as a military hospital-ship and that our principal medical officer should be an Englishman of such standing in the army as to give him ample authority. On this subject we did not at first get much encouragement from headquarters. In a letter to me, Lord Wolseley, the commander-in-chief, deprecated the idea, and rather hinted that as we were going to be *so* independent, we had better be entirely so. But later he changed his mind, and wrote:

I am only too anxious to help you in this matter to show you how thoroughly our army, and indeed the nation, appreciate this evidence of the interest that American ladies take in our sick and wounded.

Surgeon Lieutenant-Colonel Hensman, A.M.D., late of the 2nd Life Guards, was eventually chosen for us, and we never had cause to regret the choice, for to a sense of duty he added tactful and courteous manners.

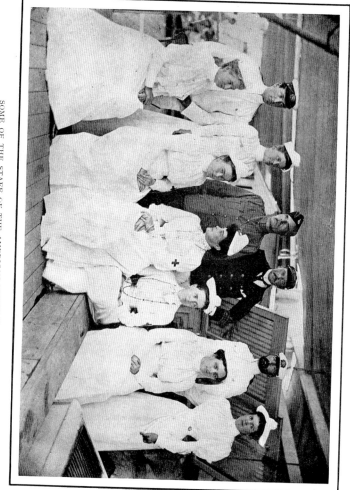

SOME OF THE STAFF OF THE AMERICAN HOSPITAL-SHIP *MAINE*

From left to right (sitting): Miss Hibbard; Sister Ruth (Miss Manly); Lady Randolph Churchill; Miss Eleanor Warrender; Sister Sarah (Miss McCean). (Standing): Dr. Weber; Sister Virginia (Miss Ludekins); Colonel H. F. Hensman, in command; Captain Stone; Dr. Dodge; Sister Margaret (Miss McPherson).

It was no easy matter to control men of two nationalities, for although they were united in a common cause, English and Americans have different ideas and methods, and it is a lasting credit to the ship that there never were any serious differences on board.

The arrival of the American staff from New York occasioned much excitement and interest not only to the committee, but in all circles. Hotels vied with one another to offer them accommodation at very reduced rates pending the departure of the ship to South Africa. Indeed, they were lionized, luncheons and dinner-parties and every sort of entertainment being given them, including one organized by the matrons and nurses of the London hospitals. They were invited to Windsor, where, after viewing the state and private apartments and having luncheon, they were personally presented to Queen Victoria by H. R. H. Princess Christian, whose interest in hospital matters is well known. Her Majesty was deeply interested, wishing them God-speed on their errand of mercy. She added: "I am very pleased to see you, and I want to say how much I appreciate your kindness in coming over to take care of my men." Before returning to London, the staff had tea with Princess Christian at Cumberland Lodge, thus getting an opportunity of seeing the Great Park as they drove through it.

Two days later I was bidden to dine and sleep at Windsor, and had a most interesting conversation with the Queen about the war. Her Majesty asked me many questions about the *Maine,* and spoke of the visit of the surgeons and nurses, whom she professed to be very pleased with; but said, "I think the surgeons look very young." "All the more energetic, therefore," I hoped. The Queen was full of inquiries about my sister-in-law, Lady Sarah Wilson, who was then reported to be a prisoner in the hands of the Boers. "They will not hurt her," she said, with a charming smile.

The next day Mrs. Ronalds and Mrs. Blow came to the Castle to be personally thanked for their work. I was asked to present them to the Queen, and felt very proud of my handsome countrywomen as they came forward with that self-possession and grace which seems inherent in them.

On the 17th of November I was paying a visit to some friends in the country, intending to go to London next day for a great fête at Claridge's Hotel on behalf of the *Maine,* when in the middle of the night I was awakened by the following telegrams:

I regret to inform you that Mr. Winston Churchill has been captured by the Boers. He fought gallantly after an armored train in which he was traveling was trapped.

Signed, EDITOR OF THE MORNING POST.

The second came from the late Mr. Oliver Borthwick, a great personal friend of ours, at that time sub-editor to the same paper, of which his father, Lord Gleneck, was proprietor:

Deeply regret Winston reported captured by Boers; no mention of his being wounded. He not only displayed great personal bravery, carrying the wounded to safety, but by his coolness and bravery encouraged the others. Our correspondent says later: "Churchill, with bravery, coolness described as magnificent, got party men clear of overturned train, subsequently fighting with Dublins and Natal Volunteers, covering retreat of engineers."

My feelings may be imagined, and I passed some terribly anxious moments. Had it not been for the absorbing occupation of the *Maine,* I cannot think how I could have got through that time of suspense. Among shoals of telegrams, I received the following from the Empress Eugénie, which touched me very much.

Farnborough: .

Prends bien part à vos inquiétudes; espère aurez bientôt nouvelle.

Signed, COMTESSE PIERREFONDS.

The committee were very desirous that President McKinley should give us the American flag we intended to fly on our hospital ship, and accordingly I cabled, asking him to do so, adding that it would carry no political significance. After some delay there came an answer through Secretary Hay, to the effect that the President thought it would not do for him to present a flag to the ship, as his "motives might be misconstrued." I cabled again: "Would not red cross on flag remove difficulty? Wounded are to be tended irrespective of nationality." But I suppose the pro-Boer feeling was running too high in America, for my request was again refused.

Meanwhile I had enlisted the kind offices of the Duke of Connaught to ask the Queen to give us a Union Jack, and never doubting that we should secure the Stars and Stripes from the President, I mentioned the fact to His Royal Highness. A few days later I received the following letter:

REMINISCENCES OF

BAGSHOT PARK, SURREY, Dec. 4th, 1899.

DEAR LADY RANDOLPH:

I am happy to be able to tell you that the Queen has consented to present a Union Jack to the Hospital Ship *Maine* as a mark of her appreciation of the generosity of those American ladies who have so nobly come forward, and have at such great expense equipped a hospital ship for wounded British officers and men. I hope to be able to bring the flag down with me on the 16th, and to present it in the Queen's name. The Duchess and I have accepted to dine at the Carlton on the 17th to meet you all, and I understand the nurses, too.

Hoping you got your telegram through to Pretoria.

Believe me,

Yours very sincerely,

ARTHUR.

The refusal from Washington placed me in rather an awkward position, as the Queen in presenting a flag, was under the impression that the President was doing the same. Under the circumstances, I thought the best policy was to preserve a judicious silence, and the American flag was not mentioned. On the appointed day the Queen's present of a huge Union Jack, embellished in the center with the red cross on a white ground was duly hoisted. This ceremony was attended with all the éclat we could ensure for it. The Duke and Duchess of Connaught, Princess Louise (Marchioness of Lorne), and a number of distinguished people came to the luncheon and witnessed the presentation.

The Duke of Connaught made a most felicitous speech, which delighted us all. In the name of her

THE AMERICAN HOSPITAL-SHIP *MAINE* IN DURBAN HARBOR

Majesty the Queen, he presented the Union Jack to the hospital-ship *Maine*

. . . as a mark of her appreciation of the generosity of those who have found the money for this ship, and also of that charity which a large number of American ladies and gentlemen have shown toward the soldiers of her kin, speaking their own language, who are now fighting gallantly in South Africa. It is a great pleasure to me to have been asked to perform what I believe is a unique ceremony. Never before has a ship sailed under the combined flags of the Union Jack and the Stars and Stripes; and it marks, I hope, an occasion which brings out that feeling of generosity and affection that the two countries have for each other. I cannot sufficiently thank those who have come forward in such a liberal manner for what they have done. As an officer in the English Army, I feel, I can assure you, most deeply what you all have done for us this day, and I am sure that the officers and men who may reap the advantage of this well-equipped ship will bless those who have done so much towards it. I should like to mention many names, but I am afraid it is impossible, and I will therefore ask Lady Randolph Churchill to accept in the name of all those who have worked with her the thanks both of the Sovereign of our country and of all English men and women for this splendid present which has been made in aid of our wounded soldiers in South Africa.

To this I replied:

Your Royal Highness, I beg to thank you in the name of my committee for your kindness in coming here to-day to present on behalf of her Majesty the Queen, her gracious gift of the Union Jack to the American ladies' hospital-ship *Maine*. I trust your Royal Highness will convey to her Majesty how deeply we feel honored by this kind and thoughtful act, which we look upon as an acknowledgment and appreciation of our efforts. It is a source of much gratification to us Americans that our compatriots have responded so generously to our call on behalf of the sick and wounded, enabling us by their sympathy and money to fit out this splendid ship. We have also had many donations from English people who have come forward most lavishly with their gifts. Indeed, all who have been interested in this work have made it a labor of love. We hope that the *Maine* will be more than useful on her errand of mercy, and that our charity will be as wide-spread as possible irrespective of nationality.

The flag was then fastened to a halyard and run up by the Duke to the mainmast, where, after an energetic pull or two, it flew out to the breeze, the band of the Scots Guards playing "Rule Britannia." This they quickly changed to the "Star-Spangled Banner" as the Stars and Stripes were run up to the mizzen, and the Red-Cross flag to the foremast. With the Admiralty's transport flag at the helm, it is not surprising that we felt much be-flagged and bedecked. It was a great moment for us all, and I confess I felt a lump in my throat. We had had an anxious moment in the morning when the Bishop of London, who was to have blessed the flag, telegraphed suddenly that he was too ill to come. London was scoured to find a divine to take his place; fortunately we secured the Bishop of Islington. But he, too, gave us a scare, as he missed his train and barely arrived in time.

On the 23rd of December, the *Maine* sailed for Cape Town. I had made up my mind some time previously to go with her, feeling that the committee should be represented by a person of authority without a salary.

Although the morning broke dark and foggy, I started with a light heart, as I had heard the day before that my son Winston, after escaping from Pretoria, where he had been a prisoner after the armor train disaster at Chieveley, was safe at Lorenzo Marquez. The news was first conveyed to me through the telephone from the office of the "Morning Post," for which paper he had been acting as war correspondent. All I could hear was "Hurrah! hurrah!" shouted by different voices, as one after another seized the instrument in their kind wish to congratulate me.

To say that the ship was in a state of chaos does not express it. On the Sunday before 10,000 people had visited her, which did not help to keep the new paint immaculate. The decks were covered with mud from the boots of the numerous workmen; painters, carpenters, plumbers, and engineers were seen in every nook and corner putting on the last touches, the wards were littered with wood-shavings, paint-pots, ropes, scaffoldings, and the thousand and one kind of débris which the conversion of a cattle boat entails. With my friend Miss Eleanor Warrender, who was going out with me, I stood on the deck as the vessel moved out of the docks, leaving family and friends behind. A gleam of sun shone on us for a moment as those on shore burst into cheers, which were taken up by the crews of the ships which lay alongside. "Mind you bring home Kruger, and we 'll eat him," and a few similar recommendations, came from grimy colliers, but these cries were soon lost in the black fog which settled down upon us. Although, owing to it, we got only as far as the outer basin, we felt we had started on our journey.

CHAPTER XVI

SOUTH AFRICA—LIFE ON THE HOSPITAL-SHIP *MAINE*—
CAPE TOWN—A REMARKABLE HAIL-STORM—DURBAN
—SOME RED-TAPE—WAR SCENES—VISIT TO CHIEVELEY
CAMP—RELIEF OF LADYSMITH.

ON my journey to South Africa in January,
1899, in the hospital-ship *Maine,* I had anticipated a certain amount of rough weather in the
Bay of Biscay, but was not prepared to meet a full gale
lasting six days, and which according to the authorities
was the worst experienced for many years. To encounter this in midwinter, in a comparatively small ship,
fitted up as a hospital, with large hatchways and sky-
lights, and with inadequate means of battening down,
was, it must be admitted, something of a trial. Indeed we lay to forty-eight hours, adding to our
physical misery the knowledge that we were making
no headway. Even to good sailors the weariness of
being buffeted from morning till night, and the impossibility of doing anything unless entrenched in a sort of
zereba, is most trying. To eat under such circumstances
one requires to be a Cinquevalli: no fiddles can restrain
your soup from being shot into your lap, or the contents
of your glass into your face. To those who are not
"Ancient Mariners" the horrors of the situation will
appeal sympathetically. I never realized before how

one can suffer by color. The green of my attractive little cabin, which I had thought so reposeful, became a source of acute suffering, and I had to find a neutral-tinted cushion on which to rest my eyes. The sound of the waves breaking on the deck with the report of cannon-balls brought to my mind our mission, and I remember thinking, as I rolled in sleepless wretchedness, that if we went to the bottom, at least we should be counted as victims of the war.

Besides the inclemency of the weather, the ship was in the greatest confusion, owing to the vast amount of goods overcrowding the holds, and to a mass of articles brought on board at the last moment. This proved a serious obstacle to getting the vessel in order, and for a time all was in chaos. I will not dwell on the discomforts, I may even say hardships, experienced more or less by all. January 2, late in the evening, we anchored off Las Palmas, and with a sigh of relief told each other the worst was now over. In the morning Mr. Swanston, the British Consul, and Captain Wintz, of H.M.S. *Furious,* who had been on the lookout for us for days, came on board, bringing the latest news and fresh flowers. The news was scanty: General French had occupied Colesberg, and there had been a fresh attack on Mafeking. Otherwise the situation was unchanged. We went on shore feeling giddy and battered, coming across in the harbor the wrecked transport *Denton Grange,* which had run ashore with three other vessels during the gale. The water was pouring through her hold, and all the engines were hopelessly ruined. We had a talk with some of her dejected officers, who were living on board.

Armed with cameras and long lists of purchases, we

lunched at the Catalina Hotel, a pretty house with low verandas covered with bougainvilleas of different shades. The air was soft and balmy, and many English visitors were lounging about, looking, if slightly bored, peaceful and comfortable. Our friends provided us with a carriage and pair in which we crawled through the two feet of mud of the one long principal street of the town. I was reminded of Monterey, California— there were the same square pink houses with green shutters and a center court or patio, tropical vegetation, and the sea at the door. But here the comparison ends, for Las Palmas is merely pretty, whereas Monterey with its seventeen-mile ocean drive, unparalleled gardens and unique storm-swept cypress groves overlooking the ocean, is perhaps one of the most beautiful spots in the world.

Excited and delighted with our day, we returned to the ship laden with spoils—birds, parrots, fruit, plants, coffee-pots, and much else. I had an opportunity of judging of the appearance of the *Maine* as we came alongside. Alas! the brilliant green stripe denoting our status as a military hospital-ship was a thing of shreds and patches, many of our stanchions were bent and twisted, and our would-be immaculate white paint was a foggy gray.

The seventeen days of our journey to Cape Town were busy ones; we were spared monotony by the work of getting the wards in order, and rescuing our hundreds of donations from the chaos of the hold. In the hurry of departure many things had been forgotten, and many were put anywhere to be out of the way. We had very little time in which to appear shipshape before arriving.

The surgeons, sisters and medical staff generally were assigned to their different wards, which reëchoed with "Be kind enough not to walk through my ward"; "Be good enough to keep your wet feet off my clean rubber"; "Pray take your things off my beds," and the like.

After crossing the line the evenings were spent in star-gazing at the Southern Cross. But I confess I felt no keenness, having seen it often before, and I thought its beauty a delusion. At first we met no ships, and the absence of news was very trying. After a few days, however, we sighted a small steamer and instantly bore down on her, signaling for intelligence. What we got was: "Buller crossed Tugela. Ladysmith rumored relieved. Continued fighting"—virtually no news, and we were fain to hold our souls in patience till our arrival in Cape Town, on the 23rd of January.

Cape Town, with its bay full of transports disembarking troops, the feverish activity of its docks, and its streets crowded with khaki-clad soldiers, seemed indeed the real thing. My first impression of the bay at 6 A.M. with innumerable vessels and forests of masts, the clouds breaking on Table Mountain, and the rising sun turning all into a pink glory, will not soon fade from my memory. Though worn and tired, and realizing that our work was all before us, we rejoiced to be in measurable distance of it. As we were rolling about outside the breakwater, by the kindness and exertions of Sir Edward Chichester who was in charge of the port, we were given a berth inside. As soon as possible I started off to see the Governor, Sir Alfred (now Lord) Milner, to get my letters and telegrams and gather what news I could. This was very meager. I have since ascertained that Lord Kitchener's first order to all officers was to practise the utmost discretion, and that any information as to war news was strictly forbidden. This was owing to the mass of spies and the disloyalty in Cape Town, much valuable information being continually transmitted to the enemy. The Standard Bank was an amazing sight of bustling activity, men in every variety of khaki-colored clothes, trousers, breeches, puttees, gaiters, sombreros, helmet and field-service caps, rushing in and out all day, till one wondered at the patience and civility of the employees. The entire staff of the *Maine* were invited to a reception at the Mount Nelson Hotel, given in their honor by a committee of American ladies. It was pleasant enough to walk in the pretty garden, eating strawberries—and a marked contrast to the melancholy which prevailed at Government House, where I dined that evening.

The day of our arrival the principal medical officer came on board and after visiting the ship, informed us that we were at once to be sent to Durban to fill up with patients and return to England. I remonstrated and explained to him the purpose and mission of the ship, pointing out the fact that were it to be treated merely as a transport for convalescents the international value of the gift would certainly suffer, and the large, expensive and efficient medical staff on board would have nothing to do and would be greatly disappointed, as of course interesting serious cases were not likely to be sent us. I pressed the point so much that at last he said the ship had better get orders from General Buller on arrival at Durban. On our arrival there the authorities came on board and told us we were to be filled up with

FIELD-MARSHAL LORD ROBERTS INSPECTING THE *MAINE* AT CAPE TOWN

drafts from the other hospital-ships and sent home at once. But with the help and influence of the Government of Natal, Sir Redvers Buller and other influential friends, I am happy to say I was able successfully to frustrate three times these endeavors to send us back. The *Maine* not only remained in the harbor of Durban but had many interesting cot cases sent down. The absence of news was making every one desperately anxious.

We had been asked by the Cape Town authorities to leave on the 25th for Durban. Although the notice was short, giving us only a couple of days after the long sea voyage of nearly a month, we were rather pleased to be able to say "Yes," and prove our readiness. A few hours after receiving our orders, however, Lord Roberts sent word that he wished to visit the ship on the following day. Accordingly he came, and gave us a thorough inspection: wards, mess rooms, dispensary, operating room, everything was visited and much approved of. The only thing wanting to prove our efficiency was beds filled with the wounded. Before starting five civil surgeons and eight army reserve sisters were added to our number, the medical authorities having asked us to take them to Durban, their ultimate destination being Mooi River. They proved very troublesome on the journey, being indeed as *exigeant* as they appeared ignorant. One or two of the nurses actually brought maids to look after them! I did not envy the hospitals which were to benefit by their services.

It was no surprise to us to repeat some of our Bay of Biscay experiences, as we knew there would be a heavy ground swell all the way. Later, however, the sea became comparatively calm, and we emerged to bask in the sun like lizards. I gazed for hours through my glasses at the shore, which was only three or four miles distant. The soft green hills and bright sandy beaches, with kraals dotted here and there, gave it such a cultivated appearance that one could hardly realize this was "Savage South Africa." As we approached Durban, the wind began to blow, and an ominous bank of gray cloud came up, with lightning flashing on the horizon. I shall never forget the astonishing storm which suddenly burst upon us. The electric barometer in my cabin dropped perpendicularly. Torrents of hailstones beat down on us as large as small plums, the wind increased to a hurricane, and was so violent that the ship stood still, although we had been going at ten knots. The awning aft was violently blown into the sea, carrying with it all its rafters and stanchions, smashing one of the big ventilators, and only just missing some of the sisters who were crouching on the deck. The sea meanwhile presented a most curious appearance, being covered with millions of little jets about a foot high, due to the force with which the hailstones fell, and as they floated for a while, in a few minutes it was quite white. Inside my deck cabin the din was terrific, the noise of the hailstones striking the skylight and windows with a sound like bullets. It was impossible to speak. One window was smashed and the water and ice poured in everywhere. The hailstones had a pattern like agate. With the decks covered with ice, the thermometer at 82 degrees seemed an anomaly, and reminded one of the Scotchman who during a rainstorm threw out his rising barometer, shouting after it, "Go and see for yourself." Luckily

LADY RANDOLPH CHURCHILL AND HER SON, MR. JOHN CHURCHILL,
ON BOARD THE AMERICAN HOSPITAL-SHIP *MAINE*

the storm did not last long, and we were soon able to emerge and look at the damage.

On the afternoon of the 29th we came in sight of Durban, the pride and glory of the Garden Colony. We rejoiced in the thought that we should soon be resting our tired eyes on the trees and flowers of the beautiful Berea, and be initiated into the delights of the unknown fruits the guide-books dilated on. Here, too, in the "active zone" our real work was to begin, and all were keen and eager.

By this time the inhabitants of the *Maine* could boast sea-legs and, notwithstanding the heavy swell, we did not mind being told that we should have to remain outside the harbor all night. Thirsting for news, however, my younger son, who had come with us from Cape Town to join the South African Light Horse in Natal, started off with one of the ship's officers in a steam-launch for the harbor and shore, little knowing that the penalty for crossing the bar was £100, and still less that, owing to the heavy sea, a small boat had no chance of getting safely over. Luckily they were hailed by a tug, with a midshipman on board from H.M.S. *Terrible,* who was the bearer of a message to me from the commandant, Captain (now Admiral Sir) Percy Scott, to the effect that my son Winston was in Durban, having come on two days' leave to meet me, and that there was no fresh news, or change in the military situation. This seemed inexplicable, as when we left Cape Town the air was full of the wildest rumors, crucial developments being expected hourly. Ladysmith, however, had neither fallen nor been relieved. The enemy's big guns were firing away with the same monotonous regularity, and the list of reverses was being steadily increased.

Pending the arrival of patients and longing for a few days' rest, I availed myself of a kind invitation from the Governor of Natal, Sir Walter Hely-Hutchinson, to go to Pietermaritzburg. Miss Eleanor Warrender and my two boys went with me, all being duly armed with passes and permissions sent us by the commandant. This made me realize that we were under martial law, and that no one could travel or be abroad after eleven o'clock at night without official permission. Two very pleasant and reposeful days were spent at Pietermaritzburg, but it was hard to say good-by to my sons, who left the next evening to join the South African Light Horse. I enjoyed talking to my host at Government House, since his long sojourn in Natal and his intimate knowledge of the people and the military situation gave particular interest to his conversation. I visited the hospitals and thought them admirably arranged. The Town Hall, a fine building, full of light and air with bright flowers decorating the tables, and soft-voiced sisters moving about, seemed an ideal ward. The four long rows of cots were full and the men liked talking about their wounds and adventures. The Fort Hospital, with its small detached cottages, was more suited to isolated cases; the officers' quarters looking particularly comfortable with rooms opening on the veranda, where thick creepers hanging from the roof shaded them from the sun. Here I visited Colonel Long, who had been desperately wounded at Colenso. Notwithstanding the terrible nature of his wounds he received me with a pleasant smile. General Buller's scathing report on Long's precipitancy must be fresh in every one's memory. The press was full of it, and naturally the hospital authorities tried to keep the knowledge from the unfortunate officer. A well-meaning though foolish visitor, however, condoled with him, and he never rested until he had read the cruel message. Colonel Long spoke of it to me quite freely, saying in the bitterness of the moment that Buller never would have dared to censure him in such terms had he not thought that he was a dead man. Leaving him lying there in pain, with agonizing thoughts of what "might have been" and what was, I pondered as I went away on the chances and fortune of war, which in a few moments can mar the reputation of the man with a gallant record, and perhaps make famous the commonplace plodder who without an idea beyond routine may happen to be in luck. A telegram from the *Maine,* announcing that some sick and wounded were arriving on the following day, hastened my departure. I traveled back by day and enjoyed the lovely scenery between Pietermaritzburg and Durban. The astonishing little railway twists in and out, round and about the ever-changing colored hills, making as many detours as the pretentious avenue of the millionaire whose palace you are allowed to see for miles before you arrive at its door.

I found the ship's staff in a pleasurable state of excitement at the prospect of the work before them. In the afternoon an ambulance train arrived, bringing us eighty-five men. The British soldier is a fine fellow, as the many thousand instances of his courage and self-sacrifice on the field and in action testify. Out of his uniform he is a big child, and wants to be kept in order and not too much spoiled. I am afraid we were inclined to do this. On the whole, I think it can only do good to give a man a higher ideal of cleanliness and comfort than he has ever had before. I had long and frequent talks with many of them. They delighted in giving their histories and experiences, and particularly the crowning one of how they received their wounds, which with the slightest encouragement they would show with great pride, as well as the extracted bullet, if they had one.

I was amused by the letters which those unable to write dictated to me. They generally began, "Dear Father and Mother, I hope this finds you well as it leaves me." Then came a great scratching of heads and biting of fingers until I would suggest, to start them off again, a description of how they were wounded. "Won't you send your love to any one?" I asked. "Not out of the family" was my answer, with a reproving look. One very gallant Tommy, who lay with a patch over his eye, an inflamed cheek, and a broken arm, asked me to add to his letter, "The sister which is a-writing of this is very nice." The compliment was fully appreciated. A few days later we received ten officers and ninety men, making us fairly full. We were busy from morning to night. Indeed one never seemed to have a moment to write or read: the one difficulty on board ship at any time, and more particularly on a hospital-ship, is to be alone, and when alone to be able to concentrate. The parties of sick and wounded men who came to us were drafted from the different hospitals of Frere, Estcourt, Mooi River and Pietermaritzburg. Apart from the surgical and operating cases, the treatment consisted principally of antiseptic dressing, electricity, and massage, the use of the gymnasium apparatus giving excellent results. The crowds of interested visitors who flocked on board became at last a source of care and worry to us, and of annoyance to the patients. They meant so well, it seemed hard to turn them away, but for one tactful, bona fide visitor who had a friend to see, twenty idlers would career over the ship, asking innumerable questions impeding the work. The practice.had to be stopped, and certain days and hours fixed. The other hospital-ship had to do the same.

It may be interesting to describe how we worked our wards. To begin with, apart from the captain and ship's company, our medical staff was comprised of the commanding officer, five surgeons, one superintending sister, four sisters, eleven male nurses, ten orderlies, and five non-commissioned officers. The personnel of each ward was composed of a head nurse, nurses, orderlies, stewards and night nurses according to the size of the ward and the number of beds in it. The surgeons did their dressings and duties in the morning, one of them being told off daily as orderly medical officer, whose duty was to make a thorough inspection of everything, report anything not correct, and to hear complaints. The superintending sister had charge of the head nurses, and was responsible for all patients according to the medical officers' instructions. The three stores—linen, personal equipment, and medical comforts, auxiliary to the nursing department—were placed under the management of the superintending sister, and were respectively in the charge of a non-commissioned officer. These N.C.O.s proved most excellent men. The staff-surgeon was employed as record clerk and acting sergeant-major. He had to keep the admission and discharge book, which showed the regiment or corps, regiment number, remarks, name of all patients, disease or disability, date of admission or discharge, number of days under treatment, ward in which treated, religion and final destination. The medical care and nursing and innumerable comforts we had to give the patients, combined with the cool fresh air on the ship, brought so many of them round that we were able to discharge them fit for duty. These did not go to the front at once, but were sent to Pietermaritzburg or elsewhere to do light duty till quite recovered.

It was astonishing how little the authorities were able to cope with the subject of clothing. At the front the men were nearly naked, their khaki hanging on them in shreds, the uniform being made of abominable stuff and having to be worn for perhaps five or six months. When one reflects on the thousands and thousands of pounds that were spent in clothing for the hospitals, not only by the Government, but by private persons, it seems incredible that the sick and wounded were allowed to leave one hospital to be drafted to another, or to a hospital-ship, in the tattered garments in which they were carried in from the battle-field. With my own eyes, I saw among a party of wounded who were being transferred from a tug to the *Maine* and another hospital-ship, the *Nubia,* a man whose khaki trousers were conspicuous by their absence, a pocket-handkerchief being tied around one of his wounded legs. This man had probably been through several hospitals, each time sent off again in his rags. Surely a reserve of uniforms or ordinary clothing might have been kept for extreme cases such as this, and the principal medical officer allowed a little discretion in the matter. But when I discussed this point with one of the authorities, he said it would be an impossibility. "You might as well have an office for recording the wishes and messages of the dying." What a happy hunting-ground the red-tape fiend has in time of war! He sits and gloats on all occasions. Think of a man in a hospital who, being on a full diet, suddenly develops fever, or some other complication needing an altered régime—say a milk diet—having to starve for twenty-four hours until the medical officer makes his rounds again and alters it! This was a fact. Incidents such as these made one admire the audacity of Major Brazier Creagh, a young and energetic ambulance officer, who, when remonstrated with for spending too much money in comforts, said his business was to bring the sick and wounded down safely, and give them everything which would further that end—"not to make accounts and count the cost."

I was very anxious to go up to the front and visit the various hospitals on the way, and after many pourparlers I received permission and a pass from General Wolfe Murray to go to Chieveley Camp. The Governor, Sir Walter Hely-Hutchinson, was kind enough to lend me his own railway carriage. Provided with food, armed with kodaks and field-glasses, not to mention a brown holland dress (my substitute for khaki) in case we should meet the enemy and wish to remain invisible, we started on our journey—Miss Warrender, Colonel Hensman, the commanding officer of the *Maine,* and myself, and, last but not least, the coxswain of the

Terrible, Porch by name. Captain Percy Scott intended taking us up, but as he was getting into the train a telegram was handed to him from General Buller, asking for two guns to be sent up immediately. This meant forty-eight hours' incessant work to get them ready, the commandant's personal and active supervision, and the loss to us of a pleasant and instructive companion. The train was full of officers and men returning to the front. Although we were traveling at night I was kept awake by the thought that I was going to pass all those well-known and to me peculiarly interesting places, Mooi River, Estcourt, and Frere, scene of the armored-train disaster.

We arrived at Estcourt in the middle of the night. I hung my head out and entered into a conversation with a friendly sergeant, who informed me that in a few moments he would have to call the railway staff officer, whose duty it was to inspect the train and see that no suspects were in it, or travelers without passes. I plied the sergeant with questions. Had they caught many spies, and what happened to them? Several had been captured, and two nights before a young lady who had been seen for a few days riding in the vicinity of the camp, had been arrested and sent through to Durban as a spy. He was full of the generosity of the Tommies, who came down in the same trains with some wounded Boers, telling how they vied with each other in attentions to their sick foes, sharing their tobacco with them, and tying up their bandages. My new-found friend was waxing eloquent when suddenly the clock struck two, and he left me abruptly, disappearing inside the station. He came forth following a smart young officer,

HIS EXCELLENCY, SIR WALTER HELY-HUTCHINSON

Governor of Natal in 1900

whose sleepy, dazed eyes showed that he had been hastily awakened. Every pass was then minutely examined, every face scanned, and I saw with keen interest two men dragged out of the next compartment, one a typical Boer, the other a small dark foreigner. Both were marched off—to what fate, one wonders!

I was asleep when we reached Frere at 5 A.M. A vigorous tap on the window awoke me. "Lady Randolph Churchill, are you there?" "Yes, very much so," I answered, as I dropped the shutter and put my head out, finding an officer of the Seaforth Highlanders on the platform. "I knew you were coming up, and thought you would like a cup of coffee," he said, "if you will accept the hospitality of my tin hut fifty yards from here," adding, "You won't get anything more for a long time." In my eagerness I was proceeding to jump down, when he remarked that I had no shoes on, and, with a glance at my disheveled locks, suggested a hat. As I walked to the hut, dawn was just breaking,— long orange-red streaks outlined the distant brown hills; through the haze of dust showing on the sky-line trains of mule-carts were crawling along, and in the plain little groups of soldiers and horsemen were moving about, emerging from the tents. My host seated me on a stool in the tiny veranda, and gave me an excellent cup of coffee. He was so delighted to have some one to speak to that the words and questions came tumbling out. Waiting for no answer, in one breath he told me how he had been there for months, broiling, with heaps of uncongenial work to do, all responsibility and anxiety, and no excitement or danger. He lived in daily hopes of getting some fighting. Meanwhile "Some one has to do the dirty work," and there it is! He showed me the hut, two cubicles opening on the veranda, one for the aide-de-camp with no bed, the other for the Colonel with a small camp stretcher.

About twenty miles after leaving Frere we slowed down, and the friendly guard, knowing who I was, rushed to tell me we were passing the place of the armored train disaster. Sure enough, there was the train, lying on its side, a mangled and battered thing, and within a few yards a grave with a cross—three sentries mounting guard—marking the place where the poor fellows killed in it were buried.

At Chieveley we were met by General Barton and an aide-de-camp, who took us all over the camp. It was a wonderful sight. The weatherbeaten and in many cases haggard men, with soiled, worn uniforms hanging on their spare figures, the horses pickeled in lines or singly, covered with canvas torn in strips to keep the flies off, the khaki-painted guns, the ambulance wagons with their train of mules, and above all the dull booming of "Long Tom" made us realize that here was war! We sat down on the outskirts of the camp near a sham gun guarded by a middy from the *Terrible*. Here also I saw the gun which the bluejackets had named after me. Six miles off, through our glasses we could see Colenso and the enemy's camp, the white tents being those captured from the British. The whole panorama spread out was a grand and thrilling sight. Major Stuart Wortley and Captain MacBean rode up and greeted us warmly, but they, like all the other officers, were terribly dejected at the news of the retreat from Spion Kop, so gloriously won and at such a sacrifice the night before. "They are

GUN AT CHIEVELEY CAMP NAMED AFTER LADY RANDOLPH CHURCHILL.

actually on their way back to Spearman's Camp: what can it mean?" The whole camp was in a state of disgust and despair and "groused" to their heart's content. We were invited by the Seventh Fusiliers to have breakfast with them, which was none the less appetizing because served in tin mugs and pewter plates. The flies, however, were a terrible plague, covering everything in an instant, besides buzzing in one's face and hair. In the hope of hearing something of my sons, I asked General Barton to let me send a letter to Spearman's Camp. He kindly consented, and installed me in his little tent. I looked around with curiosity and interest at the General's quarters: a camp-stool, a washing-basin, a box—nothing more. Sitting on the camp-stool with my feet on a tin box, I was scribbling away, when a rider galloped up, calling out in a cheery voice, "General! are you there?" His look of blank astonishment when he caught sight of me was most amusing. A woman in the camp, and in the General's tent! I explained, and after a few laughing remarks he rode off. This was General Thorald, who alas! poor man, was killed the following week. Major Stuart Wortley asked us to stay and dine, but I thought discretion was the better part of valor, and not wishing to abuse the General's kindness in letting us come up, we departed, wishing these brave men good luck and the speedy relief of Ladysmith.

The return journey was fearfully hot. At Mooi River we had two hours to wait, and were met there by Colonel Stevenson, the remount officer, who had arranged to show us his great horse farm where about 2000 horses were at that moment resting before being sent to the front, hundreds of them having just arrived from South America. What a fate! To be penned up for days on a rolling ship, then crammed into an open truck under a blazing sun, to be taken out, stiff, sore and dazed, given two days' rest, and then sent up to the front only to be food for the Boer bullets. Poor things—so understanding—such good friends—the hardships they suffered, and the lingering death many had to undergo, was one of the most hideous features of the war. Colonel Stevenson had brought two Cape carts, with a capital pair of ponies in each, which galloped at full tilt along the hill road to the farm, some miles distant. A few weeks before, when the Boers were within thirty miles of Pietermaritzburg, the farm was in nightly danger of being raided, and it is surprising that it was not, considering the prize to be hauled in. But for some reason best known to themselves the enemy kept off. On reaching our destination we found to our delight the most welcome shade, a small house buried in trees, tents agreeably dotted about under them, and horses everywhere. Here a group was waiting to be examined; there a row were being lunged; further on some were rolling in the dust, stretching their weary limbs in blissful ignorance of the fate awaiting them. They could barely be given time to recover from their long journeys before they were hurried to the front. The demand was enormous, the cry for more, and the supply limited. In vain two continents were scoured to provide for the cavalry, its importance having been too tardily recognized. For months Colonel Stevenson had been living on the railway, rushing off to Durban to meet a consignment from India, South Australia, America or Australia, supervising their debarkation, then flying back to despatch others to the front. Meanwhile time was pressing. A hasty cup of tea and a gallop back to the train, and so to Durban and duty.

On returning from Chieveley I found a telegram from my sister-in-law, Lady Sarah Wilson, who was in Mafeking. With considerable difficulty I had managed to get one to her.

Received by runner from Mafeking.

Feb. 27.

Very grateful your wire. First direct news family received. All well here but bombardment continues daily. Health town fairly good. Rations strict but sufficient. We receive very scanty news. Please wire again. Congratulate you Winston's plucky escape.

SARAH.

(Mafeking)

Life on board became a round of daily duties, varied only by excitement in regard to war news. It was interesting to distribute newspapers to the soldiers. They were so keen and eager in discussing every point. Even those who were bedridden and too ill to read would clutch you as you passed, "Any news? Ladysmith? Nothing? What, back again, Chieveley Camp? That Buller 'e 's unlucky; better try another; and we wants to get to them poor chaps." I argued on the principle that perhaps the general hoped to *reculer pour mieux sauter,* but the heads would wag sagely. I had a large map framed and hung in one of the wards, and with much assiduity placed the flags according to the situation; but daily the Union Jacks were made to fly at

21

Pretoria, Johannesburg, or Ladysmith, while the Boer flags were carefully stuck in the frame. One night the news of Cronje's surrender was signaled from the station. As soon as they were told of it a grand cheer went up from the men. Lights were flashed, messages heliographed from Captain Percy Scott's electric shutter on board the *Terrible* to all the ships in the harbor. The band played itself out, the men sang themselves hoarse, and at last after a bouquet of fireworks we went to bed. The next day Durban was *en fête,* the harbor dressed, and every one wreathed in smiles. We dined at the Royal Hotel to celebrate the event, finding there a motley crowd, principally men in worn uniforms who had just come down from the front for a few days' needed rest, others just returning. There were scarcely any ladies, a few refugees or officers' wives struggling to get up nearer to the front, all in the inevitable shirt, skirt, and sailor hat; none of the glories of Cape Town here! A few of those present were suspects and not allowed to leave Durban, having to report themselves to the commandant's office twice a week. He was dining with us, and seemed rather to enjoy the black looks cast on him, bowing with much unction to a formidable Boer lady, large in proportions and rasping as to tongue, with whom he had had a stormy interview that morning, she wanting and insisting on getting a pass to Delagoa Bay, and he refusing, knowing her to be a spy, who had given much information already. After dinner we sat in groups in a pleasant conservatory, getting into such heated discussions as to the progress of the war, and the merits and demerits of the generals, that we were in danger, like Cinderella, of forgetting the hour, and had to rush off in our jinrikishas for fear of being caught out after eleven o'clock, and marched off to prison!

As an evidence of the severity with which the press censorship was enforced, I may mention that I received a letter from General Barton from Chieveley Camp, which had been opened and the usual pink paper pasted on it: "Opened under Martial Law." I felt rather aggrieved, but was told that during the three or four days in which everything coming from the front was opened, the movements of the British troops were kept entirely dark from the enemy.

On the 29th came the news of the relief of Ladysmith, and the town went mad. A great demonstration was organized for the next day, opposite the Town Hall, under the queen's statue. The proceedings were brief, as the continuous cheering prevented any of the speakers from being heard, but we took for granted that they said all the right things. We had now been in the harbor six weeks, and the authorities after the relief of Ladysmith, being anxious to free the various hospitals in Natal, to meet the pressure of the sick and wounded who were coming down, filled the *Maine* up with convalescents, and ordered us to prepare for return to England.

Before leaving I had the good luck to go up to Ladysmith, General Buller kindly giving me a pass. It was no easy matter to get permission, as there was naturally a great struggle to get people down, only one hundred a day being taken, and every place counted. The railway was frightfully congested, and all the wounded had to be carried in litters across the Tugela at Colenso, on a bridge consisting of three planks. Miss Warrender and I, escorted by my son Winston and Captain Tharp of the Rifle Brigade (one of our discharged patients), arrived at Colenso at 6 A.M., and after a breakfast of "bully beef," which I did not appreciate, crossed the bridge of planks. After viewing and kodaking the terrible scene of ruin and devastation, where among other horrors we saw the carcasses of Colonel Long's horses in front of the trenches, we got on a trolley pushed by natives, and left for Ladysmith. This was an excellent way of seeing everything, as the whole of the last two months' fighting had been along the line. One must see it all to realize the stupendous difficulties; the harsh impossible ground to get over, the gaining of it inch by inch, the smallest mistake costing hundreds of lives. The masses of shell and bullets on either side of the line, the dead horses, and the newly made graves, testified to the fierceness of the struggle. At one point we crossed a small bridge built up with sandbags, over which the men had to run singly under a terrible fire from three kopjes. After two hours we came to an open plain glistening with the discarded food tins of the advancing army, and further on went through Intombi Camp, broiling in the blazing sun, a place of desolation and misery, and so on into Ladysmith.

Blinding dust up to one's ankles, scorching sun, shut-up empty houses, an expression of resigned martyrdom on every one's face—such was my first impression of Ladysmith. Sitting on the top of our gripsacks on a Scotch cart drawn by mules, we drove through the town, presenting as we thought a strange appearance; but no one noticed us. We drove to the Convent, General Buller's headquarters, where his aide-de-camp, Lord Gerard, received us. The building showed conspicuous signs of its bombardment. Sir Redvers invited Miss Warrender and myself to dine, and offered us beds, though he did not promise sheets! We accepted gratefully, having vainly tried to get a room, and the prospect of food had not appeared on the horizon. We visited the Tin Camp, turned into a hospital. It was wonderfully well-arranged, considering the difficulties, but seemed a hopeless place to get well in. Lord Dundonald, who commanded the South African Light Horse, lent us a spider and a wild horse which had never been in harness before, and driven by a sergeant we careered over rocks and dongas four miles to the camp of the Light Horse, where we had tea out of bottles and tin mugs. By this time I was too tired to take in any more, and the hazardous drive back in the semi-darkness quite finished me. Making a hasty and apologetic toilet we dined with the general in a tent commanding a fine view of the town. The dinner was good and the company better. Sir Redvers (who was in good spirits) was most interesting and pleasant. He told me that he expected one more big fight and that it would be the following week, if he could get his commissariat up, but that for the time being, the line was hopelessly blocked.

While in Ladysmith besides the scathing criticisms I heard passed on the recent operations, some amusing stories and incidents were related. This message from the chief of the staff to the officer commanding Cæsar's Camp is worth recording:

The General Officer commanding has left to visit you *via* Wagon Hill; he intends to resume former position as soon as *dead* and *wounded* are buried, but will strengthen Cæsar's Camp by Rifle Brigade!

REMINISCENCES OF

Programme

❋

SIEGE THEATRE OF VARIETIES, LADYSMITH

❋

SECOND GRAND PROMENADE CONCERT

UNDER THE AUSPICES OF

THE NAVAL VOLUNTEERS

Tuesday, Dec. 25, 1899

UNDER THE BOOMING PATRONAGE AND IN THE PRESENCE OF

'Silent Sue'

'Bulwan Bill'

'Pom-Pom'

'Weary Willie'

and others who since last concert—through circumstances over which
they had no control—are unable to take any active part.

Concert to commence at 7:45 P. M.   Bunny Holes at 9:45

448

Some interesting mementos, including the following letters found on two dead Boers, and the program of a concert held on Christmas Day:

(1) Translation of a letter from a Boer gunner found inside the breastwork on Gun Hill by the storming party on December 7, 1899:

MY DEAR SISTER,

. . . It is a month & seven days since we besieged Ladysmith, & I do not know what will happen further. The English we see every day walking about the town & we are bombarding the town every day with our cannon. They have erected plenty of breastworks outside the town. It is very dangerous to attack the town. Near the town they have two naval guns from which we receive very heavy fire which we cannot stand. I think there will be much bloodshed as Mr. Englishman fights hard, & is well, & our burghers are a bit frightened. I would like to write more, but the sun is very hot, & still further the flies are so troublesome, that I don't get a chance of sitting still.

YOUR AFFECTIONATE BROTHER.

(2) Extract from a Boer letter found in the trenches at Colenso:

Don't forget to bring me a d....d Englishman tied by the leg like a goat, in order that I may have the pleasure of killing him myself.

This from a daughter to her father—sweet child!
I brought back various trophies—Pom-Poms, soft-nosed bullets with murderous slits; a grain of Long Tom an inch square; Boer bandoliers; a Queen's chocolate box taken off a dead Boer; and last, but not least, the casing of a shell, fired at Chieveley by the gun named

after me, which the Bluejackets sent with this inscription:

4.7 gun mounted in a railway truck by H.M.S. *Terrible* and christened the "Lady Randolph Churchill" Extract Chieveley: We took Lady Randolph Churchill down past Gun Hill to-day & opened fire on the low copj at 5,300 yards, the first named flushed a lot of Boers & the second (a lyddite) went right in among them, causing terrible havoc; the bluejackets would like to send the cartridge case to her ladyship.

We returned next morning in the Red Cross train with the wounded, Major Brazier Creagh, the ambulance officer already mentioned, being in charge. We had a busy week in Durban before leaving. The *Maine* had a good send-off and the ships inside and outside the harbor cheered us vociferously. I was sorry to leave Durban, where every one had been so hospitable and kind to us, and so generous to our patients, but home meant much to all on board. Sir George White [1] came on board before we started, looking very ill after his hardships and anxieties. He was tremendously cheered by our men, who look upon him as a hero and a lovable man.

Owing to the relief of Ladysmith the authorities were anxious to send home as many patients as possible in order to free the various hospitals in Natal to meet the pressure of the sick and wounded who were coming down. Six thousand had to be conveyed to England somehow. The five large hospital-ships lying in Durban Harbor were to be filled, and the *Maine* was asked to assist and return at once. This time it would have been

[1] Defender of Ladysmith.

450

ungracious to refuse, although to do transport work was not the mission we had intended for the ship. On our return to Cape Town to our dismay the war authorities sent to say that the committee from London had cabled to the effect that the *Maine* was *not* to return, and therefore all the sick and wounded were to be drafted to the different hospitals in Cape Town, and we were to remain to receive *in time* other cases. Great was the consternation on board. The officers and men, with whom every berth was filled, thought that they were going home at once and were in despair at the prospect of being detained at Cape Town. Being certain that the committee did not realize the situation, I flew on shore and bearded the Principal Medical Officer, telling him that I intended the *Maine* to leave at daybreak the next morning, as previously arranged, and that I was cabling to the minister of war to back me up. Remonstrances were in vain, for before the day was out I received a welcome answer from Lord Lansdowne confirming me in my decision.

Before leaving I paid a flying visit to Groote Schuur, unfortunately missing Mr. Cecil Rhodes, who had left that afternoon for England. But Colonel F. Rhodes was there, fresh from Ladysmith, a host in himself, whose praises could not be sung loud enough by all who were in the besieged city. His cablegram on Christmas Day to his brother Cecil in Kimberley was characteristic: "Happy Christmas! How thoroughly you have misunderstood the situation."

I was too late to see the Portland Hospital, which I regretted, as I heard it was quite a model and had been doing wonders. I dined at the Mount Nelson Hotel, where I must own to having been much astonished—the dresses, the babble of both men and women, were bewildering, and seemed under the circumstances rather out of place, and a great contrast to the realities of Durban. But too much has perhaps already been said about it, and it would be a pity, and I hope impossible, if the appearance and conduct of some inconscient and frivolous beings should efface the splendid and self-sacrificing work done by many noble women who deserve to be long remembered both in Natal and in Cape Colony.

On our return journey, favored with delicious weather, the sick and wounded soon picked up. They used to sit within a few yards of my cabin singing and chattering all day about their destinations and plans. We stopped at St. Helena to get water, which we did in such primitive fashion that it took 48 hours instead of 24. But it gave us a chance of visiting the island. We had thought to find Cronje and his defeated army there, but they were still waiting at Cape Town for the arrival of the militia regiment from England deputed to guard them. St. Helena, with its bare rocks, looked formidable and awe-inspiring as we approached. With difficulty I procured a conveyance, a high curricle which, from its antiquated appearance, must have done duty for Sir Hudson Lowe in 1820. With Eleanor Warrender I drove up to Longwood, taking two hours, as the road was rough and hilly and we could only go at a foot's pace. A long low wooden building on the top of a bleak mountain, without any vegetation, the sea the only horizon, this was where the great Napoleon lived for years and ended his days. What torture! I could not shake off the impression. "Think," I said, to some young officers with whom we had tea in the camp hard by, "of a man who has conquered the world ending his days in exile in this dreadful spot." "But I assure you," answered one of them, a rosy-cheeked young fellow of twenty, "we are no better off. There is absolutely nothing to do here, and I too find the scenery hideous." I ventured to remark that he was not Napoleon, but he did not see any difference, or why the others laughed. Deadwood Camp was pointed out to me, where the Boer prisoners were to be quartered. It was surrounded with barbed wire in imitation of the manner in which the English prisoners were kept in Pretoria. I visited Government House, where Napoleon wanted to live, but was refused. The beauty of the grounds, which were cultivated and abounded in beautiful trees and rare shrubs, was in marked contrast to the arid desolation of Longwood. A pilgrimage to Napoleon's tomb brought our visit to a close.

Stopping at Madeira, we had the misfortune to lose from acute phthisis one of our non-commissioned officers. Poor fellow, he had so hoped to live to see home and his wife and children, but the end came suddenly. He was buried on shore, the governor, the Marquis de Funchal, sending an A.D.C. to represent the garrison, many residents joining in the procession and sending beautiful flowers. Never having witnessed a military funeral before, I thought it very impressive, and the volley firing and the "Last Post" with its long-drawn unfinished note most pathetic.

It can be imagined with what emotion we entered Southampton Water, all expecting to see relations and friends on the quay, as I had telegraphed the probable hour of arrival. Unfortunately the telegram arrived too late, and the Committee and all those who were anxious to welcome us arrived an hour after the officers had more or less dispersed and the men been removed to Netley Hospital. So ended the first voyage of the *Maine*. Before leaving I received the following gratifying letter:

April 22, 1900.

DEAR LADY RANDOLPH,

We wish before we leave to express our sincere gratitude to the donors & committee of the American Hospital Ship *Maine* for their great generosity & kindness in sending the *Maine* to South Africa. It is impossible to express in a few words adequate thanks for all the comforts we have received on board, but we hope you will convey to the Committee, &, as far as possible, the donors, our heartfelt thanks for what they have done for us. Their goodness will be long remembered. We would also wish to express our extreme gratitude to you, and the staff of the *Maine* for all the kind care and attention we have received. We hope the next voyage of the ship will be as pleasant to you, as this one has been to all of us.

ERIC STREATFIELD, Capt. Gordon Highlanders.

C. BLACKBURNE TEW, 14th Yorkshire Regt.

W. WINGFIELD, 19th Hussars.

R. T. MEIKLEJOHN, 1st Royal Warwickshire Regt.

H. R. GUNNING, 1st Devonshire Regt.

E. G. CAFFIN, Lieut. 19th (P. W. O.) Yorkshire Regt.

A. S. CAMPBELL, Lieut. 19th (P. W. O.) Hussars.

H. CAPEL CURE, Major Gloster Regt.

E. M. GLOSTER, Capt. 1st Devonshire Regt.

J. S. BYRNE, Lieut. 21st Royal Inniskillen Fusiliers.

A. WISE, Lieut. 21st Connaught Rangers.

M. CARBERY, Lieut. 1st Royal Irish Fusiliers.

THE HOSPITAL-SHIP *MAINE*, WITH THE COMBINED BRITISH CHANNEL, AND MEDITERRANEAN SQUADRONS, OFF NAUPLIA, GREECE

The *Maine* is the white vessel in the foreground

Later at a meeting of the general committee of the *Maine,* I explained to their satisfaction my reasons for bringing the ship back, notwithstanding their cable.

During the *Maine's* absence of four months Mrs. Adair, the Vice-Chairman, went to America in the interest of the Fund, and succeeded in enlisting the active coöperation of a number of ladies in New York and elsewhere, who by their generous exertions materially aided us. Mrs. Ronalds, our indefatigable Treasurer, was able to give a good account of our budget and Lord Lansdowne wrote, "The *Maine* is doing great work for us; we cannot be too grateful to those who have contributed to the comfort of the sick and wounded." Queen Victoria also sent us a message through Princess Louise, Duchess of Argyll:

WINDSOR, April 8, 1900.

DEAR MRS. RONALDS,

The Queen desires me to say that she is much gratified to hear what good work the *Maine* has been doing among the wounded in South Africa, and I am to express Her Majesty's great appreciation of this generous undertaking. The Queen trusts that the *Maine* is making a good and successful voyage home, and that she will be able to land her patients much benefited from the care they will have had on their homeward journey.

Yours very sincerely,

LOUISE.

The ship started on its second voyage to South Africa on the 3d of May, 1900, with everything organized and settled, the outcome of the experience we had gained in the months of active work. After her return she was sent to Chinese waters (where hostilities were just beginning), under the command of Major Meek, M.D., R.A.M.C., who proved the most excellent and conscientious officer. The committee wisely thought that, owing to the British and Americans having no hospital-ship, the *Maine* could be of greater use in China than in South Africa, where by that time the transport and care of the wounded had been organized on a very large scale.

It would take too long here to give a detailed account of the *Maine's* doings in the Far East. Suffice it to say that during the China cruise twenty-one officers and 333 men, irrespective of nationality, were treated on board during the five months of her stay. The British, American, and European forces having withdrawn from Tientsin, and Taku being frozen in as the winter came on, the committee ordered the vessel home, thinking that she had fulfilled her mission.

In appreciation of her service I received among many others letters of thanks to the American Ladies' Committee from the Hon. Elihu Root, American Secretary of War, the Lords Commissioners of the Admiralty, and Vice Admiral Seymour, giving official testimony to the gratitude in which he held her work.

THE WAR DEPARTMENT,

WASHINGTON, Dec. 11, 1900.

DEAR MADAM,

I beg you to convey to the Ladies of the Executive Committee of the American Hospital Ship *Maine* the thanks of the Army of the United States for the humane and effective service rendered by that ship in caring for wounded countrymen in China during the past summer.

Faithfully yours,

ELIHU ROOT,

Secretary of War.

ADMIRALTY, 14th Jan., 1901.

DEAR MADAM,

I am commanded by my Lords Commissioners of the Admiralty to transmit for your information, herewith a copy of a letter received from the Commander-in-Chief, China Station, relating to the American Hospital Ship *Maine* recently employed on that station, and to express their Lordships' thanks and appreciation of the generous action of the American Ladies' Committee in thus placing their ship at the disposal of the sick and wounded in Chinese waters.

I am, Madam,

Your obedient servant,

EVAN MACGREGOR.

ALACRITY AT SHANGHAI, 21st Dec., 1900.

To the Secretary of the Admiralty,

SIR,

The Hospital Ship *Maine* being about to leave China for England, I cannot let the occasion pass without asking their Lordships to give expression to the gratitude which the officers and men of the China Squadron all feel towards the American ladies for their generosity and thoughtful kindness in endeavouring to mitigate the suffering of the sick and wounded of all nations during the recent hostilities, by fitting up and maintaining that ship. The attention paid to the sick and wounded, and the arrangements made for their comforts on board, must have greatly alleviated the hard lot of many who suffered, and have helped and hastened others on their road to recovery of health. This action of the American ladies cannot fail to have a good effect in helping to draw together the civilized nations of the world, especially their nation and ours.

I have the honour to be, Sir,

Your obedient servant,

E. H. SEYMOUR,
(Vice Admiral).

On her return from China the President of the Atlantic Transport Company, Mr. Bernard Baker, presented the ship to the British Government, the Ladies' Committee giving all the hospital fittings and equipment. The ship had been in commission fifteen months, during which time the ship and crew were with great generosity provided by the Company. Mr. Baker was publicly thanked in both Houses of Parliament, and the Committee had a gold medal struck to commemorate the work of the *Maine,* which was presented to the King. In accepting it his Majesty said that "the fact that it had been intended for his beloved mother made it specially valued and that the culminating present of the ship to the British Government he trusted would always remain as a lasting link of friendship between the two countries."

Thus ended a most successful enterprise which I think I may claim reflected the greatest credit on all concerned. As I am not writing the history of the A.H.S. *Maine,* it stands to reason that much has been left unsaid, and that where all worked with such splendid zeal it would be invidious to single any one out. There may

SALISBURY HALL, ST. ALBANS

(Present home of the writer)

have been some mistakes, but on the whole it can but be a pleasant memory to those who participated in what may undoubtedly be called an historical episode. To me it was one of the most thrilling experiences of my life, certainly the most important public work I have ever tried to do.

A few months later (July, 1900) I bade farewell to Lady Randolph Churchill, who then took the name of the chronicler of these Reminiscences.

THE END

APPENDIX

APPENDIX

APPENDIX

TRANSLATIONS OF FRENCH LETTERS

Page 16

VIENNA, June 8, 1891.

DEAR LADY RANDOLPH:

I have just received a letter in which you express a desire to have the pantomime ballet "Puppenfee" performed in aid of a charitable society.

I am greatly flattered that you should do so; for we are its authors. The "Puppenfee" was acted for the first time under our roof in the country in Bohemia.

I shall ask the ballet-master at the Opéra to send me the libretto containing all the necessary notes and indications. So far as costumes are concerned, nothing could be simpler, for you are at liberty to choose whatever you want. Only—for the solo dances—it is necessary to provide Japanese, Spanish, Styrian or Tyrolese, and Chinese women, and a baby like the dolls that cry "Papa" and "Mama." In other respects, give rein to your fancy.

The awakening of the dolls takes place at midnight when the shop is closed, so that when she is roused by the witches' Sabbath going on, the shop-woman enters, and then faints away from fright, after being swept along in the crazy rounds of the dolls come to life. When she revives from her swoon, she finds everything once more in perfect order and all the dolls absolutely motionless.

Then it is that the shop-woman steps to the footlights and in dumb show gives the spectators to understand that evidently she has been the victim of a dream.

As you perceive, the plan is very simple, and no great imagination was required to invent it.

Accept, dear Lady Randolph, assurances of my best and most affectionate regards.

P. METTERNICH.

Page 33

OSTEND, Oct. 21, 1870.

MY DEAR DUKE:

I arrived in Ostend four days ago, and found your address at our mutual friends', the Dureaus.

Since our separation on the 7th I have remained in Belgium, and should have asked for news of you during that time if I had known where to send a letter. I now seize eagerly the opportunity which is offered me through meeting the excellent prefect of Orléans, to have a few moments' chat with you.

Being threatened with arrest on September 4, I departed that evening, and

APPENDIX

sought refuge first at Namur where twenty-four hours later I was joined by my wife and daughters.

My chief aim in journeying to Namur was to be near Sedan, that I might learn the fate of my son, for whom I had great anxiety. After several days of inquiry, I at last learned that my son, after having been wounded at Sedan (a horse having been killed under him), was a prisoner at Cologne, as he would not accept for himself the capitulation.

I left Namur for Spa, and a sojourn there not being very comfortable in the winter, I established myself at Ostend, where I await events, the issue of which I cannot foresee.

How I wish, my dear Duke, that my pen were clever enough to convey to you all the impressions I have received since the fatal Sedan. I have come to the point of asking myself how a disaster of such dimensions could be produced without the principal author of this lugubrious drama being buried under the corpses of his army.

I had thought that it was easier to die than to suffer dishonor.

The death of the Emperor at Sedan would have saved France, as well as his son; the capitulation has lost everything.

Now that France has become the prey of foreign and domestic Vandals, how can this desolation of our unhappy country be brought to an end!

Unless there should be a general war creating a division in Prussian politics, I do not see to what side we can turn. England appears to have abandoned us, and however the circumstances which cemented our alliance of 1856 might be reproduced for her, even then she could not count on our help, we have fallen so low!

I had offered my services to the government of the National defence, but I withdrew my offer as soon as I saw the government, to the eternal shame of France, call a Garibaldi to defend her.

On the other hand, accusations of treason reach all the generals who have served the Empire, and I am not willing to have my name bandied among all these ignominies.

Adieu, my dear Duke. If you will be so good as to send me news of yourself, my family and I will be happy indeed . . . for our hearts are full of gratitude.

Ever yours,

GÉNÉRAL DE PALIKAO.

Page 35

WILHELMSHÖHE, Jan. 7, 1871.

MY DEAR PERSIGNY:

I have received your letter of the first of January, and thank you for the prayers you offer for a better future. Without desiring to enter into a discussion of the ideas you express, I will say to you that nothing good can come from the confusion which is the result of individual efforts, made without discretion, and without authority. In fact I find it somewhat singular that any one should busy himself with the future of my son, without taking account of my own intentions.

I know you have written to M. de Bismarck, who naturally has demanded of me if you have done so with my authority and in full accord with me. I have answered him that I have authorized nobody to busy himself with my interests, and those of my son, without first obtaining my consent.

Believe, my dear Persigny, in my friendship.

NAPOLEON.

468

APPENDIX

Page 198

SHEEN HOUSE,

EAST SHEEN, SURREY, July 25, '88.

MY DEAR LADY RANDOLPH:

You have been so kind as to interest yourself somewhat in our attempts at a league in France, and I take the liberty of sending you the two circulars which we shall have printed and distributed in a few days. I hope you will read them indulgently, and keep them, so that, if we should in time attain to happy results, we shall be able later to talk them over together. You know that it is you who first gave me the idea of doing something similar in France, and so I think of you always in this great undertaking, and already I owe to you, even before beginning, the firm faith I have that we shall succeed by following your example.

The Rose League will never be the equal of the Primrose League; but perhaps they may meet often in the future.

If I have not mentioned the Primrose League in the circular, it is solely because I have not dared compare the immense success of the first flower with the modest beginnings of the second; but in private letters, and in speaking to all those who are willing to work with me, I have always mentioned it, in order to give every one the same idea: to succeed as you have.

Forgive me for my ambition, and believe me, until I shall have the pleasure of meeting you again,

Yours very affectionately,

ISABELLE, COMTESSE DE PARIS.

Page 201

SHEEN HOUSE,

EAST SHEEN, SURREY, October 7, 1888.

MY DEAR LADY RANDOLPH:

I do not know whether you are in London, but I send you a line there to say that I received last night a number of the "Primrose League Gazette," with a very kind article on the Rose League. I want to thank you for sending it, and for the article, for I feel quite sure that you had a very great part in it. If I am wrong pray express my thanks to the author. The Primrose League is indeed kind to welcome so cordially its younger sister—the Rose League.

I sent you, day before yesterday, a number of the "Soleil," so that you might see our new paper in its entirety. You doubtless recognized certain phrases, and I hope you will approve of what I have done; I have, I think, followed your advice. I hear good reports from every side; it appears that the Rose is progressing excellently; I hope this enthusiasm will continue, and it will be to you, above all, that we shall owe our success.

I hope soon to have the pleasure of seeing you again; and in the meantime pray believe me

Yours very affectionately,

ISABELLE, COMTESSE DE PARIS.

469

APPENDIX

Page 247

CHESHAM HOUSE,

CHESHAM PLACE, S. W., October 31, 1902.

DEAR MADAME AND FRIEND:

Here is the very old face of a very old man who is half-dead but who likes you very much.

Do not receive it too unkindly.

Sincerely yours,

STAAL.

Page 270

DEAR MADAME:

For a long while I have been wishing to write to you. Will this letter reach you? I shall not know unless you will kindly send me a few words to say you have received it. I have nothing good to tell you of myself. After having devoted myself body and soul to my son, he has played me the trick of marrying a perfectly impossible woman who is fourteen years older than himself,—to the great scandal of the country and the whole of Europe.

I am not willing to accept the situation and here I am, high and dry not knowing what I shall do. Pardon me for speaking of these matters to you, but in my old age, and with my hair nearer white than gray, it is too hard. I have deserved better than this.

MILAN.

Page 272

My life is saddened by the difficulty of writing "A Tragic Idyll." It is a beautiful subject on which I should write you 20 pages. With patience I will come to the end of it—but it is terribly hard. Arrived at a certain point in life, one knows too much of it, wishes to do too much, and is not able to express what one has to say. Do you know that Tourguéniew has summed it all up when he said "Life is a brutal affair."

470